MICHIGAN PROFICIENCY

FINAL COUNTDOWN

ECPE PRACTICE TESTS

DIANE FLANEL PINIARIS

REVISED EDITION 2013

Australia • Brazil • Japan • Korea • Mexico • Singapore • Spain • United Kingdom • United States

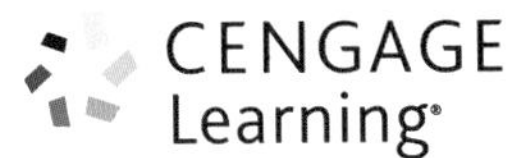

Michigan Proficiency Final Countdown Practice Tests Student's Book Revised Edition (2013)

Diane Flanel Piniaris

Publishing Manager: Sue Trory

Development Editor: Kayleigh Buller

Editorial Assistant: Georgina McComb

Marketing Manager: Charlotte Ellis

Project Editor: Tom Relf

Manufacturing Buyer: Eyvett Davis

Text Design: Vasiliki Christoforidou

Cover Design: Natasa Arsenidou/Adam Renvoize

Compositor: MPS Limited

Acknowledgments

The author would like to extend her heartfelt thanks to everyone behind the scenes who helped to bring this project to fruition. Special mention goes to Margaret Brooks for her invaluable work on the Speaking Tests and model compositions in the original edition, and Sue Trory, Tania Psatha, Kayleigh Buller and others at Cengage Learning for the role they played in making this latest revision a reality.

Recording and production by Rockwell Audio Media, New York, NY, USA

ISBN: 978-1-4080-9267-5

National Geographic EMEA
Cheriton House, North Way, Andover, Hampshire, SP10 5BE United Kingdom

Cengage Learning is a leading provider of customized learning solutions with office locations around the globe, including Singapore, the United Kingdom, Australia, Mexico, Brazil and Japan. Locate our local office at **international.cengage.com/region**

Cengage Learning products are represented in Canada by Nelson Education Ltd.

Visit National Geographic Learning online at **ngl.cengage.com**
Visit our corporate website at **cengage.com**

Photo credits
The publishers would like to thank the following sources for permission to reproduce their copyright protected photographs:

Cover photos: cover1 (Heejin/Shutterstock), cover2 (Daboost/Shutterstock), cover3 (Franck Boston/Shutterstock), cover4 (PhotoAlto/Alamy)

33 tl (Ivan_Sabo/Shutterstock), 33 bc (Ruud Morijn Photographer/Shutterstock), 33 bc (Sunny Forest/Shutterstock), 33 br (RZ Design/Shutterstock), 33 tc (A.S. Zain/Shutterstock), 33 tc (Galyna Andrushko/Shutterstock), 33 tr (Matej Hudovernik/Shutterstock), 33 cl (Picsfive/Shutterstock), 33 cc (Martin Muránsky/Shutterstock), 33 cr (Christophe Testi/Shutterstock), 33 cr (Dainis Derics/Shutterstock), 33 bl (Fouquin Christophe/age fotostock/National Geographic Learning), 55 tc (Equilibrium Photographers/Shutterstock), 55 tr (Diego Cervo/Shutterstock), 55 bl (Andrey_Kuzmin/Shutterstock), 55 bc (Stokkete/Shutterstock), 55 br (Monkey Business Images/Shutterstock), 55 tl (Creatista/Shutterstock), 77 tl (Dominique Lavoie/Shutterstock), 77 tc (Krasowit/Shutterstock), 77 tc (Anna Omelchenko/Shutterstock), 77 tr (Carlos E. Santa Maria/Shutterstock), 77 bc (Yakobchuk Vasyl/Shutterstock), 77 bc (Kletr/Shutterstock), 77 bt (Nejron Photo/Shutterstock), 77 bl (aslysun/Shutterstock), 98 l (Lucky Business/Shutterstock), 98 l (Vera Volkova/Shutterstock), 98 r (Mykhaylo Palinchak/Shutterstock), 98 c (Pressmaster/Shutterstock), 98 c (Wai Chan/Shutterstock), 99 tr (Kruglov_Orda/Shutterstock), 99 bc (@cam/Shutterstock), 99 br (absolutimages/Shutterstock), 99 tl (iofoto/Shutterstock), 99 tr (Blend Images/Shutterstock), 99 bl (Adam Gregor/Shutterstock), 99 bl (A1Stock/Shutterstock), 99 br (Lisa F. Young/Shutterstock), 99 tc (3445128471/Shutterstock), 103 t (Maxx-Studio/Shutterstock), 103 t (A.Krotov/Shutterstock), 103 c (Ammit Jack/Shutterstock), 103 c (Foxterier playing on the beach, summer/Shutterstock), 103 b (Galina Dreyzina/Shutterstock), 103 b (marylooo/Shutterstock), 121 tl (Ljupco Smokovski/Shutterstock), 121 br (isak55/Shutterstock), 121 tl (Hydromet/Shutterstock), 121 tc (Albo003/Shutterstock), 121 tr (mashe/Shutterstock), 121 tr (Sukharevskyy Dmytro (nevodka)/Shutterstock), 121 bl (Suzanne Long/Shutterstock), 121 bl (ethylalkohol/Shutterstock), 121 br (Eric Isselee/Shutterstock), 121 bc (aastock/Shutterstock), 143 tl (K. Miri Photography/Shutterstock), 143 cl (Regien Paassen/Shutterstock), 143 tc (Hallgerd/Shutterstock), 143 tr (Simon Krzic/Shutterstock), 143 cc (Natalia D./Shutterstock), 143 cr (Anneka/Shutterstock), 143 bl (Gemenacom/Shutterstock), 143 bc (Feng Yu/Shutterstock), 143 br (Gelpi JM/Shutterstock), 143 tr (Lorraine Swanson/Shutterstock), 143 cl (JHDT Stock Images LLC/Shutterstock), 143 cc (dotshock/Shutterstock), 143 cr (zimmytws/Shutterstock), 143 bl (Alex Valent/Shutterstock), 143 bc (Pixel Embargo/Shutterstock), 143 br (Lisa F. Young/Shutterstock), 143 cl (3445128471/Shutterstock), 143 tc (Pressmaster/Shutterstock), 164 tl (AVAVA/Shutterstock), 164 tc (Larry Powell/Shutterstock), 164 tr (Jim Parkin/Shutterstock), 164 bl (Monkey Business Images/Shutterstock), 164 bc (Teresa Levite/Shutterstock), 164 br (MSPhotographic/Shutterstock), 164 tl (Alta Oosthuizen/Shutterstock), 164 bl (Dragon Images/Shutterstock), 165 tl (Johanna Goodyear/Shutterstock), 165 tc (TTphoto/Shutterstock), 165 tr (Petrenko Andriy/Shutterstock), 165 tr (T-Design/Shutterstock), 165 cl (Elena Elisseeva/Shutterstock), 165 cl (Vasiliy Koval/Shutterstock), 165 cc (arek_malang/Shutterstock), 165 cr (justasc/Shutterstock), 165 cr (PHB.cz (Richard Semik)/Shutterstock), 165 bl (Brian Daly/Shutterstock), 165 bl (Zacarias Pereira da Mata/Shutterstock), 165 bc (freelanceartist/Shutterstock), 165 br (Alexander Kalina/Shutterstock), 165 br (patrimonio designs ltd/Shutterstock), 165 tl (Maciej Oleksy/Shutterstock), 186 tl (berna namoglu/Shutterstock), 186 bl (Benjamin Howell/Shutterstock), 186 bl (WilleeCole/Shutterstock), 186 bc (red rose/Shutterstock), 186 br (Kinetic Imagery/Shutterstock), 186 tl (Dmitry Kalinovsky/Shutterstock), 186 tc (potowizard/Shutterstock), 186 tr (dinozzaver/Shutterstock), 186 tr (bikeriderlondon/Shutterstock), 186 cl (Tyler Olson/Shutterstock), 186 cl (Stephen Coburn/Shutterstock), 186 cc (Andre Dobroskok/Shutterstock), 186 cr (dean bertoncelj/Shutterstock), 186 cr (RexRover/Shutterstock), 186 br (Paul Turner/Shutterstock), 187 l (Hasloo Group Production Studio/Shutterstock), 187 C (Stephen Finn/Shutterstock), 187 C (Glenda/Shutterstock), 187 R (William Casey/Shutterstock), 189 (Mazzzur/Shutterstock), 191 t (Roman Sigaev/Shutterstock), 191 c (Bruce Amos/Shutterstock), 191 b (Tischenko Irina/Shutterstock), 191 b (GVictoria/Shutterstock)

Illustrations:
101 l (Panyiotis Angeletakis), 101 c (Panyiotis Angeletakis), 101 c (Panyiotis Angeletakis), 101 r (Panyiotis Angeletakis), 218 l (Cengage Learning (EMEA) Ltd), 218 c (Cengage Learning (EMEA) Ltd), 218 r (Cengage Learning (EMEA) Ltd)

All other illustrations by George Alexandris

Printed in United Kingdom by Ashford Colour Press Ltd.
Print Number: 05 Print Year: 2019

Contents

Introduction

The 2013 revised edition of *Michigan Proficiency Final Countdown ECPE Practice Tests* consists of eight complete practice tests plus supporting exercises, activities, and test-taking advice for the most recent version of the ECPE (Examination for the Certificate of Proficiency in English).

What's New in This Revision?

In keeping with minor changes made to the format of several sections of the ECPE since 2009, the 2013 revised edition includes changes in the following three areas:

- **Listening Part III:** Printed questions now appear above the answer choices.
- **Cloze sections:** Two 10-item passages now replace the single 20-item passage in each GCVR.
- **Grammar sections:** These have been updated to reflect the movement away from conversational grammar items based on short dialogues. All grammar items are now based on a single gapped sentence followed by four answer choices.

Unique Features

As with the other books in the author's Michigan ECPE series, *Final Countdown* is based on the implicit philosophy that practice tests should be teachable, educational, stimulating, and enjoyable. As such, *Final Countdown* contains several unique features.

1. Thematic Continuity with Other Books in the Series

The practice tests in this book are specially designed to provide students with exposure to topics that frequently appear on the ECPE. Anyone who has followed the ECPE over the years will be aware that certain topics appear in the Cloze, Reading, and Listening sections with surprising regularity. Chief among these topics are **plants and animals, health and medicine, the environment,** and **technology** – all topics which students who have used the author's *Michigan Proficiency First Steps* and/or *Michigan Proficiency Skills Builder* have been systematically exposed to. Students who have used one or both of these will especially benefit from these practice tests. This is because the texts that appear in the Cloze, Reading, and Listening sections have been carefully chosen to reinforce and build on the topic-related material that students have already met.

2. Delving Deeper Questions to Reinforce Key Themes and Foster Comfort and Confidence

Themed passages, however, are a mere frill – unless, of course, we push our students to do something more with them than just check their answers and move on. For those of you who feel the need to have your students slow down and explore the Reading passages, we have included a section with comprehension questions and other tasks (pages 217-224) designed to offer students the chance to really think about what they have read. We realize that not everyone will have time to utilize all the material in this section, but even occasional use of it will add a rich dimension to your lessons.

3. Special Emphasis on Vocabulary Enrichment and Consolidation

Item Selection – Another major feature is that the large majority of the words tested in the Vocabulary sections come from a master list compiled by the author from ECPE testing materials (e.g., now-obsolete Preliminary and Final Tests) made available over the years by the developers of the ECPE. This ensures that students have the opportunity to expand their vocabulary with words at the appropriate level of difficulty. Also, it is important to note that students who have used the author's *Michigan Proficiency First Steps* and/or *Michigan Proficiency Skills Builder* will already have encountered many of the words in the Reading, Cloze, and Vocabulary tasks in those books. The Vocabulary sections included in this volume will thus serve as a valuable tool for recycling, reviewing, and reinforcing lexical items that have previously been introduced.

Recycling in Final Tests 4 and 8 – The Vocabulary sections in Practice Tests 4 and 8 introduce no new material. Instead, they intentionally recycle words that have already been introduced in the Vocabulary sections of the previous three tests so that students can catch their breath and consolidate what they have met before. To aid consolidation, students should be encouraged to do a complete revision of the relevant practice tests before attempting the Vocabulary sections in Tests 4 and 8.

Vocabulary Enhancements – Immediately following each practice test is a supplementary two-page section called Vocabulary Enhancement. Focusing on specific words or themes that students encounter in the Cloze or Reading passages, these sections clearly embody the philosophy mentioned above: that practice test books should be "teachable, educational, stimulating, and enjoyable." Students will especially enjoy the photo tasks as they explore a wide variety of frequently tested lexical areas.

Vocabulary Consolidations – To ensure immediate reinforcement of the 160 Vocabulary items in each test, there is also a four-page Consolidation. The Consolidations after Practice Tests 1–3 and 5–7 contain exercises that allow students to focus on the meanings and usage of many of the words they have met in the corresponding Vocabulary sections. For variety (and also because the Vocabulary sections in Tests 4 and 8 are themselves review tests), the Consolidations after Practice Tests 4 and 8 review high-frequency items that students have seen in the Reading passages and Vocabulary Enhancements.

4. Special Emphasis on Composition Writing

A hurdle that every ECPE candidate faces is the 30-minute Writing time limit. When students begin ECPE-level work, it is logical for teachers to focus on making students aware of different composition types and on teaching strategies for organizing and developing their ideas. As exam time nears, however, another element must be added, and that is helping students develop the "lightning reflexes" they need to succeed on the Writing section. *Final Countdown* addresses this with the help of two unique sections:

Writing Tutorial *(Student's Book/Teacher's Book)* – This section consists of 16 optional mini-lessons that correspond to the 16 Writing topics students will encounter in Practice Tests 1–8. Each tutorial is broken into two parts: **Before You Begin**, which contains discussion and brainstorming activities designed to provide younger students with the raw material they need to develop competent compositions; and **Suggestions for Development**, which includes step-by-step guidance for building up each paragraph. How teachers use these mini-lessons depends, of course, on how much time is available and how good the students' composition skills already are. Teachers may want to rely heavily on the tasks in the first month or so of using *Final Countdown* and then gradually allow students to work more independently once the main message of using clear topic sentences and linking devices has been driven home. The main objective, of course, is to provide students with a method for organizing and developing each composition type so they know exactly how to approach the 30-minute Writing task on the day of the exam.

Model Compositions *(Teacher's Book only)* – Supporting the 16 mini-lessons in the Writing Tutorial are 16 annotated models that demonstrate how the step-by-step guidance provided in the mini-lessons can be put into practice. The models are intended to be used as follow-ups to be shared and discussed with the class after students have attempted one or both of the compositions in each test.

5. Special Emphasis on Test-Taking Strategies

In addition to a special section entitled "Tips and Strategies for the Day of the Exam," there is also a liberal sprinkling of test-taking strategies scattered throughout each practice test.

Relation to Other Books in the Author's ECPE Series

Michigan Proficiency Final Countdown ECPE Practice Tests is designed to be used in the final stages of a student's preparation for the ECPE – either on its own or in addition to one or both of the other books of full-length practice tests in the author's ECPE series: *Michigan Proficiency Practice Tests* and *Michigan Proficiency All-Star ECPE Practice Tests.* As the tests in all three of these books review and recycle the thematic, lexical, grammatical, and skills content of *Michigan Proficiency First Steps*, *Michigan Proficiency Skills Builder*, and *Michigan Proficiency Listening and Speaking*, they are an invaluable tool for the final months of preparation for both first-time candidates and re-takers alike.

It is the author's sincere hope that the material in these tests will go a long way towards making your students into competent test-takers and more confident users of the language.

The ECPE: Overview

THE ECPE: OVERVIEW*

The Examination for the Certificate of Proficiency in English (ECPE) is administered in many countries around the world at test centers authorized by Cambridge Michigan Language Assessments (CaMLA).

As of spring 2013, the ECPE consists of the following four sections administered in the following order:

1	**Writing (30 minutes)** Candidates must choose one out of two topics and write an argumentative or expository composition (about 250-300 words).
2	**Listening** (approximately 35-40 minutes) – Audio CD 50 multiple-choice items divided into three parts: • Part 1 – Interpret short dialogues (17 items) • Part 2 – Choose the appropriate response to a question (18 items) • Part 3 – Answer questions about three extended listening passages (15 items)
3	**Grammar, Cloze, Vocabulary, Reading (GCVR)** (75 minutes) 120 multiple-choice items divided into 4 parts: • 40 multiple-choice Grammar items • 20 multiple-choice Cloze items, based on two passages • 40 multiple-choice Vocabulary items • 20 multiple-choice Reading items, based on four passages of five items each.
4	**Speaking – as of June 2009** (usually 25-35 minutes) Two or three candidates participate in a decision-making task that allows candidates to demonstrate the full range of their speaking ability while performing a multi-stage semi-structured task consisting of the following: introduction and small talk; summarizing and recommending; reaching a consensus; presenting and convincing; justifying and defending. Two examiners will be present during the Speaking Test. In the rare event that three candidates are examined together, the test will last 35-45 minutes. For more information, see page 192.

For information on the current scoring policy of the ECPE, please see the CaMLA website referred to in the footnote below.

* Adapted from the Cambridge Michigan Language Assessments website, retrieved August 13, 2013 from: http://www.cambridgemichigan.org

CRITERIA FOR WRITING AND SPEAKING*

Writing

In general, candidates are rated on four main criteria: **rhetoric** (organization, topic development, linking); **grammar and syntax; vocabulary;** and **mechanics** (punctuation and spelling). A candidate who receives a grade in the C range displays the following characteristics:

Rhetoric	Grammar/Syntax	Vocabulary	Mechanics
• Topic clearly developed, but not always completely or with acknowledgment of its complexity. • Organization generally controlled; connection sometimes absent or unsuccessful.	• Both simple and complex syntax present. • Features may be cautious but accurate, or more fluent but less accurate. • Morphological control sometimes inconsistent.	• Adequate range. • Words may sometimes be used inappropriately.	• Spelling and punctuation errors may at times be distracting.

Speaking

In general, candidates are rated on three main criteria:

- Discourse and interaction: production of independent, spontaneous speech; contribution to extended interaction; ability to comprehend what is said in order to engage effectively in conversation
- Linguistic resources: range and accuracy of vocabulary and grammar
- Deliverability and intelligibility: fluency of delivery, rate of speech, register, ability to be understood

A candidate who receives a grade in the C range displays the following:

Discourse and Interaction	Linguistic Resources	Deliverability and Intelligibility
• Summarizes concisely and accurately; may sometimes rely on written material. • Elaborates, often without prompting, and offers coherent explanations. • Often presents decisions clearly; is sometimes limited in extending discourse. • Often contributes to development of interaction; aware of listener. • Usually understands information in order to engage in interaction.	• Uses moderate range of vocabulary accurately and appropriately. • Sometimes uses incorrect collocations that may lead to vagueness. • Often uses a variety of basic and complex grammatical structures accurately and effectively. • Gaps and/or errors in vocabulary and grammar, sometimes self-corrected, usually do not hinder communication.	• Often fluent, usually articulate; may require some listener effort. • Fluency may decline with more challenging speech events, but this does not stop the flow of discourse. • Pace usually consistent, may occasionally be relatively slower. • An increase in rate of delivery may occasionally lead to decrease in clarity of speech or ability to be understood.

* Adapted from the Cambridge Michigan Language Assessments website, retrieved August 13, 2013 from: http://www.cambridgemichigan.org

Tips and Strategies for the Day of the Exam

TIPS AND STRATEGIES FOR THE DAY OF THE EXAM

Here is a section-by-section rundown offering tips and strategies for the day of the exam. The sections are presented in the order that you will encounter them on the exam.

WRITING (30 minutes)

- In the days before the exam, review the Summary of Main Composition Types on page 9, and read over the Writing Tutorial (pages 201-216). Then read through your own work and any models your teacher has given you. Pay careful attention to any advice you've been given about organizing and developing your paragraphs and on using clear topic sentences and linking devices.
- Review the Scoring Criteria for Writing on page 7. Remember that you are being graded on four main criteria: rhetoric, grammar and syntax, vocabulary, and mechanics. Keep these in mind as you plan your composition.
- Although handwriting is not one of the grading criteria, do your best to write neatly and legibly. You may write with pen or pencil. If you tend to change your mind a lot, use pencil and a clean eraser!
- Remember that you've only got 30 minutes, which means that you cannot possibly delve into every single aspect of a subject. What you can do in that time is to treat a topic by mentioning and developing two or three points in each paragraph ... and that limit should be uppermost in your mind as you begin to work.

Here's what we recommend:

Focus → → → → → → → → → ***How to handle the 30-minute composition***

1. **Study the two topics** and decide which one you can develop more effectively.
2. **Read the question carefully.** Make sure you are clear on what it asks you to do and what type of composition it is (see **Summary of Main Composition Types**, page 9).
3. **Take about 5 minutes to plan out the composition on scrap paper.** Jot down a quick paragraph plan and make brief notes about points to include in the Introduction, each paragraph of the Main Body, and the Conclusion. Also jot down any impressive vocabulary or phrases that you might like to fit in. All this may seem like a waste of time, but it could be a life-saver if your mind goes blank while you're writing.
4. **Remember to start each paragraph with a clear topic sentence.**
5. **Use linking devices wherever possible** as you develop your ideas with reasons and examples.
6. **Take a few minutes to read over your work.** When you have finished, proofread what you have written, looking for omitted words and obvious errors in grammar, spelling, and punctuation.

COMPOSITION CHECKLIST

✓ Introduction - Main Body - Conclusion

✓ Clear topic sentences

✓ Linking words for logical development

✓ General ideas supported with reasons/examples

✓ Good range of vocabulary and grammar

SUMMARY OF MAIN COMPOSITION TYPES

PROTOTYPE

Introduction → Tell them what you're going to tell them
Main Body → Tell them
Conclusion → Tell them what you told them

For compositions that don't quite fit the mold, see Tip on page 82.

TYPE 1	**Narrative**
Introduction	Restate the topic in your own words and briefly introduce the person or incident you will be writing about.
Main Body	• Establish background to what you are about to describe (e.g., how you met someone, where you were going, what you were doing). • Narrate what happened. Break into 2-3 paragraphs: the lead-up to the key moment and the key moment itself in 1-2 paragraphs and the aftermath in a separate paragraph. Use time links where possible.
Conclusion	Discuss the influence the person/incident has had on you and what you learned.

TYPE 2	**Problem/Solution**
Introduction	Restate the situation in the topic in your own words. State simply that the situation involves problems (name them, if appropriate), but solutions do exist.
Main Body	Devote a separate paragraph to each problem. • Start with a clear topic sentence announcing the problem, and then analyze the problem with a series of reasons, examples, and results. • Using a clear transition statement (e.g., "One way to remedy this would be to ..." or "If I were in charge, I would ..."), present one or more solutions. Use links and elaborate with reasons, examples, and/or results.
Conclusion	Summarize by restating message in introduction. Close, if possible, with a thought-provoking statement about putting solutions into effect.

TYPE 3	**For and Against**
Introduction	Briefly restate the issue in the topic. State simply that the issue has advantages and disadvantages or reasons to be "for" or "against" it. (Save your opinion for the end.)
Main Body	Devote a separate paragraph to each side of the argument. • Start with a clear topic sentence announcing one side of the argument. • Develop with 2-4 aspects. Use linking words and elaborate, if needed, with reasons and examples.
Conclusion	End by weighing both sides and expressing your opinion.

TYPE 4a/4b **Opinion**

This type may ask your opinion about something or it may ask you whether you agree or disagree with a statement. You will be more convincing if you acknowledge the complexity of the issue and discuss both sides.

Introduction	Briefly restate the topic and your opinion.
Main body	Discuss your opinion: **(a)** by examining two aspects of it (one in each paragraph), or **(b)** by devoting one paragraph to your opinion and one to the opposing point of view. In either case, start each paragraph with a clear topic sentence and develop with reasons and examples. If you choose (b), discuss your opinion in one paragraph and the opposing view in the other, ending (if desired) with 1-2 reasons why this view is flawed.
Conclusion	End by restating your opinion and leaving readers with a thought-provoking idea.

LISTENING (approximately 35–40 minutes)

- Keep in mind that items are *not* repeated on the ECPE. You will hear each part only *once*!
- Try to stay cool, even if a question goes by you too quickly. If you allow yourself to panic, you might miss the next question as well!
- Finally, pray that the exam room has a good sound system *and* good acoustics ... and that there are no dogs barking or workers drilling just outside the window! If anything irregular occurs (e.g., if the volume is distorted or needs adjusting), immediately raise your hand and bring it to the examiners' attention.

Tackling Part III

Use the months before the exam to experiment with both of the methods below. On the day of the exam, use the one you feel most comfortable with.

Method 1 – The Traditional Way: Taking Notes

The instructions to Part III suggest that you may want to make notes in your test booklet. This is fine if you are an experienced note-taker in English, but if you aren't, you may find it unhelpful. Needless to say, the purpose of note-taking is defeated if writing down one thing causes you to miss the next thing the speaker says. The only way to know if note-taking will work for you is to try it. You'll undoubtedly improve with practice, but – if you're like many of our past students – you'll probably find that you listen better if you don't write! If that's the case, forget note-taking and try Method 2.

Method 2 – Our Way: Using the Questions and Choices in the Test Booklet

A method that many of our students have had great success with in the past is to concentrate on the questions and choices while listening to the segment. Here are some tips you may find helpful:

1. Use the time before each segment begins to skim the questions and underline key words. This will give you a better idea of what the radio segment is about.
2. Remember that the questions almost always follow the order of the information in the text.
3. As the segment begins, reread the first two questions and focus on the first set of choices. If you hear something that repeats or, more likely, paraphrases a choice, put a mark next to it. (That is usually the answer.) If you hear something that relates to the next question, quickly shift your focus to the next set of choices. (At the end, you have 10 seconds to reconsider each question, so don't panic if you can't answer one or more questions as you listen.)
4. Do the same for the remaining questions, always keeping in mind the next question in case you miss an answer.
5. At the end, as the narrator reads each question, check your answer and transfer it to the separate answer sheet. If you left anything blank the first time around, carefully consider the choices again, guess if you have to, and mark the answer sheet. Remember that you are not penalized for wrong answers.

THE GCVR: GRAMMAR – CLOZE – VOCABULARY – READING (75 minutes)

USE YOUR TIME WISELY – A word about overall strategy

The GCVR is the last, longest, and most demanding section. Even native speakers have trouble finishing it in 75 minutes!

To maximize your score, you must use your time wisely.

We recommend that you spend as much time as you can on Grammar, Cloze, and Reading and proportionately less time on Vocabulary. Our reasons are as follows:

- If you slow down on Grammar and read each item carefully, you will avoid making careless mistakes and you'll accumulate a solid base of points. There are few surprises here, so a few more seconds per question means fewer mistakes! (13 minutes is ideal.)
- Spending more time on Vocabulary will not improve your score. Go through the questions as quickly as possible without wasting time on items you don't know. This will give you a few more minutes for the Cloze and Reading passages. (10-11 minutes for Vocabulary is ideal.)
- The more time you have for the Cloze and Reading sections, the more time you have to work with the texts and find the answers. Staying within the recommended limits for Grammar and Vocabulary leaves you 50 minutes for the Cloze and Reading passages. That gives you about five minutes for each of the two Cloze passages and ten minutes for each of the four Reading passages, which is tight but achievable.

GRAMMAR

- Remember that every question tests one or more specific grammar topics (e.g., conditionals, wishes, modals, tenses, subject-verb agreement, word order, inversion, reported speech, and the subjunctive). Use the list in the box below as a basis for review.
- Watch out for "avoidable errors" on question types that you've seen a thousand times before. To do this, open your eyes (it really does help!), read the entire question stem, and consider all four choices carefully.
- Expect six to eight "killer" questions. These questions often test emphatic phrases, complex sentence structure, or fine points of grammar that you may not have seen. How to cope? Admit you don't know, guess, and then cut and run! Staring at the question doesn't help, and you'll be taking valuable time away from the Cloze and Reading passages.

Frequently-Tested Grammar Topics

subject-verb agreement	constructions of probability	word forms and derivatives
verb tenses	modal verbs + functions	participles/participial phrases
active vs. passive voice	inversion	countable/uncountable nouns
reported speech	word order	relative clauses
embedded questions	subjunctive mood	connectors and conjunctions
tag questions	causative form	adjective and adverb forms
wishes	infinitives vs. gerunds	compound adjectives
conditionals	verbs + dependent prepositions	*so*/*such* vs. *too*/*enough*

CLOZE

Remember that to do well on Cloze passages, it's vital that you understand that the examiners are testing you on two different levels:

- **The sentence level,** where you focus on a single sentence in order to:

  a) determine what its structure is and what is missing grammatically; or
  b) check whether or not the missing item is part of a phrasal verb or other collocation.

- **The text (or discourse) level,** where you must consider the overall meaning, organization, and development of a passage. Unlike sentence-level questions, text-level questions cannot be answered by focusing on single sentences. They require you to understand what the writer is saying and how the ideas unfold sentence by sentence from one paragraph to the next. Text-level questions often ask you to:

  a) choose appropriate vocabulary, as determined by the context;
  b) supply pronouns or other referent words that refer to other parts of the text;
  c) choose appropriate linking words and discourse markers.

Here is a suggested approach that will help you answer Cloze questions at both levels.

Focus → → → → → → → → → → → → *How to handle a Cloze passage*

1. **Read the passage quickly without looking at the choices.**

   This will give you a feel for what the text is about, which in turn will make it easier for you to recognize and answer questions concerning vocabulary, referent words, and overall meaning.

2. **Glance quickly at the verbs in each paragraph and get a feel for the tenses.**

   Does one tense dominate or are a variety of tenses used? Are the verbs active or passive voice? This will help you make choices about sentence-level grammar-based questions.

3. **Notice the function of each paragraph.**

   Some paragraphs contain a topic statement supported by reasons and examples, while others may contain a procedure or sequence of events, a list of reasons, or contrasting ideas. You will be better able to answer questions related to linking words and discourse markers if you are sensitive to the kind of information in each paragraph and to how a sentence relates to the ones before and after it.

4. **Work through the passage, item by item and choice by choice.**

   As you come to each blank, decide whether the item is testing you at sentence level or at text level by quickly studying the choices. Do they suggest that a verb or part of a collocation is missing at sentence level? Or are you being asked to supply a linking word, vocabulary item, or pronoun that depends on your understanding of the wider context? Whatever the question type, remember to consider all four choices and use process of elimination to narrow down the choices.

5. **Remember that the clock is ticking.**

   Don't spend too much time on any one question. If you're not sure of an answer, guess and move on. You should plan to spend about five minutes on each ten-item Cloze passage.

6. **When you have completed all the items, read the passage again as a final check to see if your answers make sense.**

VOCABULARY

This is the "Achilles' heel" of students taking the ECPE. No matter how many thousands of words you know, chances are there will be words on the exam that you haven't seen. But don't despair! Believe it or not, there is plenty of "room for error" on the Vocabulary section of the GCVR. If you get a good base of points on Grammar (say, 30 out of 40) and do fairly well on both the Cloze (say, 13 out of 20) and the Reading sections (say, 13 out of 20), then all you need is 22 out of 40 on Vocabulary to achieve a Low Pass on the GCVR.

You have a good chance of achieving this if you follow these simple tips:

- **Don't panic!** Expect to encounter unknown words and remember that there is room for error. Don't allow yourself to lose even a second worrying about 5,10, or even 15 questions that you don't know. The math is still on your side!
- **Remember that your goal is to do this section as quickly as possible.** Don't waste time staring at the test booklet when you encounter trouble. Read each sentence carefully, rule out the choices that you know are wrong, **guess**, and move on. Answer all 40 questions, and do not leave blanks. The time you save by "being done" with Vocabulary can be used to much better advantage on the Cloze and Reading sections.
- **Don't lose points on items with words that you do know**! Here are two things to keep in mind so you don't make silly errors in the heat of the moment:
  - Make sure you read the main sentence all the way to the end so you have a clear idea of the meaning before making your choice.
  - Check to see if a preposition or particle follows the blank and make sure your choice agrees with it. Test-makers often include questions with prepositions or particles to try and catch you off guard. Don't fall into the trap of choosing the synonym of a phrasal verb when it's the main part of a phrasal verb that's missing!
- **As a final review, go over the Vocabulary sections, Vocabulary Enhancements, and Vocabulary Consolidations** in this book to keep the words you've encountered fresh in your mind.

A little knowledge is a great thing, so don't give up because you don't know one of the choices!

When all seems lost, remember to use process of elimination. This may seem obvious, but you'd be amazed at how many times we've seen students throw up their hands and say they're not sure of the answer to a question when three of the four choices are words they surely know! The fact that the remaining choice is unknown does not mean that you should feel unsure. If you know enough about the other three choices to know they are clearly wrong, then you've brought hard-earned knowledge to the exam and deserve to be awarded a point for it!

Remember: The more choices you can rule out based on the knowledge you have, the more you increase your chance of getting the correct answer. This is educated guessing, not wild guessing ... and there's a world of difference between the two!

I know 3 out of the 4 words but none of them fit!
No sweat! The 4th is the answer. Move on and stop worrying!

READING

If you follow the suggested time guidelines for Grammar, Cloze, and Vocabulary, you'll have 40 minutes to work on Reading. Bear in mind that 10 minutes per passage isn't a lot (especially as you'll be nearing exhaustion by the end of the exam!), but if you work carefully and efficiently, you'll still be able to pick up a good number of the available 20 points. Here are some suggestions to help you cope.

Before you begin

- Glance at all four passages. If one seems overly technical or difficult, consider leaving it for the end. This will let you get the most out of the passages that seem easy to you.

As you work through the questions

- Remember that you will be pressed for time on this part. Your goal is to work accurately and efficiently, which means not getting hung up on any one question. If need be, guess and move on. You need to "mine" this section for all the right answers you can ... and there may be easier questions just ahead of one you may get stuck on. Don't let time run out without giving yourself a chance to answer them!

- Don't panic if you see technical terms. Remember that such terms are usually explained the first time they are used. If you find yourself getting hung up because of the technical nature of a passage, skim the questions to see which parts of the text you need to focus on. If that fails as well, guess and move on!

- Remember that ECPE Reading questions tend **not** to be in the order that facts are presented in the text.

- Expect most questions to be straightforward. If you can't justify an answer by pointing to specific details in the text, don't let that work against you. As soon as you feel you're in trouble, shift gears and start eliminating choices that are clearly wrong. If all else fails, **guess** and move on.

- Keep your eyes open for common **distractors**, such as:

  Truth statements: choices that are true but do not answer the question posed in the stem.

  Opposite statements: choices that look like exact paraphrases of details in the text but may include a word or phrase that makes them exactly the opposite of the expected answer.

  Absolute statements: choices that contain words like *always* or *never* that subtly conflict with text phrases such as *sometimes, most of the time, in the majority of cases, hardly ever.*

Tip

Learn to approach each question as if it were four "True or False" statements.

This is one of the wisest test-taking strategies that we have ever come across. We strongly advise you to try it out, as it might be just the strategy you need to turn yourself into a "world-class" test-taker!

The logic behind the technique is simple but elegant! If you test the "truth" of each of the four choices, you will end up with one statement that is "True" and three statements that are "False." This ensures that you carefully consider all four choices until you have ruled out the three that are false and are left with the one that is true.

Try it! It may feel like slow-going at first, but you'll soon pick up speed *and* accuracy!

SPEAKING

Here are a few pointers for handling the Speaking Test.

Several Days before the Test

- Read over the introduction to the Speaking Tests section on pages 192-193 so you know exactly what to expect. Go over the Scoring Criteria for the Speaking Test on page 7 and the "Fluency Builders" chart on page 194 so they are fresh in your mind.
- Review the Speaking Tests at the back of the book to remind yourself of the kinds of information that might be included in the options.
- If you feel you'd benefit from extra practice, invite one or more of your classmates to a practice session and redo some of the tasks that you're already familiar with.

During the Test

Take advantage of the friendly atmosphere that the examiners try to establish. Those butterflies in your stomach will fly away if you take a few deep breaths and try to relax.

Try not to be too dominant or too passive. Remember that you're being tested on your ability to participate in an extended interaction. Being a good listener and building on what your partner says are important, but so are sensing when to give up your turn and inviting your partner to speak.

Remember to maintain eye contact with your partner and the lead examiner. It's all right to refer occasionally to your information sheet as you're speaking, but try not to rely on it. If you do, you'll wind up speaking to it and not to your partner and the examiner.

Don't be afraid to ask your partner to repeat or clarify. If you do, you're demonstrating that you have the skills you need to keep the interaction moving. If you don't, communication may break down.

Speak clearly, confidently, and naturally, and don't panic if you make an occasional mistake in verb tense, structure, or vocabulary. Fluency and overall intelligibility (i.e., how well you make yourself understood) are more important than 100% accuracy.

SPEAKING TIPS

- ✓ Be an active participant.
- ✓ Speak - Know when to give up your turn - Listen!
- ✓ Don't worry about making minor mistakes.

FINAL CHECKLIST: Before you leave home ...

Use this checklist to make sure you have everything you need.

- ✓ **Your official "Receipt / Testing Program"**
  (sent to you or your school by the official test center before the examination)
- ✓ **Your identity card, passport, or equivalent official document**
- ✓ **A good supply of pencils, erasers, and pens**
- ✓ **A watch (your teacher has only one, and she/he can't lend it to everybody!)**

1 Practice Test 1

Writing 30 minutes

- You may write in pen or pencil.
- You will have 30 minutes to write on one of the two topics. If you do not write on one of these topics, your paper will not be scored. If you do not understand the topics, ask the examiner to explain them.
- You may make an outline if you wish, but your outline will not count toward your score.
- Write about one-and-a-half to two pages. Your essay will be marked down if it is extremely short.
- You will not be graded on the appearance of your paper, but your handwriting must be readable. You may change or correct your writing, but you should not recopy the whole essay.
- Your essay will be judged on clarity and overall effectiveness, as well as on topic development, organization, and the range, accuracy, and appropriateness of your grammar and vocabulary. Your essay will be graded at the University of Michigan.

TOPICS For help in writing these compositions, see *Writing Tutorial,* pages 201-202.

1. As Wendell Berry, an American poet, farmer, and essayist, once said, "The right local solutions are often the right global ones." Consider the area that you live in (i.e., your neighborhood or your town), and discuss two changes that you think could be made to help raise the quality of people's life in your community. What global implications might these local changes have?

2. All students in secondary school should be required to study music and art. Do you agree or disagree with this statement? Use specific reasons to support your answer.

FIRST THINGS FIRST

1. Read both topics carefully and decide which you can develop more effectively.
2. Underline key words in the question.
3. Make sure you identify everything the question wants you to do.

Don't be caught sleeping! Some topics have more than one part! If you fail to address any part of the task, you will be marked down.

Listening approx. 35-40 minutes

This section of the examination tests your understanding of spoken English. The listening section has three parts. There are 50 questions. Mark all your answers on the separate answer sheet. Do not make any stray marks on the answer sheet. If you change your mind about an answer, erase your first answer completely.

Part I

In this part, you will hear short conversations. From the three answer choices given, choose the answer which means about the same thing as what you hear, or that is true based upon what you hear.

For problems 1 through 17, mark your answers on the separate answer sheet. No problems can be repeated.

Please listen carefully. Do you have any questions?

Part I of the test examines your ability to interpret short conversations between two speakers. Most items will focus on your ability to recognize the choice that provides an accurate summary or explanation of what you hear. Such questions are similar to gist or main idea questions that you find in the Reading section.

1. **a.** He doesn't object to Chinese food.
b. He's too tired to go out for Chinese.
c. He likes the idea of eating at home.

2. **a.** She's surprised he remembered.
b. She loves what he's given her.
c. The gift is exactly what she wanted.

3. **a.** The medication takes a while to get used to.
b. He plans to stop taking the medication.
c. His doctor was concerned about his reaction.

4. **a.** She frequently travels in the winter.
b. She never arrived at her destination.
c. Her flight took off despite the weather.

5. **a.** Marge has offered to treat her to lunch.
b. Her plans for lunch aren't firm yet.
c. He wants her to help him hang a picture.

6. **a.** She agrees with the court's verdict.
b. She was pushed as she left the court.
c. She was shocked at the outcome.

7. **a.** They're not sure why the door is open.
b. They hope the lock isn't broken.
c. They're relieved that nothing is missing.

8. **a.** She had a lot of money in college.
b. She couldn't afford to have a car back then.
c. She had a bike in college, but never used it.

9. **a.** He thinks his friend will try to cheat him.
b. He's upset because he's been lied to.
c. She thinks his friend is a bit slow.

10. **a.** She doesn't want to make the sauce for him.
b. The tomatoes she has aren't ripe enough.
c. She'll use canned tomatoes in the sauce.

11. **a.** They're at a hotel.
b. They're at a library.
c. They're at a supermarket.

12. **a.** She's been having trouble sleeping.
b. She has to stay late to talk to the boss.
c. She stayed up late to meet a deadline.

13. **a.** Al refuses to take no for an answer.
b. Al is hoping Janet will send him a message.
c. Al is discouraged by Janet's actions.

14. **a.** The film was better than they expected
b. The film didn't live up to its positive reviews.
c. The film was even worse than the critics said.

15. **a.** She's not sure if she's free to come.
b. She'd like to visit if it isn't a problem for him.
c. She's not sure if his invitation is sincere.

16. **a.** If she moves, it will be to a house nearby.
b. She's not interested in moving yet.
c. She needs to have her alarm system fixed.

17. **a.** He'll use a credit card to buy a new laptop.
b. He doesn't really need a new laptop.
c. He's ruled out buying a used laptop.

Part II

In this part, you will hear a question. From the three answer choices given, choose the one which best answers the question.

For problems 18 through 35, mark your answers on the separate answer sheet. No problems can be repeated. Please listen carefully. Do you have any questions?

This part tests your ability to understand the way questions are used in English. Most commonly, we use questions to ask for information or advice. But we can also use them to suggest, offer, request, invite, and complain, as well as to express a wide range of emotions, such as concern, surprise, or anger. As you listen to each question, try thinking about the speaker's purpose. Doing so should help you zero in on the correct printed response.

18. **a.** Have I done something wrong?
b. No, I never said I would do it.
c. I'm not sure. Ask me later.

19. **a.** I didn't realize you had left.
b. I wish you had.
c. Is it really necessary?

20. **a.** I couldn't have.
b. I didn't really have a choice.
c. I'm sure he'll be back soon.

21. **a.** Actually, I'm planning to walk.
b. No, they must not be home.
c. Yes, can I give you a lift?

22. **a.** Even better.
b. I thought so, too.
c. Far from it. In fact, it was fascinating.

23. **a.** The dishwasher was broken.
b. That's why you can't see anything.
c. You're right. Have you got a lens cloth?

24. **a.** Maybe next year.
b. No, I work from home now.
c. No, today I'm driving.

25. **a.** For a few minutes.
b. I had no idea.
c. It's been at least ten years.

26. **a.** I'm not sure. I haven't voted yet.
b. I was ill, so I didn't vote last year.
c. It's hard to say. It could go either way.

27. **a.** Good idea. Let's eat out.
b. I'd rather you didn't.
c. Tonight's out. How about tomorrow?

28. **a.** Because he overslept again.
b. I don't know, but he'd better mend his ways!
c. It's too early to say.

29. **a.** Isn't it yours?
b. Not me. I'll be at the convention.
c. That was your idea. Not mine.

30. **a.** Why don't you call him and see?
b. Speak for yourself.
c. It really is none of his business.

31. **a.** I'm not sure. Is that him over there?
b. No. Are you looking forward to it?
c. Actually, it's been a while.

32. **a.** No, but several people were injured.
b. We all pulled through without a scratch.
c. I'm not sure. I was in the back seat.

33. **a.** No, I thought you did.
b. I was going to, but I changed my mind.
c. I don't think so. Are you sure?

34. **a.** Why do you ask?
b. I don't think you did.
c. Tomorrow would be better

35. **a.** I just got a raise!
b. I'm so hungry, I could eat a horse!
c. I'm tired, that's all.

Use the time before each radio segment begins to skim through the question and answer choices. This will give you a rough idea of what the program is about even before it begins.

Part III

In this part, you will hear three short segments from a radio program. The program is called "Learning from the Experts." You will hear what three different radio guests have to say about three different topics.

Each talk lasts about two minutes. As you listen, you may want to take some notes to help you remember information given in the talk. Write your notes in the test booklet.

After each talk, you will be asked some questions about what was said. From the three answer choices given, you should choose the one that best answers the question according to the information you heard.

Remember, no problems can be repeated. For problems 36 through 50, mark all your answers on the separate answer sheet. Do you have any questions?

SEGMENT 1

36. What is the main focus of the study under discussion?
- **a.** the nuisance potential of personal music devices
- **b.** noise leakage in personal music devices
- **c.** the risks faced by users of personal music devices

37. What point does the study make about the high-volume setting of some music devices?
- **a.** It should only be used for five hours a week.
- **b.** It can be just as loud as a plane taking off.
- **c.** It is just below the limit established by law.

38. What is true about youngsters who regularly listen to personal music devices at high volumes?
- **a.** They will probably suffer hearing loss, but not right away.
- **b.** They will notice serious hearing loss almost immediately.
- **c.** They are less likely to suffer hearing loss than older people.

39. According to the report, which allows the greatest sound exposure and is therefore riskier to use?
- **a.** headphones
- **b.** earbuds
- **c.** portable speakers

40. What does the European Union intend to do, now that the risk has been identified?
- **a.** hold an EU-wide conference to discuss the problem
- **b.** pass a law to impose limits on manufacturing
- **c.** plan further action with the EU's Consumer Affairs Department

SEGMENT 2

41. What is the main focus of the radio segment?
- **a.** animals that can be trained using Pavlov's methods
- **b.** the honeybee's amazing sense of smell
- **c.** a unique military defense project

42. What insects were used in earlier training experiments?
- **a.** dogs
- **b.** wasps
- **c.** bees

43. What have scientists trained bees to do?
- **a.** buzz violently when explosives are present
- **b.** distinguish between different types of explosives
- **c.** detect the presence of a wide range of explosives

(Segment 2 continues at top of next page)

44. What did scientists find significant about the ability of the bees to detect TATP?
 a. It showed that they can detect some scents better than specialized equipment.
 b. It meant that they might be trained to identify and attack suicide bombers.
 c. It proved they were effective even when explosives were masked by other scents.

45. Why are scientists so enthusiastic about their research?
 a. because they are nearing the final stages of the project
 b. because bees are predictable and so easy to train
 c. because they feel their research will help save lives

SEGMENT 3

46. What term does Gene Shaw use to describe misleading claims about a product's environmental benefits?
 a. green credentials
 b. greenwashing
 c. consumer affairs

47. Why are more and more companies so eager to appear green?
 a. because they are genuinely concerned about the environment
 b. because they realize there is a lot of money to be made by doing so
 c. because the government has still not set high enough standards

48. According to Gene Shaw, what might happen if the Federal Trade Commission does not act in a timely fashion to establish stricter standards for green advertising?
 a. The term "green" will become meaningless.
 b. Green products will flood the market.
 c. The demand for green products will vanish.

49. Which of the following is NOT true of the Greenwashing Index website?
 a. It disapproves of the Federal Trade Commission's greenwashing hearings.
 b. It illustrates how consumer awareness can be raised via the Internet.
 c. It provides examples of greenwashing for consumers to evaluate.

50. What point does Gene Shaw leave his listeners with?
 a. There is no such thing as a truly "green" product.
 b. Don't spend your hard-earned money on "green" products.
 c. Many "green" companies are just out to get your money.

Grammar – Cloze – Vocabulary – Reading 75 minutes

This section of the examination contains 120 problems, numbered 51 through 170. There are 40 grammar, 20 cloze, 40 vocabulary, and 20 reading comprehension problems. If you do not understand how to do the problems, raise your hand, and a proctor will explain the examples to you. None of the actual test problems can be explained.

Each problem has only one correct answer. Do not spend too much time on any one problem. If you do not know the answer to a problem, you may guess. Work quickly but carefully. You have one hour and 15 minutes (75 minutes) to answer all 120 problems. If you finish before the time is over, you may check your answers within the GCVR section only. Do not go back to the Listening section of the exam.

The GCVR is long, demanding, and difficult to finish in the allotted time. To maximize your score you must use your time wisely. See page 11 for suggestions on time management.

GRAMMAR

51. The bank has over 100 branches, _____ in a major urban area.
- **a.** each locating
- **b.** each located
- **c.** the location of which
- **d.** and are located

52. There's been a rash of burglaries in our area _____ the last few months.
- **a.** since
- **b.** through
- **c.** over
- **d.** while

53. _____ is someone who can reduce spending without hurting morale.
- **a.** What is needed
- **b.** What needs
- **c.** Being needed
- **d.** That which needs

54. The boss left firm instructions: under no circumstances _____ unattended.
- **a.** should the office leave
- **b.** is the office to be left
- **c.** we are to leave the office
- **d.** should leave the office

55. Ed loves to get books for his birthday, so I'm going to let him choose one of _____ .
- **a.** exciting new two spy novels
- **b.** two spy exciting new novels
- **c.** new two exciting spy novels
- **d.** two exciting new spy novels

56. The guidance counselor urged _____ a foreign language.
- **a.** all of us studying
- **b.** us all to study
- **c.** all that we study
- **d.** that all we study

57. We regret _____ that your rent is three months in arrears.
- **a.** to inform you
- **b.** you to inform
- **c.** you having informed
- **d.** that we informed you

58. I hope he won't be disappointed. He seems _____ confident for his own good.
- **a.** so very
- **b.** much too
- **c.** extremely
- **d.** more than

59. She has a 12-year-old and a 5-year-old, so I guess I spoke to the _____ two.
- **a.** older one out of
- **b.** one who is older than the
- **c.** older of the
- **d.** older than the

60. I thought we would need to have another meeting on the issue, but now I _____ .
- **a.** think so
- **b.** think not
- **c.** don't think
- **d.** think it isn't

61. _____ could only have been made by someone totally incompetent.
   a. How serious a mistake
   b. So serious a mistake
   c. Such serious mistake
   d. So serious is this mistake

62. The student was making so much noise in the library that he _____ to leave.
   a. told him
   b. was being told
   c. asked
   d. was asked

63. It's urgent _____ of the problem as soon as humanly possible.
   a. to be informed the boss
   b. the boss be informed
   c. the boss's being informing
   d. informing the boss

64. The _____ section of our supermarket has a wide range of fresh fruits and vegetables.
   a. production
   b. productive
   c. produce
   d. product

65. Those flowers must have cost a fortune; he really _____ them for her.
   a. needn't have to buy
   b. shouldn't have bought
   c. mustn't have bought
   d. ought not have to buy

66. We stopped at a motel _____ we wouldn't arrive in Chicago in the middle of the night.
   a. so that
   b. because
   c. for fear that
   d. in case

67. Global warming has progressed _____ glaciers everywhere are shrinking.
   a. too much that
   b. enough to cause
   c. to such an extent that
   d. so great an extent that

68. You said you were leaving, _____ you're still here. Is everything all right?
   a. yet
   b. while
   c. so
   d. even if

STEP 1: Analyze the stem and choices.

STEP 2: Figure out what grammar topic is being tested.

STEP 3: Work through each item choice by choice.

69. _____ a small creature that defends itself with lobster-like claws and a poisonous sting.
   a. Scorpions are
   b. Many a scorpion is
   c. The scorpion is
   d. A scorpion, which is

70. Jonathan still has the accordion his grandfather gave him, but _____ .
   a. he has years to play it
   b. it has years to have not been played
   c. it hasn't played for years
   d. it's been years since he played it

71. She insisted that the reporter _____ her as his source of information.
   a. not mention
   b. not to mention
   c. don't mention
   d. not mentioning

72. It's unlikely that two students would write identical compositions without _____ .
   a. one who copies the other
   b. one copying from the other
   c. one to copy the other's
   d. each other's copying

73. Allowing students to do most of the talking in class is a common _____ strategy.
   a. instructive
   b. instructional
   c. instructing
   d. instruct

74. _____ traveling is educational, it can also be stressful and expensive.
   a. Since
   b. Providing
   c. While
   d. As though

75. We've been walking for hours, so _____ break for a few minutes, shall we?
   a. let's
   b. why not a
   c. how about a
   d. maybe we should

76. _____ factories continue to comply with the law, improved air quality will not diminish.
   a. As soon as
   b. As far as
   c. As long as
   d. As little as

77. Company policy states that, upon arrival, all employees are _____ at the front desk.
   a. to sign in
   b. signing in
   c. having to sign in
   d. going to have to sign in

78. Such _____ that none of the students in the class could solve it.
   a. a difficult problem it was
   b. a difficult problem was it
   c. difficult a problem was it
   d. was the problem difficult

79. They arrived home only _____ the house had been burgled in their absence.
   a. upon finding
   b. to find that
   c. after having found
   d. then did they find

80. He may or may not come with us, but I'm not sure _____ depends on.
   a. that it
   b. what it
   c. whether or not he
   d. about what he

81. There were three eye witnesses. Is it possible he'll deny _____ the crime?
   a. he committed
   b. he commits
   c. to commit
   d. to committing

82. _____ the Coast Guard, not a single life was lost in the ferry accident.
   a. Were it not for
   b. Regardless of
   c. As a result of
   d. Thanks to

83. At the current rate, the company's sales _____ $3 million by the end of the year.
   a. are exceeding
   b. will have exceeded
   c. had exceeded
   d. would be exceeded

84. The boss won't be able to see you today as he's got several _____ meetings.
   a. two hours
   b. two-hour
   c. two hours'
   d. two hour's

85. When deciding on a new computer, you should buy _____ you can afford.
   a. the one whichever
   b. which one that
   c. whichever one
   d. the one that which

86. Unfortunately, you're required to take the exam _____ you want to or not.
   a. either
   b. what if
   c. whether
   d. in case

87. The accountant broke the law, so it would be irresponsible of the firm _____ .
   a. if they won't fire him
   b. not to fire him
   c. that they not fire him
   d. for not firing him

88. I hope everything's OK. They _____ several hours ago.
   a. were to have called
   b. would have called
   c. must have called
   d. supposed to call

89. If he _____ a doctor's appointment, he would have been at work yesterday.
   a. wouldn't have had
   b. hasn't had
   c. didn't have
   d. hadn't had

90. The two men were never friendly in the past; _____ get along in the future.
   a. nor are they likely to
   b. and still won't they
   c. neither won't they
   d. and yet they won't

STEP 1: Skim whole passage for gist.
STEP 2: Think about what is missing and what is tested.
STEP 3: Work through the passage, item by item, choice by choice.
STEP 4: Reread the passage with your answers in place.

CLOZE

Passage 1 is about global warming.

For many years, global warming was portrayed in the media as an issue with two sides. Some scientists argued that global warming was occurring, and others argued that it was __(91)__ . However, this portrayal was an oversimplification of the debate. Skeptics of global warming, __(92)__ some scientists, __(93)__ to lingering scientific uncertainties that caused them to question whether global warming was actually occurring. However, there is now __(94)__ evidence that global temperatures are increasing, based __(95)__ direct temperature measurements and observations of other impacts such as __(96)__ glaciers and polar ice, rising sea levels, and changes in the life __(97)__ of plants and animals.

As the scientific evidence on rising global temperatures became indisputable, skeptics began to focus on whether human activities are in fact the __(98)__ of global warming. They argued that the observed warming could be caused by natural processes such as changes in the energy __(99)__ by the sun. However, the sun's influence has been found to have contributed only __(100)__ to observed warming, particularly since the mid-20th century. In fact, there is now overwhelming evidence that greenhouse gas emissions from human activities are the main cause of the warming.

91. a. false b. mistake c. not d. so

92. a. containing b. including c. comprising d. composing

93. a. pointed b. showed c. leading d. indicated

94. a. unacceptable b. invalid c. inconceivable d. undeniable

95. a. by b. in c. from d. on

96. a. fading b. melting c. sinking d. expanding

97. a. cycles b. style c. histories d. expectancy

98. a. reason b. fault c. cause d. result

99. a. emerging b. emitted c. radiating d. production

100. a. slightly b. vaguely c. vastly d. significantly

Passage 2 is about acupuncture.

A key component of traditional Chinese medicine, acupuncture is most commonly used, both in the East and the West, as a means of alleviating pain. Some people are __(101)__ by the thought of acupuncture and may feel __(102)__ takes a great deal of courage to __(103)__ treatment on themselves. The first and probably most important fact to understand about acupuncture is that it is not a frightening experience. It __(104)__ , however, involve the __(105)__ of fine needles through the skin; most acupuncturists use __(106)__ six and twelve acupuncture needles at each session. The needles __(107)__ are smaller than injection needles; in __(108)__ , an acupuncture needle can fit into the central hole of a normal injection needle. Acupuncture needles do not __(109)__ a cutting end like most hypodermic needles, which means they are far less __(110)__ to cause tissue damage or bruising when inserted.

101. a. afraid b. fearful c. frightened d. horrifying

102. a. like b. that c. one d. it

103. a. afflict b. inflict c. conflict d. inject

104. a. may b. always c. does d. is

105. a. insertion b. installation c. interjection d. intervention

106. a. among b. about c. approximately d. between

107. a. that b. used c. they d. points

108. a. all b. spite c. fact d. case

109. a. have b. make c. inject d. involve

110. a. going b. likely c. due d. painful

VOCABULARY

STEP 1: Read each stem carefully, so you have a clear idea of the meaning before making your choice.

STEP 2: Check to see if a preposition or particle follows the blank.

STEP 3: Consider the choices one by one. Rule out any you know are wrong; then guess if you have to.

111. I'm shocked that he had the nerve to tell such an _____ lie.
- **a.** outright
- **b.** enigmatic
- **c.** obscure
- **d.** abundant

112. The company is famous for making sturdy work clothes that can _____ hard wear.
- **a.** stand up to
- **b.** stand up for
- **c.** stand in for
- **d.** stand out against

113. Employees are advised to take _____ of the changes in company policy.
- **a.** hold
- **b.** notice
- **c.** root
- **d.** effect

114. The day their first child was born, the new parents were _____ with joy.
- **a.** overpowered
- **b.** overtaken
- **c.** overthrown
- **d.** overcome

115. The audience was _____ by the dancer's brilliant performance.
- **a.** detained
- **b.** dazzled
- **c.** detested
- **d.** diversified

116. Keeping a journal is an excellent way to give _____ to your feelings.
- **a.** voice
- **b.** rise
- **c.** way
- **d.** pause

117. Laughter is often _____ . If one person begins to laugh, everyone else joins in.
- **a.** contagious
- **b.** contingent
- **c.** conspicuous
- **d.** conceivable

118. The writer's _____ is prodigious: he's written more than 20 best-selling novels.
- **a.** produce
- **b.** harvest
- **c.** output
- **d.** manufacture

119. The _____ child is forever asking questions. He's incredibly curious.
- **a.** acquisitive
- **b.** acquitted
- **c.** inquisitive
- **d.** exquisite

120. He's head over heels in love with her. It's as if she has cast _____ over him.
- **a.** a pall
- **b.** a spell
- **c.** an eye
- **d.** doubt

121. They're asking $5,000 for the used car, but the price is _____ .
- **a.** negligible
- **b.** negotiable
- **c.** unconditional
- **d.** underhanded

122. Police have not yet managed to _____ the stolen goods.
- **a.** apprehend
- **b.** redeem
- **c.** recover
- **d.** interrogate

123. The optimistic manager saw the drop in sales as a temporary _____ .
- **a.** backdrop
- **b.** comeback
- **c.** downfall
- **d.** setback

124. If you think you're right, then _____ . Don't let him bully you into changing your mind.
- **a.** stand your ground
- **b.** stand still
- **c.** stand clear
- **d.** stand corrected

125. At the end of the broadcast, the TV station received a _____ of complaints.
  a. hurricane
  b. current
  c. torrent
  d. tide

126. The doctors made every _____ effort to save the patient's life.
  a. conceivable
  b. imaginative
  c. available
  d. knowledgeable

127. The controversial new film has caused quite a _____ in the national press.
  a. sensation
  b. publicity
  c. spectacle
  d. reception

128. The lecturer gave several examples to _____ her point.
  a. sharpen
  b. illustrate
  c. debate
  d. conclude

129. The comedian's subtle quips caused everyone to _____ .
  a. exaggerate
  b. pant
  c. sob
  d. chuckle

130. Much to his _____, his efforts to find employment have been fruitless.
  a. amusement
  b. dismay
  c. benefit
  d. credit

131. Monica's sense of humor is a bit _____ . Sometimes I wish she were more upbeat.
  a. fragile
  b. buoyant
  c. grim
  d. impending

132. Her voice is so _____ that she's often mistaken for a man.
  a. low-key
  b. low-pitched
  c. downcast
  d. downtrodden

133. Students were chosen to participate in the study _____ .
  a. by accident
  b. in sequence
  c. at random
  d. on impact

134. Clinical trials show that the vaccine _____ immunity against the disease.
  a. boosts
  b. lowers
  c. formulates
  d. resists

135. The senator believes that national security must take _____ over health care.
  a. advantage
  b. precedence
  c. place
  d. control

136. Despite the rising cost of tuition, college _____ continue to increase each year.
  a. entrances
  b. permits
  c. admissions
  d. entries

137. The situation is more _____ than we originally believed.
  a. perplexed
  b. sophisticated
  c. eminent
  d. complicated

138. Recent outbreaks signify that the disease has not yet been _____ .
  a. repealed
  b. extinguished
  c. overthrown
  d. eradicated

139. The team has come up against some _____ opponents this year.
  a. elaborate
  b. devastated
  c. formidable
  d. oppressive

140. How can you work with all the _____ coming from the construction site?
  a. squeals
  b. trumpeting
  c. racket
  d. groans

141. The old, run-down house was _____ with mice and cockroaches.
   a. affected
   b. inflicted
   c. infested
   d. afflicted

142. You'll need a(n) _____ dictionary if you want to find the meaning of such a technical word.
   a. unabridged
   b. lengthy
   c. elongated
   d. expanded

143. The child's _____ questions were beginning to get on her nerves.
   a. consistent
   b. recurrent
   c. pertinent
   d. persistent

144. You'll have to speak up. Grandmother is rather _____ of hearing.
   a. difficulty
   b. impaired
   c. hard
   d. deaf

145. I was depending on you to help me move this weekend. You can't _____ now.
   a. back out
   b. back away
   c. pass up
   d. pass away

146. The popular politician won the election by a(n) _____ majority.
   a. overwhelming
   b. ruthless
   c. contagious
   d. unanimous

147. I've been feeling fatigued and run-down the past few days. I must be _____ something.
   a. coming out with
   b. coming down with
   c. coming up with
   d. coming in for

148. As Christmas approached, she couldn't help but find the children's enthusiasm _____ .
   a. infectious
   b. catchy
   c. deadly
   d. restrained

149. He spent the morning in the yard, _____ the hedges.
   a. truncating
   b. shortening
   c. contracting
   d. trimming

150. If a solution cannot be reached through diplomacy, military _____ may be necessary.
   a. interaction
   b. intervention
   c. intersection
   d. integration

STEP 1: Skim for gist.

STEP 2: As you do each item, read the question and underline key words.

STEP 3: Scan to find info; read surrounding text carefully.

STEP 4: Reread the question; consider all four choices.

READING

Passage 1 is about a papyrus expert.

Dirk Obbink is the University Lecturer in Papyrology at Oxford University and, as such, helps curate the university's papyrus collection, the largest in the world. By any measure, his job stretches the meaning of "painstaking." Aided by computer technology and a humble pair of tweezers, Obbink spends his days piecing together postage-stamp remnants of papyrus, the material that was used as paper by Egyptians, Greeks, and Romans from the sixth century B.C. until the eighth century A.D.

Obbink is best known for his clever deciphering of papyri from Herculaneum, a settlement in Italy which along with Pompeii was buried under ash when Vesuvius erupted in A.D. 79. Excavators in the 1750s had retrieved some 1,500 papyri from a single villa, but over the years scholars had done more harm than good. At times they had to split the hardened scrolls apart, as if cutting into a charred onion to get at its undamaged core. The result was thousands of badly labeled fragments, which became further scrambled when moved to Naples. Over time, little progress was made until Obbink arrived and began to sort things out. Building on the work of previous scholars, he noticed a syntax match between the end of one page and the start of another. He put more bits in order by using numbers jotted on the fragments by 19th-century copyists. More fell into place when he figured out the labeling system used by the scholars who had cut the scrolls apart. And then he devised a formula that enabled him to reconstruct a halved papyrus by assuming that its pieces would get larger as they approached the outermost layer of the scroll. The work, which made accessible a great library of writings and the lost world they represented, dazzled his colleagues.

Obbink and his colleagues now spend their time attempting to restore and interpret Oxford's cache of more than 50,000 scraps of papyrus – including lost works by Sappho and Sophocles – from Oxyrhynchus, a Greek settlement that thrived more than 2,300 years ago 200 miles south of Cairo. When asked to predict when they might finish, Obbink chuckled: "There's enough here for 40 lifetimes."

151. Which quality does Obbink's job **not** require?
- **a.** a knowledge of ancient languages
- **b.** a tolerance for intense pain
- **c.** patience and discipline
- **d.** scrupulous attention to detail

152. What is true of Obbink's work on the papyri of Herculaneum?
- **a.** He figured out how to split the hardened scrolls.
- **b.** He had access to better libraries than his predecessors.
- **c.** He benefited from clues left by previous scholars.
- **d.** It took him years to repair the damage of his predecessors.

153. How long had the Herculaneum papyri remained buried under ash?
- **a.** almost 300 years
- **b.** more than 1,600 years
- **c.** since the 18th century
- **d.** for more than two thousand years

154. What do the papyri from Herculaneum and the papyri from Oxyrhynchus have in common?
- **a.** They are from the same period of history.
- **b.** They were written in the same language.
- **c.** They are in storage at Oxford University.
- **d.** They must be reassembled piece by piece.

155. What is true of the status of Obbink's current project?
- **a.** Work on the papyri is not likely to be finished any time soon.
- **b.** He and his colleagues are on the verge of an important discovery.
- **c.** Work has been hampered by the age of the fragments.
- **d.** The scrolls are in even worse shape than the Herculaneum papyri.

Passage 2 is about cacao production.

Today 70% of all chocolate beans come from west and central Africa, where growers use so-called pioneer farming. They strip patches of forest of all but the tallest canopy trees and then plant cacao, using temporary plantings of banana to shade the cacao while it's young. With luck, such groves produce annual yields of 50 to 60 pods per tree for 25 to 30 years. But eventually pests, disease, and soil exhaustion take their toll and yields diminish. Then the growers move on and clear a new forest patch – unless farmers of other crops get there first. "But they can't keep cutting tropical forest, because the forest itself is endangered," says one expert. "Global chocolate demand increases on average by 3 percent a year. With a lack of land for new plantings in tropical forests, how do you meet that?"

Since deforestation is a problem wherever cacao is grown, sustainability is now the mantra on many people's lips. Sustainable farming involves land rehabilitation – reclaiming old farms and recycling weedy spaces into cacao fields – and adopting practices that extend a farm's productive life, such as planting enough shade trees to help recycle nutrients and maintain overall soil fertility. While this arrangement produces fewer beans than a plantation with more light and fewer shade trees, farmers can increase the potential value of their efforts by planting other tree crops along with cacao. Cacao trees dispersed in a woody mix take more time to care for and harvest; but the resulting diversity helps stabilize a farmer's income and keep diseases at bay.

Agroforestry experts push this thinking even further, believing that creating new forest is the way to go. "Take a despoiled area on the fringe of pristine forest," says another expert. "Replant it to create a buffer for the forest and a foundation for expansion. If things are done right, it will mimic a wild cacao forest in Ecuador. What you want is a multi-layered cacophony of trees, not just canopy and undergrowth. You want ground cover, shrubs, small trees, intermediate ones, and canopy, plus a robust soil life underneath it all to help maintain and expand things." Besides cacao, experts also envisage fruit trees, spice shrubs, and income-producing timber trees as being vital factors, depending on local growing conditions and markets.

156. What is the writer's main idea?
- **a.** However farmers grow cacao, they can't meet global demand.
- **b.** Cacao farming is inherently devastating for the environment.
- **c.** The future of cacao farming lies in reclaiming old cacao farms.
- **d.** Cacao growers would reap many benefits by embracing sustainability.

157. What does the writer imply about pioneer farming?
- **a.** It contributes to deforestation and soil depletion.
- **b.** It is a sustainable form of cacao cultivation.
- **c.** It can easily keep up with global cacao demand.
- **d.** It results in increased crop yields as time goes on.

158. How would it benefit cacao farmers to plant a mix of other tree crops along with cacao?
- **a.** It would increase the yield of their cacao trees.
- **b.** The cacao beans would be easier to pick.
- **c.** Their income would not depend on a single crop.
- **d.** It would eliminate all risk of disease.

159. What is true about the presence of shade trees on a cacao farm?
- **a.** It is not a necessary component of pioneer farming.
- **b.** It prevents the soil from becoming less fertile.
- **c.** It guarantees that the cacao plants will remain pest-free.
- **d.** It is strongly discouraged by supporters of sustainability.

160. According to one of the experts cited, cacao farming is most desirable when it …
- **a.** is done in areas with canopy trees and low undergrowth.
- **b.** recreates the conditions of an unspoiled tropical forest.
- **c.** takes place on the edge of an endangered forest.
- **d.** finds a way to keep up with growing global demand.

Passage 3 is about cars and highway safety.

You don't have to hoist yourself into a 14-mile-per-gallon, gas-guzzling sport utility vehicle (SUV) to be safe on the highway. While that's been the hunch of many an accident-free driver, it's now the conclusion of U.S. Department of Energy researchers, who performed a "risk analysis" using crash data from the Insurance Institute for Highway Safety. Their neatly graphed results, which unblinkingly chart annual deaths per million vehicles sold for 40 different models, show that drivers of many small cars are statistically safer than drivers of the average SUV. That will alarm SUV drivers who assumed that, if nothing else, they could guarantee their own protection on the interstate. But more than a dozen passenger cars, including the subcompact, fuel-efficient Volkswagen Jetta and Honda Civic, protect drivers better than SUVs.

The study also found that most passenger cars are safer than the average sport utility vehicle or pickup truck when the risk posed to other drivers is taken into account, a figure the researchers call "combined risk." Even the safest SUV on the road, the mammoth Chevrolet Suburban, is bested by much smaller Honda Accords and Toyota Camrys. The safest vehicles of them all? Minivans and imported luxury cars. The worst: full-size Chevrolet, Ford, and Dodge pickup trucks.

So much for the conventional wisdom that large cars are inherently safe and small cars inherently dangerous. A wide disparity in results among small cars like the front-running Jetta and Civic and the relatively risky Ford Escort and Dodge Neon suggests that vehicle design is more important than sheer mass. "The argument that lowering the weight of cars to achieve high fuel economy has resulted in excess deaths is unfounded," says one of the authors of the report. "Safety is a challenging concept. It includes the design of the car itself, driver demographics, and behavior, the kinds of roads, the time of day – a whole host of factors." While highway safety is complex, one thing is clear: A safety-conscious driver need not purchase a vehicle by the pound.

161. What commonly believed idea has the study disproved?

- **a.** SUVs are more fuel efficient than smaller cars.
- **b.** SUVs are more dangerous than small cars.
- **c.** SUVs are safer than smaller cars.
- **d.** SUVs are heavier than smaller cars.

162. According to the passage, which of the following received the best safety rating?

- **a.** full-size pickup trucks
- **b.** subcompacts
- **c.** minivans
- **d.** SUVs

163. How do the Ford Escort and Dodge Neon differ from the Volkswagen Jetta and Honda Civic?

- **a.** They weigh considerably more.
- **b.** They are not as fuel efficient.
- **c.** They are much less massive.
- **d.** Their design makes them less safe.

164. Of the following, which is the largest?

- **a.** the Chevrolet Suburban
- **b.** the Honda Accord
- **c.** the Toyota Camry
- **d.** the Volkswagen Jetta

165. Which of the following best sums up the main idea of the passage?

- **a.** Drivers should think twice about fuel economy.
- **b.** Fuel economy has resulted in fewer accidents.
- **c.** The smaller the model, the safer the driver.
- **d.** Cars can be both fuel efficient and safe.

Passage 4 is about bird feathers.

The feathers of birds, collectively called plumage, play several roles. Brightly colored plumage, sometimes including ornamental feathers called plumes, is often influential in attracting a mate, but display of such plumage is used with equal frequency by males to try to intimidate other males competing for females or for territory. Some birds are camouflaged to resemble their surroundings, thus escaping the notice of possible predators. They sometimes even take on a pose that enhances the protective coloration. The marsh-dwelling herons called bitterns "freeze" with their striped necks and long bills pointing straight up, emphasizing their resemblance to the surrounding reeds. The screech owls, which have a plumage pattern that resembles tree bark, close their large eyes and stretch very thin, thus often passing for a stubby, broken branch. In many species of birds, including most ducks and pheasants, adult males are brightly colored, whereas the more vulnerable females and young blend into the background.

Most adult birds molt at least once a year, with the exception that molting of the flight feathers of the wings can extend over two years in a few very large birds such as eagles and cranes. Feathers are subject to physical wear and become faded and brittle with long exposure to sunlight. During molting, new feathers grow within follicles in the skin, pushing out the old feathers, which are dead structures. Molt cycles often go hand in hand with other cycles. In most migratory species, the new plumage is grown after breeding and before autumn migration.

The importance of a bird's feathers is reflected in the amount of time each bird spends preening (that is, cleaning and arranging its plumage with its bill). The preen or uropygeal gland, situated at the base of the bird's tail, secretes oil that is used in preening. The oil keeps the feathers in good condition but also waterproofs them and so is particularly important for sea and water birds.

166. What is true about protective coloration?
- **a.** It is rarely, if ever, found in adult female birds.
- **b.** It allows weaker birds to avoid their enemies.
- **c.** It is ineffective unless the bird adopts a pose.
- **d.** It serves to help birds intimidate predators.

167. How does brightly colored plumage benefit certain male birds?
- **a.** It helps them fight off aggressive females.
- **b.** It helps them avoid predators.
- **c.** It helps them compete for females.
- **d.** It serves as protective coloration.

168. What does the writer imply about reeds (line 7)?
- **a.** They are long, thin, woody plants that grow in marshes.
- **b.** They are striped plants that grow in icy marsh water.
- **c.** They are birds that very closely resemble bitterns.
- **d.** They are an effective form of protective coloration.

169. What is **not** true about preening?
- **a.** It keeps the feathers waterproof and in good condition.
- **b.** It involves an oil produced at the base of the tail.
- **c.** It helps to keep the feathers properly arranged.
- **d.** It is necessary only on a very infrequent basis.

170. What does the molting process involve?
- **a.** the preening and waterproofing of old feathers
- **b.** the replacement of old feathers with new ones
- **c.** the production of oils in the uropygeal gland
- **d.** a resting phase between breeding and migrating

Vocabulary Enhancement

A Planet Is A Terrible Thing To Waste

While working through Cloze Passage 1 on page 24, did you encounter environmental words you hadn't seen before? Let's see how good your awareness of environment-related vocabulary is.

A **Odd One Out** – In groups 1-3, each four-element grouping contains three words or phrases that have something in common and a fourth word or phrase that is related but essentially different. Study each grouping and underline the word or phrase that is the "odd one out." Then match the number of each grouping with its explanation below. Some of the words may be unfamiliar, so use a dictionary and share what you find with your classmates.

GROUP 1: Physical Features

1.	glacier	ice cap	reef	iceberg
2.	dam	pond	lake	reservoir
3.	promontory	peninsula	cape	island
4.	canyon	cavern	gorge	ravine
5.	swamp	wetland	desert	marsh
6.	habitat	biosphere	ecosystem	environment
7.	plains	mountain	plateau	volcano

Now identify the grouping (1-7) that contains ...

a. _______ – three areas of land that are "spongy" with water and another that is extremely arid (i.e., dry)

b. _______ – three areas of land that extend out into the sea and a land mass totally surrounded by water

c. _______ – three freshwater bodies and a wall that holds back water

d. _______ – three frozen masses of ice and a natural "wall" of coral, sand, etc., below the surface of the sea

e. _______ – three kinds of deep narrow valleys cut by a river and a large, dark hollow place in the earth

f. _______ – three landforms that rise well above sea level and a large area of low flat land

g. _______ – three ways to refer to the place an animal/plant lives and a general term for the entire area that supports life on and surrounding the earth

GROUP 2: Natural Catastrophes

1.	tidal wave	deluge	flood	avalanche
2.	hurricane	blizzard	tornado	gale
3.	lava	earthquake	fault	tremor
4.	drought	famine	humidity	starvation

Now identify the grouping (1-4) that contains ...

a. _______ – three things of interest to a seismologist and one related to volcanic eruptions

b. _______ – three conditions related to a prolonged lack of rain and one that means "moisture in the air"

c. _______ – three weather events that are "watery" and one that is "snowy"

d. _______ – three violent wind storms and one windy snowstorm

GROUP 3: Manmade Catastrophes

1.	overpopulation	food shortages	birth control	dwindling natural resources
2.	global warming	greenhouse effect	air pollution	hole in the ozone layer
3.	intensive logging	erosion	deforestation	desertification
4.	landfill	garbage dump	recycling bin	trash can
5.	oil spills	acid rain	factory fumes	car exhaust

Now identify the grouping (1-5) that contains ...

a. ________ – three causes of pollution and one result

b. ________ – three places where waste is put and never used again, and one where it awaits treatment for reuse

c. ________ – a major world problem and its ramifications, plus something that could help minimize it

d. ________ – a human activity and its devastating environmental results

e. ________ – three broad environmental problems and a natural phenomenon that has always been with us

B **Photographic Recall** – Study the photos and label each one with one of the featured words or phrases in Groups 1-3 above. More than one answer may be possible.

1
____

2
____

3
____

4
____

5
____

6
____

7
____

8
____

9
____

10
____

11
____

12
____

Vocabulary Consolidation

VEXING VERBS

A Common Collocations – Complete each phrase with a word from the box.

apprehend | *be overcome with* | *cast* | *come in for* | *extinguish* | *pass up* | *resist* | *sob*

1. ________________ like a baby
2. ________________ emotion
3. ________________ temptation
4. ________________ a shock
5. ________________ a fire
6. ________________ doubt on a theory
7. ________________ a promotion
8. ________________ an escaped prisoner

B Fine-Tuning Your Knowledge – The numbers below refer to questions in the Vocabulary sections of Practice Test 1. After reviewing the words, fill in each blank with the correct form of the appropriate verb.

112. stand up to **stand up for** **stand in for** **stand out**	**a.** Our math teacher is ill today, so another teacher is ________________ him. **b.** The moon ________________ clearly against the cloudless night sky. **c.** This diver's watch is specially designed to ________________ hard wear. **d.** If you knew I was right, why didn't you ________________ me? Then the two of us could have ________________ the boss together.
115. detain **dazzle** **detest** **diversify**	**a.** I ________________ the way the boss's wife orders us around. **b.** The talented rock star has been ________________ audiences for decades. **c.** Financial advisors recommend that their clients ________________ their holdings. **d.** The police have ________________ several suspects for further questioning.
122. apprehend **interrogate** **recover** **redeem**	**a.** Only by solving the difficult case could he ________________ his tarnished reputation. **b.** It took them time to ________________ from the shock of finding a burglar in the house. **c.** Can anyone fully ________________ the criminal mind? **d.** Whenever he comes home late, his parents ________________ him as if he were a suspect in a murder case.
128. conclude **debate** **illustrate** **sharpen**	**a.** To ________________ his point, the speaker gave several interesting examples. **b.** After ________________ the issue for several hours, a decision has still not been made. **c.** The threat of terrorism has ________________ everyone's awareness. **d.** The commission has ________________ that the mayor acted inappropriately.
134. boost **formulate** **lower** **resist**	**a.** Let's meet on Wednesday to ________________ a plan of action. **b.** To ________________ the economy, Congress plans to ________________ taxes. **c.** White blood cells help the body ________________ disease. **d.** Lack of sleep can ________________ one's resistance to disease. Exercise and proper diet, however, are good ways to ________________ the immune system.
138. eradicate **extinguish** **overthrow** **repeal**	**a.** Tighter security helps, but the terrorist threat has not been ________________ . **b.** If a law is found to be unconstitutional, it must be ________________ . **c.** The blaze proved difficult to ________________ . **d.** If the dictator is ________________ , who will take his place?

NOTORIOUS NOUNS

A Amusing Associations – Find the word in the box that is suggested by each prompt.

a pall	*a spectacle*	*a current*	*notice*	*produce*	*publicity*	*way*	*your downfall*

1. ______________ – If you're lucky, your friends won't cast one of these over your next party.
2. ______________ – Fresh is best: from avocadoes and bananas to yams and zucchini.
3. ______________ – If you embarrass easily, you don't want to make this of yourself.
4. ______________ – You don't want to get stuck in one of these when swimming at the beach.
5. ______________ – When actors crave this, they call up a few of their favorite paparazzi.
6. ______________ – A piece of chocolate cake might be this if you're struggling to lose weight.
7. ______________ – You'll want to give this if you see a truck heading straight at you.
8. ______________ – You'll want to take this if your teacher says something is important.

B Fine-Tuning Your Knowledge – The numbers below refer to questions in the Vocabulary sections of Practice Test 1. After reviewing the words, fill in each blank with the appropriate word.

118. harvest **manufacture** **output** **produce**	**a.** This year's grape ______________ was devastated by heavy rainfall. **b.** She prefers to buy ______________ at the farmers' market every Friday. **c.** Until 1990, the firm was engaged in the ______________ of manual typewriters. **d.** Unexpected demand has forced the factory to increase their ______________ .
120. doubt **eye** **pall** **spell**	**a.** Could you cast a(n) ______________ over Tom's report? Something seems wrong. **b.** The director's gloomy announcement cast a(n) ______________ over the employees. **c.** She's been very absent-minded lately, as if someone's cast a(n) ______________ on her. **d.** The new findings cast ______________ on the notion that SUVs are safer than smaller car models.
125. current **hurricane** **tide** **torrent**	**a.** A ______________ of political unrest could be felt throughout the capital. **b.** I'm shocked he disagreed with them. It's not like him to go against the ______________ . **c.** Suddenly the sky blackened and rain began to fall in ______________ . **d.** Ed blew through here like a ______________ a while ago, but I haven't seen him since.
130. amusement **benefit** **credit** **dismay**	**a.** The proposed tax deductions would be to everyone's ______________ . **b.** To everyone's ______________ , the clown slipped on the banana peel. **c.** To everyone's ______________ , the test was extremely difficult. **d.** I didn't think he'd succeed but, to his ______________ , he managed to pay for his own college education.
136. admission **entrance** **entry** **permit**	**a.** If you want to learn to drive, you need to apply for a learner's ______________ . **b.** Hospital ______________ skyrocketed during the heat wave last summer. **c.** Every ______________ in a learner's dictionary has at least one example. **d.** The building's main ______________ is on Fifth Avenue.
140. groan **racket** **squeal** **trumpet**	**a.** Who's making all that ______________ ? I can't think straight. **b.** The child let out a ______________ of delight when he opened the present. **c.** Suddenly we heard a ______________ of pain coming from the bushes. **d.** Everyone at the zoo could hear the ______________ of the elephants.

AUDACIOUS ADJECTIVES

A Common Collocations – Complete each phrase with a word from the box.

available *conspicuous* *contagious* *exquisite* *formidable* *negotiable* *perplexed* *unconditional*

1. be _______________ by one's absence
2. demand an enemy's _______________ surrender
3. try every means _______________
4. pose a(n) _______________ threat to someone
5. suggest that a price is _______________
6. contract a(n) _______________ disease
7. have _______________ taste in music
8. have a(n) _______________ look on one's face

B Fine-Tuning Your Knowledge – The numbers below refer to questions in the Vocabulary section of Practice Test 1. After reviewing the words, fill in each blank with the appropriate word.

111. abundant **enigmatic** **obscure** **outright**	**a.** South Africa is a country with _______________ natural resources. **b.** What he told you is an _______________ lie! Do you really believe him? **c.** Why are you being so _______________? Why don't you just tell us? **d.** The scholar has spent years studying an _______________ 17th-century writer who few people have heard of.
119. acquisitive **acquitted** **exquisite** **inquisitive**	**a.** _______________ children are always asking questions. **b.** Everyone agreed that the bride looked _______________ in her wedding gown. **c.** We live in an _______________ materialistic society. **d.** The _______________ defendant walked out of the courtroom a free woman. It was an _______________ victory for the defense attorneys.
121. negligible **negotiable** **unconditional** **underhanded**	**a.** The general says he will accept nothing less than _______________ surrender. **b.** You'd be OK with either car; the difference in their safety ratings is _______________ . **c.** He has my _______________ trust. He's never done anything that I consider _______________ . **d.** The terms of the contract we're offering you are not _______________ . Either you accept them as they are, or the deal is off.
126. available **conceivable** **imaginative** **knowledgeable**	**a.** He's an _______________ artist who is also extremely _______________ about art history. **b.** If you're _______________ tomorrow evening, I'd love to have dinner with you. **c.** If you need computer advice, Ed is the most _______________ person I know. **d.** It's simply not _______________ that he stole the money.
132. downcast **downtrodden** **low-key** **low-pitched**	**a.** His _______________ gaze was proof that he was ashamed of his actions. **b.** She was attracted to his _______________, resonant voice. **c.** Marx and Engels were champions of the _______________ working class. **d.** The boss was in a good mood, so the meeting was relatively _______________ . When he's _______________ , you never know how things will turn out.
137. complicated **eminent** **perplexed** **sophisticated**	**a.** The _______________ physicist has been nominated for a Nobel Prize. **b.** You look _______________ . What can I do to help? **c.** The deluxe hotel had a(n) _______________ ambience that made her feel out of place. **d.** The story is too _______________ to explain in a few minutes. Call me later.

PRICKLY PREPOSITIONS AND PARTICLES

The following extracts are taken from passages that you have encountered in Practice Test 1. Read each one quickly, and then fill in each blank with an appropriate preposition or particle.

1. As the scientific evidence ________ rising global temperature became indisputable, skeptics began to focus ________ whether human activities are ________ fact the cause ________ global warming. They argued that the observed warming could be caused ________ natural processes such as changes ________ the energy emitted by the sun. However, the sun's influence has been found to have contributed only slightly ________ observed warming, particularly since the mid-20th century. ________ fact, there is now overwhelming evidence that greenhouse gas emissions ________ human activities are the main cause ________ the warming.

2. Over time, little progress was made until Obbink arrived and began to sort things ________ . Building ________ the work ________ previous scholars, he noticed a syntax match ________ the end of one page ________ the start ________ another. He put more bits ________ order ________ using numbers jotted ________ the fragments ________ 19th-century copyists. More fell ________ place when he figured ________ the labeling system used ________ the scholars who had cut the scrolls ________ .

3. Since deforestation is a problem wherever cacao is grown, sustainability is now the mantra ________ many people's lips. Sustainable farming involves land rehabilitation – reclaiming old farms and recycling weedy spaces ________ cacao fields ... While this arrangement produces fewer beans than a plantation ________ more light and fewer shade trees, farmers can increase the potential value ________ their efforts ________ planting other tree crops along ________ cacao. Cacao trees dispersed ________ a woody mix take more time to care ________ and harvest; but the resulting diversity helps stabilize a farmer's income and keep diseases ________ bay.

4. The study also found that most passenger cars are safer than the average sport utility vehicle when the risk posed ________ other drivers is taken ________ account. Even the safest SUV ________ the road, the mammoth Chevrolet Suburban, is bested ________ much smaller Honda Accords and Toyota Camrys. The vehicles with the worst safety record ________ them all? Full-size Chevrolet, Ford, and Dodge pickup trucks. A wide disparity ________ results among small cars suggests that vehicle design is more important than sheer mass. "The argument that lowering the weight ________ cars to achieve high fuel economy has resulted ________ excess deaths is unfounded," says one ________ the authors. "Safety is a challenging concept. It includes the design ________ the car itself, driver demographics, and a whole host ________ other factors." But while highway safety is complex, one thing is clear: A safety-conscious driver need not purchase a vehicle ________ the pound.

5. Feathers are subject ________ physical wear and become faded and brittle ________ long exposure ________ sunlight. ... Molt cycles often go hand ________ hand ________ other cycles. ________ most migratory species, the new plumage is grown after breeding and ________ autumn migration. The importance ________ a bird's feathers is reflected ________ the time each bird spends preening (that is, cleaning and arranging its plumage ________ its bill).

Practice Test 2

Writing 30 minutes

- You may write in pen or pencil.
- You will have 30 minutes to write on one of the two topics. If you do not write on one of these topics, your paper will not be scored. If you do not understand the topics, ask the examiner to explain them.
- You may make an outline if you wish, but your outline will not count toward your score.
- Write about one-and-a-half to two pages. Your essay will be marked down if it is extremely short.
- You will not be graded on the appearance of your paper, but your handwriting must be readable. You may change or correct your writing, but you should not recopy the whole essay.
- Your essay will be judged on clarity and overall effectiveness, as well as on topic development, organization, and the range, accuracy, and appropriateness of your grammar and vocabulary. Your essay will be graded at the University of Michigan.

TOPICS For help in writing these compositions, see *Writing Tutorial,* pages 203-204.

1. In many countries, teenagers take on part-time jobs while they are still students. Do you think this is a good idea? Support your opinion using specific reasons and examples.

2. Some people insist that the main emphasis in foreign language teaching should be on speaking and writing correctly, while others feel that teaching learners how to communicate and express their ideas fluently should be the main goal. What's your opinion? Support your ideas with reasons and examples from your own language-learning experience.

Responses to opinion tasks are usually more convincing when writers:

(a) acknowledge the complexity of the issue, and

(b) take time to examine the opposing side of the argument.

The key is to weigh both sides of the issue in the main body of your composition. Devote one paragraph to fully exploring your own opinion and the other to a brief survey of one or more aspects of the opposing view. Finish the second paragraph by giving 1-2 reasons why this view is flawed.

Listening approx. 35-40 minutes

This section of the examination tests your understanding of spoken English. The listening section has three parts. There are 50 questions. Mark all your answers on the separate answer sheet. Do not make any stray marks on the answer sheet. If you change your mind about an answer, erase your first answer completely.

Part I

In this part, you will hear short conversations. From the three answer choices given, choose the answer which means about the same thing as what you hear, or that is true based upon what you hear.

For problems 1 through 17, mark your answers on the separate answer sheet. No problems can be repeated.

Please listen carefully. Do you have any questions?

Expect at least one item to test your ability to infer something based on context-specific vocabulary (e.g., where the speakers are or what they're doing). Such items are easy to spot, as the choices are usually three different places or activities: e.g., *They're at the supermarket. / They've just arrived at a hotel. / They're at an airport.* To answer correctly, you need to listen carefully to the speakers' choice of words in order to pick up on context-specific clues. Be careful, though. The examiners may try to distract you by referring to several contexts at once.

Take a minute to preview the answer choices. Can you spot the questions that fall into this category?

____

1. a. She's just been to see a musical.
   b. She's happy about the outcome of a game.
   c. Neither of them like opera very much.
2. a. She likes the ring he gave his fiancée.
   b. She thinks Tina should give back his ring.
   c. His former girlfriend is engaged.
3. a. She's determined to find a new job.
   b. She agrees she's being mistreated.
   c. She's decided to fight for her rights.
4. a. They're at a bank.
   b. They're still at home.
   c. They're on their way to the airport.
5. a. He thinks they'll find the right person.
   b. He's sure a few people will come to the interview.
   c. He thinks they should interview everyone.
6. a. Her son still lives at home.
   b. Her son hates his new job.
   c. Her son has just started college.
7. a. Rita never means what she says.
   b. She's not sure how Rita took the news.
   c. She thinks Rita is not telling the truth.
8. a. They're watching a trial in a courtroom.
   b. They're at home watching a film.
   c. They're law students attending a lecture.
9. a. He doesn't think the Smiths got the message.
   b. He'd rather she be his guest tomorrow.
   c. She'll call to see when the Smiths are available.
10. a. They're almost out of gas.
    b. She's afraid the car will break down.
    c. She thinks they should take another route.
11. a. She thinks he's repeating himself.
    b. She doesn't believe him.
    c. She thinks he travels too much.
12. a. There's going to be an election soon.
    b. Their candidate was hurt in an accident.
    c. Their candidate won by a narrow margin.
13. a. They're in the garden.
    b. They're cooking in the kitchen.
    c. They're out shopping for fresh herbs.
14. a. He'd rather not tell Mary himself.
    b. He thinks Mary can't keep a secret.
    c. He doesn't object to Mary being told.
15. a. He wants her to see who's at the door.
    b. He wants her to answer the telephone.
    c. He's happy with their current phone service.
16. a. They were surprised Mike didn't panic.
    b. They think Mike behaved inappropriately.
    c. They think Mike's a strange character.
17. a. The boss won't like his long-term solution.
    b. He has no idea what to tell the boss.
    c. He wishes she would talk to the boss for him.

Part II

In this part, you will hear a question. From the three answer choices given, choose the one which best answers the question.

For problems 18 through 35, mark your answers on the separate answer sheet. No problems can be repeated. Please listen carefully. Do you have any questions?

Don't jump to conclusions! Just because a choice repeats words, phrases, or grammatical elements that you hear in the speaker's question, it doesn't mean that the choice is an appropriate answer. As we said in Practice Test 1, your best defense is to think about the purpose or function behind the speaker's question and then find a response that's suitable.

18. **a.** This Saturday? I'd love to.
b. Most of the time I go out with friends.
c. I stayed home as usual.

19. **a.** Yes, you're there.
b. Not that I know of.
c. To be honest, I'm not sure.

20. **a.** I'll let you know.
b. Actually, he was on time today.
c. Not for a while. Have you?

21. **a.** No, aren't you?
b. No, I called in sick.
c. No, I work from home.

22. **a.** It's not my decision.
b. Yes, I think so.
c. It's not for me to say.

23. **a.** It completely slipped my mind.
b. Sorry, something's come up.
c. I wish I could.

24. **a.** As long as it takes.
b. As soon as I hear from him.
c. The sooner the better.

25. **a.** Of course, I'm coming. See you later!
b. Yes, I am. Isn't everyone?
c. I just got a raise.

26. **a.** Good idea.
b. No, I didn't. He never answers them.
c. I would, but I don't know his address.

27. **a.** She's having a bad day, that's all.
b. Yes, she got it yesterday.
c. Because her boyfriend broke up with her.

28. **a.** I'd rather not, but I guess I should.
b. Because I already did.
c. Something told me not to.

29. **a.** Next time I see you.
b. You should have seen his reaction.
c. As soon as the words were out of my mouth.

30. **a.** It's a matter of pride.
b. She doesn't think it's necessary.
c. He doesn't think so.

31. **a.** I'm fresh out of good ideas.
b. I've been under the weather for days.
c. No, something's come up.

32. **a.** Yes, but I fail to see the humor in it.
b. No, he hasn't called me yet.
c. Sorry, I haven't seen him lately.

33. **a.** When's it playing?
b. It was most informative.
c. No, do you know where you put it?

34. **a.** How should I know?
b. I'm sure she didn't
c. I knew she would.

35. **a.** Thanks. I'd appreciate it.
b. No, but we're out of milk again.
c. I had them delivered yesterday.

Part III

In this part, you will hear three short segments from a radio program. The program is called "Learning from the Experts." You will hear what three different radio guests have to say about three different topics.

Each talk lasts about two minutes. As you listen, you may want to take some notes to help you remember information given in the talk. Write your notes in the test booklet.

After each talk, you will be asked some questions about what was said. From the three answer choices given, you should choose the one that best answers the question according to the information you heard.

Remember, no problems can be repeated. For problems 36 through 50, mark all your answers on the separate answer sheet. Do you have any questions?

SEGMENT 1

36. What misconception do many people have about the Venus flytrap?
- **a.** that it's able to trap flies and other living prey
- **b.** that it's a tiny plant only a few inches tall
- **c.** that it is found in many parts of the world

37. Which of the following is NOT mentioned as a potential threat to the plant?
- **a.** the area's lack of nature reserves
- **b.** logging and wildfire control
- **c.** population growth and building

38. What point does Helen Hall make about poachers?
- **a.** They no longer pose a threat to the plants.
- **b.** Their activity frequently goes unpunished.
- **c.** They have worked hard to protect the plant.

39. According to a representative of the U.S. Fish & Wildlife Service, why is it so difficult to get people excited about protecting Venus flytraps?
- **a.** The plants aren't as soulful as furry animals with big, brown eyes.
- **b.** Many people simply don't care enough to bother pushing for stronger laws.
- **c.** The plants are low priority for most legislators and law enforcement agents.

40. What common problem is referred to by two of the agencies that Helen spoke to?
- **a.** the absence of protective state laws
- **b.** the lack of manpower to enforce state laws
- **c.** fines and jail sentences that are too lenient

Not good at taking notes? Few of us are! Instead, try using the questions and choices to organize your listening. See the box at the bottom of page 10 for tips.

SEGMENT 2

41. What prevents a penny from gathering deadly speed when it is thrown from a great height?
- **a.** the height of the fall
- **b.** the air resistance generated
- **c.** the material the coin is made of

42. What is the grain of truth contained in the first urban legend that Mark Constantine discusses?
- **a.** People who stand on tall buildings shouldn't throw pennies.
- **b.** It's best to avoid walking on the sidewalk near the Empire State Building.
- **c.** Getting hit by an object falling from a great height may prove fatal.

43. What point does Mark make about derailments caused by pennying train tracks?
- **a.** His research has failed to turn up any reported occurrences.
- **b.** They could never result from such an innocent action.
- **c.** They have resulted in a disturbing number of deaths.

(Segment 2 continues at top of next page)

44. Why does Mark mention his grandfather?
   - **a.** He was seriously injured waiting for a streetcar to flatten a penny.
   - **b.** He led a long, happy life, despite the risky practices of his youth.
   - **c.** He taught his grandson a safe way to penny streetcar tracks.

45. What thought does Mark leave his listeners with?
   - **a.** Children should be taught the value of saving money.
   - **b.** Something must be done to stop people from pennying tracks.
   - **c.** Playing near train tracks is a potentially deadly pastime.

SEGMENT 3

46. According to John Seaberg, what was so scary about the MIT professor's findings?
   - **a.** the fact that thawing permafrost in Siberia will release gigatons of carbon dioxide
   - **b.** the fact that even bright students are ignorant about preventing global warming
   - **c.** the fact that the professor's students scored so poorly on a test about global warming

47. What is it that John Seaberg feels most people don't understand about carbon emissions?
   - **a.** the relationship between the carbon we emit and the carbon water and plants can absorb
   - **b.** the fact that humans are emitting much too much carbon dioxide and other greenhouse gases
   - **c.** the sad reality that global warming has already begun and nothing can be done to stop it

48. Of the carbon dioxide emitted the previous year, how much of it remained trapped in the atmosphere?
   - **a.** almost all of it
   - **b.** only a tiny fraction of it
   - **c.** slightly more than half of it

49. What simple fact should the MIT students have understood?
   - **a.** that emissions should be capped
   - **b.** that emissions must be decreased radically and quickly
   - **c.** that global warming is already spinning out of control

50. In John's opinion, what does the problem require?
   - **a.** a commonsense solution to global warming
   - **b.** drastic change in how we travel and use energy
   - **c.** a better comparison to replace the "bathtub" analogy

Grammar – Cloze – Vocabulary – Reading 75 minutes

This section of the examination contains 120 problems, numbered 51 through 170. There are 40 grammar, 20 cloze, 40 vocabulary, and 20 reading comprehension problems. If you do not understand how to do the problems, raise your hand, and a proctor will explain the examples to you. None of the actual test problems can be explained.

Each problem has only one correct answer. Do not spend too much time on any one problem. If you do not know the answer to a problem, you may guess. Work quickly but carefully. You have one hour and 15 minutes (75 minutes) to answer all 120 problems. If you finish before the time is over, you may check your answers within the GCVR section only. Do not go back to the Listening section of the exam.

GRAMMAR

51. We all agreed that the restaurant was _____ we expected it to be.
- **a.** so good that
- **b.** even better than
- **c.** the best that
- **d.** good as

52. He was too tired to mow the lawn, so he _____ one of his sons to do it.
- **a.** had
- **b.** let
- **c.** made
- **d.** got

53. In case he asks, tell him that I've already read his e-mail and _____ .
- **a.** wrote back him
- **b.** written him back
- **c.** have written back him
- **d.** wrote to him back

54. You'll feel more relaxed _____ you finish that research paper.
- **a.** until
- **b.** since
- **c.** once
- **d.** afterwards

55. _____ the accident he had ten years ago, he might have been a great athlete today.
- **a.** Had it not been for
- **b.** Not having
- **c.** Until he had
- **d.** Because of

56. Of the two jackets he owns, one is made of cotton and _____ of polyester.
- **a.** the other
- **b.** other
- **c.** another
- **d.** a second

57. He bought the car of his dreams after coming _____ a lot of money from a wealthy uncle.
- **a.** across
- **b.** by
- **c.** into
- **d.** of

58. They're having _____ a car that is within their price range.
- **a.** it difficult to find
- **b.** difficulty finding
- **c.** difficulty to find
- **d.** it difficult finding

59. He'd be _____ happier if he were able to extend his vacation by another week.
- **a.** a lot more
- **b.** plenty
- **c.** extremely
- **d.** a great deal

60. I doubt she'll accept his proposal, but you can't blame _____ .
- **a.** him for trying
- **b.** him to try
- **c.** that he tried
- **d.** trying on him

61. They're early risers, so they're unlikely _____ at this hour.
- **a.** that they are sleeping
- **b.** having slept
- **c.** to sleep
- **d.** to be sleeping

62. He regrets _____ harder during his high school years.
- **a.** that he not worked
- **b.** not to have worked
- **c.** not having worked
- **d.** not to work

63. The _____ champions have had another strong season this year.
   a. two-time
   b. twice-winning
   c. two-timing
   d. twice-won

64. After a month-long investigation, police are still not sure who _____ .
   a. is blamed by them
   b. do they blame
   c. to lay the blame on
   d. to be blamed

65. His appointment with the dentist went well, so he _____ worried.
   a. must not have
   b. couldn't have
   c. needn't have
   d. wouldn't have

66. It's freezing outside, so _____ to stay home and be warm.
   a. we'd do well
   b. we might as well
   c. we'd better
   d. we're better off

67. Something definitely _____ about the rising price of gasoline.
   a. needs to be done
   b. needs to do
   c. must have been done
   d. must be doing

68. The band was so good that they soon had everyone _____ in the aisles.
   a. dancing
   b. dance
   c. to dance
   d. was dancing

69. The doctors did _____ to save the old man, but their efforts were in vain.
   a. the best
   b. their best
   c. better than
   d. better

70. He's tried apologizing to her, but _____ he does, she refuses to speak to him.
   a. no matter what
   b. in case
   c. regardless of
   d. in as much as

Think about it!

Grammar is one section of the ECPE where it's worth spending a few more seconds on items that you find difficult.

71. She saw the play just last month, so _____ that she'll want to see it again.
   a. she isn't likely
   b. unlikely is it
   c. it's unlikely
   d. it doesn't like her

72. The food wasn't bad, but I'd _____ to go somewhere else next time.
   a. rather
   b. prefer
   c. better
   d. liked

73. It is believed that _____ students will pass the exam with flying colors.
   a. each and every
   b. each one of the
   c. all of
   d. every

74. It's been ages since he saw his favorite cousin, so he _____ for him to visit next week.
   a. can't wait
   b. isn't going to wait
   c. hasn't been waiting
   d. won't have been waiting

75. She said she would lend him the money _____ to repay it next week.
   a. on condition that he promises
   b. so that he promised
   c. if only he had promised
   d. as long as his promising

76. He said he would study hard for the exam, and he has every intention _____ .
   a. on doing so
   b. that he does it
   c. of doing so
   d. to do it

77. It isn't certain _____ tonight as he may have to work late.
   a. Dan can come
   b. of Dan's coming
   c. for Dan to come
   d. that Dan comes

78. It's crucial _____ late, or the tour bus will depart without you.
   a. your not being
   b. that you won't be
   c. that you not be
   d. to be not

79. Believing he would pass the test without opening a book was wishful _____ .
   a. thought
   b. thinking
   c. think
   d. thinker

80. During the meeting with his superiors, _____ to believe that he was in line for a promotion.
   a. it led him
   b. it was led
   c. he led them
   d. he was led

81. It's clear that the child _____ by an older brother or sister.
   a. influenced
   b. has been influencing
   c. is being influenced
   d. is under the influence

82. Air quality in the city is at its worst at rush hour due to the increase in _____ fumes.
   a. exhaust
   b. exhaustion
   c. exhaustive
   d. exhausted

83. By the end of the meal, she was so full that she felt _____ .
   a. as though to burst
   b. like having burst
   c. as if she would burst
   d. that she had burst

84. The manager expects them _____ by the end of the week.
   a. to have the report finished
   b. the report to be finished
   c. that they'll finish the report
   d. having to finish the report

85. I know I had my wallet a few minutes ago, which means, if I'm not mistaken, _____ .
   a. I was just picked from my pocket
   b. someone just my pocket picked
   c. I just had my pocket picked
   d. my pocket was just picked from me

86. She was afraid to get a checkup _____ she was seriously ill.
   a. due to
   b. as though
   c. for fear that
   d. in case

87. He left the office an hour ago, so he's bound _____ here soon.
   a. that he'll be
   b. to be
   c. to have been
   d. for being

88. She's looking for a roommate as she can't get used to _____ everything on her own.
   a. have to do
   b. have been doing
   c. having done
   d. having to do

89. _____ she got home, her husband had dinner ready and waiting for her.
   a. By the time
   b. As soon as
   c. Once
   d. Until

90. It was obvious that she was cold, so I asked _____ the window for her.
   a. her if I closed
   b. if she would like me to close
   c. her to close
   d. to close

Take time to notice the flow of each paragraph. Does it contain a topic sentence followed by reasons or examples? Does it describe a sequence or present contrasting ideas? Being sensitive to this will help you answer questions related to linking words and discourse markers.

CLOZE

Passage 1 is about hibernation.

Hibernation seems simple enough. Animals fatten up in the summer, disappear into their dens during the winter, ___(91)___ food is scarce, and then emerge in the spring alive and alert, if a lot ___(92)___ . But if you could peek inside a hibernating ground squirrel, you'd witness a physiological wonder. The animal's metabolism slows to ___(93)___ nothing. Its body temperature plummets to a few ___(94)___ warmer than outside. Its heartbeat slows from 300 beats per minute to ___(95)___ than 10. And other, more mysterious changes protect the squirrel in a state that would kill many other animals.

It's that self-protection that ___(96)___ medical researchers. ___(97)___ out how mammals survive such extreme conditions offers clues to how humans might be protected against their own health threats such as stroke, which causes restricted blood flow in the brain, and trauma-induced hemorrhaging. Fueling interest in the field ___(98)___ a recent paper showing that mice, which don't hibernate, ___(99)___ induced to do so by a carefully measured-out whiff of a normally toxic gas. When the gas was removed, the mice emerged apparently unharmed from their sluggish state. ___(100)___ human applications are years away, hopeful investors have already put up more than $10 million in a start-up company.

91. **a.** and **b.** when **c.** so **d.** although

92. **a.** warmer **b.** survive **c.** have **d.** thinner

93. **a.** hardly **b.** near **c.** almost **d.** next

94. **a.** degrees **b.** levels **c.** points **d.** grades

95. **a.** lesser **b.** fewer **c.** under **d.** smaller

96. **a.** disturbs **b.** observes **c.** intrigues **d.** repels

97. **a.** Ruling **b.** Understanding **c.** Checking **d.** Figuring

98. **a.** that **b.** is **c.** because **d.** when

99. **a.** they **b.** which **c.** were **d.** have

100. **a.** While **b.** If **c.** Because **d.** Since

Passage 2 is about Mark Twain, the American writer.

Samuel Clemens, better known by his pen name of Mark Twain, grew up in the Mississippi River frontier town of Hannibal, Missouri. Ernest Hemingway's famous ___(101)___ – that all of American literature comes from one great book, Twain's *Adventures of Huckleberry Finn* – indicates this author's towering place in American ___(102)___ tradition. Early 19th-century American writers ___(103)___ to be too flowery, sentimental, or ostentatious – partially because they were still trying to prove that they ___(104)___ write as elegantly as the English. Based on vigorous, realistic, colloquial American speech, Twain's style gave American ___(105)___ a new appreciation of their national voice. Twain was the ___(106)___ major American author to come from the interior of the country, ___(107)___ he captured its distinctive slang, humor, and character. ___(108)___ Twain and other American writers of the late 19th century, realism was ___(109)___ just a literary technique, but rather a way of speaking truth and exploding worn-out conventions. As such, it was profoundly liberating, though potentially at ___(110)___ with society.

101. **a.** reputation **b.** novel **c.** statement **d.** philosophy

102. **a.** literary **b.** literal **c.** literate **d.** literacy

103. **a.** hated **b.** tended **c.** inclined **d.** had

104. **a.** not **b.** and **c.** to **d.** could

105. **a.** writers **b.** public **c.** novels **d.** critics

106. **a.** most **b.** first **c.** other **d.** next

107. **a.** as **b.** however **c.** and **d.** which

108. **a.** For **b.** Despite **c.** If **d.** Since

109. **a.** only **b.** not **c.** always **d.** plainly

110. **a.** conflict **b.** risk **c.** fault **d.** odds

VOCABULARY

Staring at the test booklet (or the ceiling!) will not help you find the answers to difficult Vocabulary items. If you don't know the choices, guess and move on. The time you save can be put to much better use on the Cloze and Reading passages.

111. If you believe his story, you're more _____ than I thought.
- **a.** voracious
- **b.** avaricious
- **c.** gullible
- **d.** opinionated

112. Eating well and getting plenty of sleep improves your _____ to disease.
- **a.** susceptibility
- **b.** opposition
- **c** resistance
- **d.** defense

113. Although almost non-existent in the West, the disease is still _____ in developing countries.
- **a.** equivalent
- **b.** prevalent
- **c.** malevolent
- **d.** ambivalent

114. The miniskirt has enjoyed a _____ of popularity in recent years.
- **a.** resurgence
- **b.** reassurance
- **c.** retaliation
- **d.** renovation

115. Surviving the car crash brought him face to face with his own _____ .
- **a.** destiny
- **b.** fatality
- **c.** mortality
- **d.** extinction

116. He twisted his ankle and fell to the ground in _____ pain.
- **a.** elaborate
- **b.** exquisite
- **c.** excruciating
- **d.** severed

117. When he finally regained _____ , he remembered nothing of the accident.
- **a.** conscience
- **b.** coordination
- **c.** consciousness
- **d.** confidence

118. The doctor says the boy will be well enough to be _____ from the hospital in a few days.
- **a.** expelled
- **b.** evicted
- **c.** dismissed
- **d.** discharged

119. She has little patience for people who spread _____ rumors.
- **a.** malignant
- **b.** malicious
- **c.** illustrious
- **d.** artificial

120. It's a miracle that they _____ from the accident without a scratch.
- **a.** emerged
- **b.** surged
- **c.** diverged
- **d.** converged

121. The Internet has become a powerful tool for _____ information.
- **a.** withholding
- **b.** distorting
- **c.** contributing
- **d.** disseminating

122. The director has a _____ schedule today. Could you possibly call back tomorrow?
- **a.** gaudy
- **b.** wispy
- **c.** fervent
- **d.** hectic

123. Unfortunately, the surgery was difficult and the patient died of _____ .
- **a.** symptoms
- **b.** obstacles
- **c.** complications
- **d.** derivatives

124. The students found it difficult to _____ all the information in the professor's lecture.
- **a.** take to
- **b.** take up
- **c.** take on
- **d.** take in

125. The managers were given _____ orders not to discuss the plans with anyone.
   a. explicit
   b. negligible
   c. irreverent
   d. indefinite

126. Not wanting to put all their eggs in one basket, most investors prefer to _____ their stock portfolios.
   a. clarify
   b. verify
   c. diversify
   d. intensify

127. Whatever you do, try to stay calm and don't lose your _____ .
   a. composure
   b. sight
   c. sensation
   d. temperament

128. The heat has been _____ lately. I'm hoping it will rain to cool things down.
   a. stagnant
   b. oppressive
   c. discernible
   d. muggy

129. The researchers are in the final stage of analyzing their _____ .
   a. assumptions
   b. data
   c. fundamentals
   d. output

130. Should he tell the police? It was a dilemma he was still _____ with.
   a. wrestling
   b. experimenting
   c. complying
   d. collaborating

131. Is the defense attorney planning to ask the defendant to _____ ?
   a. stand trial
   b. stand clear
   c. take the stand
   d. stand on principle

132. As a result of the four-car pile-up, traffic was at a total _____ .
   a. standstill
   b. roadblock
   c. detour
   d. bottleneck

133. The child is a pleasure to be around because she has such a sunny _____ .
   a. complexion
   b. disposition
   c. tantrum
   d. outlet

134. The divorce will be nasty. Neither parent is willing to _____ custody of the children.
   a. garnish
   b. embellish
   c. relinquish
   d. extinguish

135. The car slowed down as it made its way up the steep _____ .
   a. decline
   b. inclination
   c. incline
   d. descent

136. The stock market has been unpredictable lately, so be _____ with your investments.
   a. reckless
   b. tolerant
   c. cordial
   d. cautious

137. I can't imagine why anyone would have done such a thing. It's simply _____ .
   a. unfaltering
   b. uneasy
   c. unfathomable
   d. unattended

138. He went to great lengths to _____ the details of the intricate plan to his co-workers.
   a. carry out
   b. speak out
   c. measure out
   d. spell out

139. The employees were _____ when they were told that the company would have to close.
   a. taken aback
   b. taken amiss
   c. taken apart
   d. taken over

140. Everyone said the play was brilliant. Even the critics were _____ in their praise.
   a. ubiquitous
   b. unappreciative
   c. undaunted
   d. unanimous

141. The manufacturer guarantees that it will replace ____ parts for one year.
   - a. deficient
   - b. deranged
   - c. defective
   - d. dejected

142. She backs up her computer files every day as a precaution against power ____ .
   - a. outrages
   - b. surges
   - c. bulges
   - d. booms

143. We didn't send you an invitation because we ____ that you were coming.
   - a. took it to heart
   - b. took it upon ourselves
   - c. took it for granted
   - d. took it in stride

144. When the test booklets have been ____ , you will be instructed to begin.
   - a. convened
   - b. apportioned
   - c. donated
   - d. distributed

145. If you need help, please don't hesitate to call me. I can be there ____ .
   - a. in a fix
   - b. in a flash
   - c. in a daze
   - d. in the bag

146. I'm worried about her. I've never seen anyone spend money so ____ .
   - a. eloquently
   - b. adequately
   - c. sporadically
   - d. extravagantly

147. I told you, there's nothing to be afraid of. Your fears are totally ____ .
   - a. unfounded
   - b. undeclared
   - c. unchecked
   - d. undying

148. Government troops have surrounded the city in hopes of ____ the rebellion.
   - a. prolonging
   - b. containing
   - c. enduring
   - d. sedating

149. They had no idea what the strange-looking ____ might be used for.
   - a. contraption
   - b. convention
   - c. confection
   - d. confession

150. He felt his heart ____ as his bride-to-be began her walk down the aisle.
   - a. fasten
   - b. quicken
   - c. expedite
   - d. heighten

READING

Passage 1 is about an amazing underground discovery.

Deep below the surface of a remote mountain range in Chihuahua, Mexico, sit two rooms of splendor: translucent crystals the length and girth of mature pine trees lie pitched atop one another, as though moonbeams suddenly took on weight and substance.

In April 2000, miners found what experts believe are the world's largest crystals. While preparing to blast open a tunnel 1,000 feet underground in a silver and lead mine, a miner climbed through a tiny opening into a 30-by 60-foot cavern choked with immense crystals. "It was beautiful, like light reflecting off a broken mirror," he said. A month later another team found an even larger cavern adjacent to the first.

Until recently, mining officials kept the discoveries secret out of concern for vandalism. Few, however, would casually venture inside: the temperature in the caverns hovers at a sweltering 150 degrees; the humidity, 100 percent. One can stay in the caves only six to ten minutes before becoming disoriented.

Geologists conjecture that a chamber of magma, or superheated molten rock, lying two to three miles underneath the mountain, forced mineral-rich fluids upward through a fault into openings in the limestone bedrock near the surface. Over time, this hydrothermal liquid deposited metals such as gold, silver, lead, and zinc in the limestone bedrock – metals which have been mined there since the deposits were discovered in 1794. In a few caves, however, the conditions were ideal for the formation of a different kind of treasure. Groundwater rich with sulfur from the adjacent metal deposits began dissolving the limestone walls, releasing large quantities of calcium. This calcium, in turn, combined with the sulfur to form crystals on a scale never before seen by humans. In addition to 4-foot-in diameter columns 50 feet (15.25 meters) in length, the cavern also contains row upon row of shark-tooth-shaped formations up to 3 feet high, set at odd angles. Fittingly, the pale, translucent crystals are made of selenite, a form of gypsum named after Selene, the Greek goddess of the moon. "To see crystals that are so huge and perfect is truly mind-boggling," says one expert. "Everyone here is on pins and needles because caverns with even more fantastic formations could be found any day."

151. What makes the crystals that were found unique?
- **a.** their enormity
- **b.** their translucence
- **c.** their volcanic origin
- **d.** their accidental discovery

152. What elements are the crystals composed of?
- **a.** bedrock and magma
- **b.** groundwater and limestone
- **c.** gold, silver, and lead
- **d.** calcium and sulfur

153. Which comes closest to having the same height as the tallest crystals?
- **a.** a small Christmas tree
- **b.** an average 10-year-old child
- **c.** an extremely tall basketball player
- **d.** 8-9 people standing on each other's shoulders

154. How would a person feel after being in a cave for about ten minutes?
- **a.** physically unaffected
- **b.** sweaty and confused
- **c.** cold and shivering
- **d.** thirsty but thrilled

155. According to one expert, how do people familiar with the discovery now feel?
- **a.** concerned that vandals will destroy the crystals
- **b.** hopeful that similar discoveries will soon be made
- **c.** nervous that casual visitors will be injured
- **d.** eager to begin commercial exploitation of the crystals

Passage 2 is about mass extinctions.

Scientists have identified two ways in which species disappear. The first is through ordinary or "background" extinctions, where species that fail to adapt are slowly replaced by more adaptable life forms. The second is when large numbers of species go to the wall in relatively short periods of biological time. There have been five such extinctions, each provoked by cataclysmic evolutionary events caused by some geological eruption, climate shift, or space junk slamming into the earth. Scientists now believe that another mass extinction of species is currently under way – and this time human fingerprints are on the trigger.

How are we doing it? Simply by demanding more and more space for ourselves. In our assault on the ecosystems around us we have used a number of tools, from spear and gun to bulldozer and chainsaw. Certain especially rich ecosystems have proved the most vulnerable. In Hawaii more than half of the native birds are now gone – some 50 species. Such carnage has taken place all across the island communities of the Pacific and Indian oceans. While many species were hunted to extinction, others simply succumbed to the "introduced predators" that humans brought with them: the cat, the dog, the pig, and the rat.

Today the tempo of extinction is picking up speed. Hunting is no longer the major culprit, although rare birds and animals continue to be butchered for their skin, feathers, tusks, and internal organs, or taken as cage pets. Today the main threat comes from the destruction of the habitat that wild plants, animals, and insects need to survive. The draining and damming of wetland and river courses threatens the aquatic food chain and our own seafood industry. Overfishing and the destruction of fragile coral reefs destroy ocean biodiversity. Deforestation is taking a staggering toll, particularly in the tropics where the most global biodiversity is at stake. The shrinking rainforest cover of the Congo and Amazon river basins and such places as Borneo and Madagascar have a wealth of species per hectare existing nowhere else. As those precious hectares are drowned or turned into arid pasture and cropland, such species disappear forever.

156. Which phrase best describes deforestation, damming rivers, and draining wetlands?
- **a.** evolutionary events
- **b.** mass extinction
- **c.** habitat destruction
- **d.** global biodiversity

157. Until recently, what was the main threat to biodiversity in Hawaii and other islands in the Pacific and Indian oceans?
- **a.** climate shift
- **b.** geological eruption
- **c.** bulldozers and chainsaws
- **d.** hunters and introduced predators

158. According to the passage, what is true of the current wave of mass extinction?
- **a.** It is unique in that it is the only one ever caused by humans.
- **b.** It will be more devastating than the others that have occurred.
- **c.** It has come about at a surprisingly slow, but steady pace.
- **d.** It is similar in many ways to the five others that preceded it.

159. Which is no longer considered a major cause of the mass extinction that is currently under way?
- **a.** the slaughter of animals for their feathers or fur
- **b.** cutting down large areas of tropical rainforest
- **c.** the practice of building dams across rivers
- **d.** unprecedented human intervention

160. What is true according to the passage?
- **a.** It is impossible for scientists to predict a background extinction.
- **b.** The most fragile ecosystems are ones that are highly diversified.
- **c.** Deforestation is only a significant problem in the tropics.
- **d.** Human development should be stopped at all costs.

Remember: Technical terms are almost always explained in simpler terms the first time they appear ... so don't panic when you see the phrase "computer-mediated stereotaxis radiosurgery system" in line 5!

Passage 3 is about bloodless surgical techniques.

High-tech bloodless surgery techniques are now being used to mend broken bones, remove tattoos, and quiet chronic snoring. But their most important application to date may be in destroying hard-to-reach brain and spinal tumors. Without sawing into the skull or so much as cutting the scalp, doctors at Stanford University Medical Center are curing patients with brain and spinal tumors that were once considered deadly. The operations are made possible by the use of Stanford's computer-mediated stereotaxis radiosurgery system, also called the cyberknife. The cyberknife is essentially a robotic x-ray gun that shoots small amounts of radiation into tumors from hundreds of directions without overexposing other parts of the body. In effect, it is a robotic arm that locks the radiation beam on the tumor and constantly readjusts its aim in response to the patient's natural small movements. This eliminates the need for the circular metal "halo" frame that previously had to be screwed into the skull to hold the head in place. The procedure takes about 45 minutes and the patient leaves the hospital the same day.

For patients requiring more powerful doses of radiation or in-tumor delivery of chemotherapy drugs, bloodless surgical techniques known as magnetic stereotaxis systems may offer a cure. Still in the trial stage, these begin with the creation of a 3-dimensional map based on MRI scans of the patient's brain. Having determined the precise location of the tumor or damaged tissue, doctors can map out the best path to reach it while avoiding blood vessels and clusters of neurons that control vital body functions. The surgeon then makes a tiny incision through the scalp and skull and places a magnetic probe on the surface of the brain. Next the patient dons a magnetic helmet that contains superconducting magnets controlled by a computer. By manipulating the attracting and repulsing forces between the tiny magnet in the patient's brain and the more powerful magnets in the helmet, the computer steers the probe to its target. After the operation, the probe can be "parked" indefinitely in a nonessential part of the brain or until it is needed for additional treatments.

Surgeons believe that the cyberknife will soon be used on small and medium-size tumors in the prostate, pancreas, lung, and liver. Also coming are techniques that repair knee injuries and arthritic joint damage. If advances keep up, the notion of a surgeon using a scalpel may someday seem as primitive as operating without anesthesia.

161. Which is **not** a benefit of treatment associated with the cyberknife?
- **a.** It delivers radiation only where it is required.
- **b.** It may involve either high or low doses of radiation.
- **c.** A special frame no longer needs to be screwed into the skull.
- **d.** Tumors can be treated without having to cut into the brain.

162. What can we conclude about procedures done with magnetic stereotaxis systems?
- **a.** They are used to treat tumors that are more difficult than those treatable by cyberknife.
- **b.** They are much less complicated than procedures that are performed by cyberknife.
- **c.** They are so effective that most patients are cured after only a single treatment.
- **d.** They involve less risk to the patient than procedures done with the cyberknife.

163. What role is played by the helmet worn by the patient during magnetic stereotaxis procedures?
- **a.** It keeps the head of the patient absolutely still while the surgeon is working.
- **b.** It allows the surgeon to steer away from blood vessels and neuron clusters.
- **c.** It contains an MRI scanner that provides the surgeon with a map of the brain.
- **d.** It contains magnets that help guide a tiny magnetic probe down into the brain.

164. What do the two systems have in common?
- **a.** Both involve the use of magnetic probes.
- **b.** Neither involve cutting into the skull.
- **c.** Both involve the use of a computer.
- **d.** Both deliver radiation from outside the body.

165. What point does the writer make in the final paragraph?
- **a.** The use of anesthesia and scalpels in conventional surgery is a barbaric practice.
- **b.** The advent of bloodless surgery is the start of a new chapter in medical history.
- **c.** It is too early to say what impact bloodless surgery will have on the medical field.
- **d.** Bloodless surgery is effective, but so far its applications are extremely limited.

Passage 4 is about a natural phenomenon called the aurora borealis.

The whole dome of the night sky was awash with color: cascades of yellow-green and blushes of crimson fanning from a darker point high overhead. As they fell in broad rays, they shifted and changed in brightness, sometimes intense in one place, then cool, then hot. It was like looking up into the heart of a flower of glorious light whose petals rippled in a breeze that could not be felt – a breath from beyond this planet.

That aurora borealis lit up the northern night sky in the Scottish Highlands on March 13-14, 1989, but to this day I can still picture its colors, shapes, and movements. The show peaked for less than an hour, but its tonal themes lingered longer. It seemed an act of magic, but of course it was science at work: electrically charged particles from the sun were making gases glow in the upper atmosphere.

Thousands of miles away in Alaska, that same aurora caught the eye of Charles Deerh at the Geophysical Institute of the University of Alaska in Fairbanks. "That display on March 13-14, 1989, was one of the best in the last 50 years," said Deehr, one of the world's leading experts in auroral forecasting. Deehr's work involves searching for patterns in the latest information sent from near-earth satellites in hopes of predicting auroral activity a day or so in advance. Such forewarning would make it possible to prepare electrical systems on earth and in space for disturbances.

Satellite monitoring of the 1989 aurora's extreme reach demonstrated to experts just how unusual that aurora was. Most are visible only in the higher latitudes (above 60 degrees), but that one showed up as far south as Key West in Florida and the Yucatán Peninsula in Mexico. Unnerved by the fiery tint in the sky, people phoned the police; others watched in awe. Within 90 seconds of the aurora's reaching the sky above Quebec, magnetic storms associated with it caused a province-wide collapse of the power grid, leaving six million Canadians without electricity for hours. At the same time, compass readings became unreliable, and there were reports of automatic garage doors opening and closing on their own. Radio transmissions and coastal navigation systems were disrupted, and information feeds from some satellites were temporarily lost. These troubles were a clear indication of why we need to hone our ability to predict the phenomenon.

166. Which word best characterizes the author's tone in the first paragraph?

- **a.** despair
- **b.** horror
- **c.** awe
- **d.** sorrow

167. Which of the following does the author find most significant about the aurora he witnessed?

- **a.** the fact that the aurora was visible so far north.
- **b.** the vividness and intensity of the aurora's colors.
- **c.** the fact that experts like Deehr still remember it.
- **d.** the extent and intensity of the disruption it caused.

168. According to information in the text, what can auroras cause?

- **a.** gases to glow in the upper atmosphere
- **b.** magnetic storms that disrupt electrical systems
- **c.** electrical storms on the surface of the sun
- **d.** the atmosphere of the earth to overheat

169. What does the writer believe?

- **a.** Scientists like Deehr will never be able to predict auroras accurately.
- **b.** It is necessary for scientists like Deehr to find a way to prevent auroras.
- **c.** Better forecasting will help minimize problems that auroras can cause.
- **d.** Scientists were negligent for not having predicted the impact of the 1989 aurora.

170. According to the text, what is Deehr's research based on?

- **a.** observing auroras with the naked eye
- **b.** searching the sky with powerful telescopes
- **c.** data sent to him from experts around the world
- **d.** analyzing data that is fed to him via satellite

2 Vocabulary Enhancement

If You Snooze, You Lose

Since hibernation for humans is still a long way off (see Cloze Passage 1), we mortals will have to content ourselves with normal sleep. But what's "normal"? As you undoubtedly know, English has a wide range of words and expressions to express fine differences in the seemingly simple act of closing one's eyes. Master the material below, and you won't ever ***get caught sleeping*** *(i.e., be found to be unprepared)!*

A The Fine Art of Sleeping – Read each sentence and underline the choice that best fits each context.

1. Shhh! Don't wake the baby. She's **taking a** sleep / nap / slumber .
2. Dana had a snooze / sleep / slumber **party**, but as usual no one slept!
3. Go to bed! Do you realize you keep nodding / napping / sleeping **off**?
4. If you don't move around, your foot will fall asleep / sleepy / sleeping .
5. Bears snooze / hibernate / snore in the winter.
6. The volcano has been hibernating / resting / dormant since it erupted in 1901.
7. I'm beat! I think I'll **get some** catnap / shut-eye / 40 winks before dinner.
8. Dad likes to **have a** snore / shut-eye / snooze after dinner.
9. I **couldn't sleep** it off / like a light / a wink all night. I hate having insomnia.
10. I was late for work today because I slept over / overslept / slept through .
11. There was a storm last night, but you slept over / overslept / slept through it!
12. The lecturer was so dull that he **put me** to rest / to sleep / to bed .
13. The rumors are false. Can't we **lay them** to rest / to sleep / to bed ?
14. I'll tell you what I've decided in the morning. I need to **sleep** on it / through it / in .
15. I can't wait till Saturday when I can **sleep** on it / through it / in .
16. I'm bushed. I need to **put my** head down / feet down / shoes off for a while.
17. You won't disturb him. He **sleeps like a** dog / log / bird .
18. I didn't dare tell him. Better to **let sleeping** dogs / logs / babies lie.

Thought for the day:
People who say they sleep like a baby probably don't have one.

B Summary – Complete each definition with a word or phrase from Part A. For verbs, use the base form.

1. take ______________ – have a short, quick sleep
2. have ______________ – have a short, quick sleep
3. get ______________ – have a short, quick sleep
4. put (sb's) ______________ – lie down (briefly)
5. put (sb) ______________ – bore (sb) to death
6. lay (sth) ______________ – put an end to sth
7. fall ______________ – (of feet, arms) go numb
8. can't ______________ – not be able to sleep at all
9. let sleeping ______________ – don't make waves
10. sleep ______________ – keep sleeping, not wake up
11. sleep ______________ – delay a decision till the next day
12. sleep ______________ – stay in bed longer than usual
13. sleep ______________ – sleep heavily
14. ______________ – fail to get up on time
15. ______________ – fall asleep, doze off
16. ______________ – inactive
17. ______________ – (animal) spend winter sleeping
18. ______________ – sleep-over, pajama party

C **Picture This!** – Underline the appropriate words and/or phrases to complete each caption, and then match the captions (**1-6**) to the photos (**a-f**).

1. Is it morning already? Ugh! I think I'll just hit the snooze / slumber / doze button and sleep through / sleep in / sleep over for a while.
2. I told her to not get caught sleeping / sleep on it / let sleeping dogs lie, but I didn't think she'd take me literally!
3. The chimps had a wild party last night and now old Zimba is dozing / sleeping / nodding it off!
4. Now that's what I call a cat snooze / catnap / cat slumber - literally and figuratively!
5. Tina invited her friends to a sleep-out / sleep-over / sleep-in last night, but none of them slept a wink / winked / caught 40 winks .
6. The meeting was so boring that one of my colleagues was laid to rest / slept through it / overslept!

a. ____________________

b. ____________________

c. ____________________

d. ____________________

e. ____________________

f. ____________________

D **What's the difference?** – Explain the differences between the words and phrases below.

1. **a sleepy baby / a sleeping baby -** ____________________
2. **sleeplessness / restlessness -** ____________________
3. **an insomniac / a somnambulist -** ____________________
4. **oversleep / sleep over -** ____________________
5. **catch some sleep / be caught sleeping -** ____________________

2 Vocabulary Consolidation

VEXING VERBS

A Common Collocations – Complete each phrase with a word from the box.

comply *distort* *donate* *extinguish* *fasten* *take on* *withhold* *wrestle*

1. ______________ the truth
2. ______________ your seatbelt
3. ______________ with rules or regulations
4. ______________ too much work
5. ______________ with your conscience
6. ______________ a fire
7. ______________ taxes from a paycheck
8. ______________ money to a favorite charity

B Fine-Tuning Your Knowledge – The numbers below refer to questions in the Vocabulary section of Practice Test 2. After reviewing the words, fill in each blank with the correct form of the appropriate verb.

121. contribute **disseminate** **distort** **withhold**	**a.** Children love to see how the mirrors in a fun house ______________ their reflection. **b.** With the aid of satellites, breaking news is ______________ globally in a matter of seconds. **c.** The police are convinced that the suspect is ______________ information. **d.** Employees may elect to ______________ 7% of their salary into a savings fund. The Payroll Department will ______________ the correct amount from each check.
126. clarify **diversify** **intensify** **verify**	**a.** When you receive your license, please ______________ your personal data. **b.** Police have ______________ their search for the missing teenagers. **c.** I don't understand your point. Could you ______________ it with an example? **d.** Not wanting to have "all its eggs in one basket," the magazine company has decided to ______________ by opening a chain of bookstores.
134. embellish **extinguish** **garnish** **relinquish**	**a.** The evening gown was ______________ with sequins. **b.** The parents' hopes were ______________ when rescuers called off the week-long search for the missing child. **c.** The fish was ______________ with chopped parsley and lemon slices. **d.** John told me the boss intends to ______________ control of the firm to his son. Is it true, or is he ______________ the truth as usual?
139. take aback **take amiss** **take apart** **take over**	**a.** It was only a friendly observation. Please don't ______________ it ______________ . **b.** The child's disruptive behavior ______________ everyone ______________ . **c.** I'm tired of driving. Would you like to ______________ ? **d.** When you finish the puzzle, please ______________ it ______________ and put the pieces back in the box.
148. contain **endure** **prolong** **sedate**	**a.** The envelope ______________ the name of the winner. **b.** It's normal for patients to be ______________ to calm them before surgery. **c.** Eve's getting married, and she's so happy that she can't ______________ herself! **d.** I think you should call and see if he's OK. Otherwise, you're just ______________ the agony. I don't see how you can ______________ it!
150. expedite **fasten** **heighten** **quicken**	**a.** The runners ______________ their pace as they approached the finish line. **b.** She ______________ her name tag to her sweater with a safety pin. **c.** The right music will ______________ the effect that the director is hoping to create. **d.** The company guarantees that orders for top clients will be ______________ .

NOTOTORIOUS NOUNS

A Amusing Associations – Find the phrase in the box that is suggested by each prompt.

an assumption *your composure* *a confection* *a confession* *a detour* *your output* *a standstill* *a tantrum*

1. ______________ – Come to this during the evening rush hour and for sure you'll be late for dinner.
2. ______________ – Avoid this if you're on a low-carb, low-fat, low-calorie diet.
3. ______________ – Increase this at work and you may get a nice bonus at Christmas.
4. ______________ – Keep this if you want to make a good impression at an interview.
5. ______________ – Avoid making this until you've got enough evidence to back it up.
6. ______________ – Take this if you want to avoid a traffic jam caused by road works.
7. ______________ – Throw (or have) this, and your parents will probably ground you for a month.
8. ______________ – Make this if you've done something wrong and you want to have a clear conscience.

B Fine-Tuning Your Knowledge – The numbers below refer to questions in the Vocabulary section of Practice Test 2. After reviewing the words, fill in each blank with the appropriate word.

123. complications **derivatives** **obstacles** **symptoms**	**a.** The road to success is full of ______________ that must be overcome. **b.** The operation was a success, but the patient died of ______________ . **c.** Shortness of breath and wheezing are classic ______________ of asthma. **d.** The words *quickness* and *quickly* are ______________ of *quick*.
129. assumption **data** **fundamental** **output**	**a.** Unfortunately, the theory was based on a series of wrong ______________ . **b.** "Not putting all your eggs in one basket" is a ______________ of business. **c.** The factory has had to increase its ______________ to keep up with rising demand. **d.** The researchers are compiling their ______________ . Our ______________ is that they will be ready to publish their findings in the fall.
133. complexion **disposition** **outlet** **tantrum**	**a.** Everyone needs to have a(n) ______________ for their emotions. **b.** Increasing terrorism in the region puts a new ______________ on the situation. **c.** The young woman had a classic "peaches and cream" ______________ . **d.** The child has a stormy ______________ and is likely to throw a ______________ without warning.
135. decline **descent** **inclination** **incline**	**a.** A ______________ in unemployment shows that the economy is recovering. **b.** Children with a(n) ______________ to be lazy need constant motivation. **c.** Most of her friends are of Greek ______________ . **d.** Some of the weaker cyclists walked their bikes up the steep ______________ . The ______________ was predictably much easier.
142. boom **bulge** **outrage** **surge**	**a.** Do you know anyone born during the population ______________ of the 1950s? **b.** A simple device can protect your computer against a power ______________ . **c.** The pregnant woman was proud of her ______________ . **d.** The latest terrorist ______________ was a devastating explosion at the city's main train station. The ______________ had been heard for miles around.
145. bag **daze** **fix** **flash**	**a.** You've been staring into nowhere as if you're in a ______________ . Are you OK? **b.** The mechanic said he'd have the car back to us in a ______________ . **c.** You've got yourself into this ______________ . Now get yourself out! **d.** He says the interview went well and he's got the job in the ______________ !

AUDACIOUS ADJECTIVES

A **Common Collocations** – Complete each phrase with a word from the box.

cordial	*defective*	*fervent*	*grim*	*reckless*	*stagnant*	*unilateral*	*wispy*

1. a ______________ head of hair

2. a ______________ hostess

3. a ______________ driver

4. a ______________ piece of equipment

5. a ______________ prayer

6. a ______________ pond/pool of water

7. a ______________ prospect

8. a ______________ declaration of war

B **Fine-Tuning Your Knowledge** – The numbers below refer to questions in the Vocabulary section of Practice Test 2. After reviewing the words, fill in each blank with the appropriate word.

116. ambivalent **equivalent** **malevolent** **prevalent**	**a.** It's sad that terrorism is so ______________ nowadays. **b.** Do you really believe that house is haunted by a ______________ ghost? **c.** I have 100 euros. Can you tell me what the ______________ amount is in U.S. dollars? **d.** The boss is ______________ about hiring the last candidate. He feels she may not have enough experience.
122. fervent **gaudy** **hectic** **wispy**	**a.** She's fond of wearing ______________ outfits, the brighter and louder the better. **b.** It's a ______________ time at the office. I wish they'd hurry up and hire more staff. **c.** The hostage's family made a ______________ plea for the return of their loved one. **d.** The sky was full of ______________ clouds.
125. explicit **indefinite** **irreverent** **negligible**	**a.** Luckily, the strike had only a(n) ______________ impact on the firm's sales. **b.** The children were punished for making ______________ comments. **c.** The boss left ______________ orders for us to complete the report before he returns. **d.** My plans are still ______________ . I'll let you know when I firm them up.
136. cautious **cordial** **reckless** **tolerant**	**a.** It's sometimes difficult to be ______________ of other people's prejudices. **b.** That ______________ comment may have just cost him his job. **c.** We couldn't have asked for a more ______________ welcome. **d.** ______________ drivers do their best to insure the safety of everyone on the road, while ______________ drivers are a danger to themselves and everyone else.
141. dejected **defective** **deficient** **deranged**	**a.** When the patient became ______________ , he had to be put in restraints. **b.** Anemia can be caused by a diet that is ______________ in iron. **c.** The players were understandably ______________ after they lost the championship. **d.** If the appliance is ______________ , you should return it to the manufacturer.
147. unchecked **undeclared** **undying** **unfounded**	**a.** Most writers stand in awe of Shakespeare's ______________ fame. **b.** The two sisters found themselves in an ______________ rivalry for the same man; both denied their interest, yet their feelings were obvious. **c.** Without evidence, your accusation is totally ______________ . **d.** As a result of ______________ government spending, the national debt has reached unprecedented heights.

PRICKLY PREPOSITIONS AND PARTICLES

The following extracts are taken from passages that you have encountered in Practice Test 2. Read each one quickly, and then fill in the gaps with an appropriate preposition or particle.

1. ________ a few caves, however, the conditions were ideal ________ the formation ________ a different kind ________ treasure. Groundwater rich ________ sulfur ________ the adjacent metal deposits began dissolving the limestone walls, releasing large quantities ________ calcium. This calcium, ________ turn, combined ________ the sulfur to form crystals ________ a scale never ________ seen ________ humans. ________ addition ________ 4-foot thick columns 50 feet ________ length, the cavern also contains row ________ row ________ shark-tooth-shaped formations ________ 3 feet high, set ________ odd angles. Fittingly, the pale, translucent crystals are made ________ selenite, a form ________ gypsum named ________ Selene, the Greek goddess ________ the moon.

2. Scientists have identified two ways ________ which species disappear. The first is through ordinary or "background" extinctions, where species that fail to adapt are slowly replaced ________ more adaptable life forms. The second is when large numbers ________ species go ________ the wall ________ relatively short periods ________ biological time. There have been five such extinctions, each provoked ________ cataclysmic evolutionary events caused ________ some geological eruption, climate shift, or space junk slamming ________ the earth. Scientists now believe that another mass extinction is currently ________ way (i.e., ________ progress) – and this time human fingerprints are ________ the trigger.

3. High-tech bloodless surgery techniques are now being used to mend broken bones, remove tattoos, and quiet chronic snoring. But their most important application ________ date may be ________ destroying hard-to-reach brain and spinal tumors. Without sawing ________ the skull or so much ________ cutting the scalp, doctors ________ Stanford University Medical Center are curing patients ________ brain and spinal tumors that were once considered deadly. The operations are made possible ________ the use ________ Stanford's computer-mediated stereotaxis radiosurgery system, also called the cyberknife. The cyberknife is essentially a robotic x-ray gun that shoots small amounts ________ radiation ________ tumors ________ hundreds of directions ________ overexposing other parts ________ the body. ________ effect, it is a robotic arm that locks the radiation beam ________ the tumor and constantly readjusts its aim ________ response ________ the patient's natural small movements. This eliminates the need ________ the circular metal "halo" frame that previously had to be screwed ________ the skull to hold the head ________ place. ... If advances keep ________ , the notion ________ a surgeon using a scalpel may someday seem ________ primitive ________ operating ________ anesthesia.

4. That aurora borealis lit ________ the northern night sky ________ the Scottish Highlands ________ March 13-14, 1989, but ________ this day I can still picture its colors, shapes, and movements. The show peaked ________ less than an hour, but its tonal themes lingered longer. It seemed an act ________ magic, but ________ course it was science ________ work: Electrically charged particles ________ the sun were making gases glow ________ the upper atmosphere.

   Thousands ________ miles away ________ Alaska, that same aurora caught the attention ________ Charles Deehr... . Deehr's work involves searching ________ patterns ________ the latest information sent ________ near-earth satellites ________ hopes ________ predicting auroral activity a day or so ________ advance. Such forewarning would make it possible to prepare electrical systems ________ earth and ________ space ________ disturbances.

3 Practice Test 3

Writing 30 minutes

- You may write in pen or pencil.
- You will have 30 minutes to write on one of the two topics. If you do not write on one of these topics, your paper will not be scored. If you do not understand the topics, ask the examiner to explain them.
- You may make an outline if you wish, but your outline will not count toward your score.
- Write about one-and-a-half to two pages. Your essay will be marked down if it is extremely short.
- You will not be graded on the appearance of your paper, but your handwriting must be readable. You may change or correct your writing, but you should not recopy the whole essay.
- Your essay will be judged on clarity and overall effectiveness, as well as on topic development, organization, and the range, accuracy, and appropriateness of your grammar and vocabulary. Your essay will be graded at the University of Michigan.

TOPICS For help in writing these compositions, see *Writing Tutorial,* pages 205-206.

1. Microsoft founder Bill Gates has suggested that the role of innovators is not just to drive breakthroughs in new products, but also to find ways to give more and more people access to these breakthroughs and their benefits. Choose one of the following areas, and discuss how innovators might fulfill the role that Gates mentions. (You may discuss the area in general or a specific breakthrough within the general area.)

   health and medicine   alternate forms of energy   computer technology   agriculture

2. Some people feel admission should be free to national museums, galleries, and major historical sites, while others disagree, arguing that admission fees are necessary. Discuss the arguments for and against establishing free admission to national treasures. Which do you feel is a better policy? Support your ideas with reasons and examples.

Managing your time on the 30-minute Writing task is crucial. Here's a plan that has worked well for many students. See the "Focus" box on page 8 for more details.

DECIDE	approx. 2 minutes
PLAN	approx. 5 minutes
WRITE	approx. 20 minutes
PROOFREAD	approx. 3 minutes

Listening approx. 35-40 minutes

This section of the examination tests your understanding of spoken English. The listening section has three parts. There are 50 questions. Mark all your answers on the separate answer sheet. Do not make any stray marks on the answer sheet. If you change your mind about an answer, erase your first answer completely.

Part I

In this part, you will hear short conversations. From the three answer choices given, choose the answer which means about the same thing as what you hear, or that is true based upon what you hear.

For problems 1 through 17, mark your answers on the separate answer sheet. No problems can be repeated.

Please listen carefully. Do you have any questions?

Some questions in Part I test your ability to understand the message and/or emotion conveyed by the speaker's tone of voice.

Questions like this are easy to spot, as one or more choices will contain an "emotion" word (e.g., **sad, amused, angry, bored**). When you see a set of choices with one or more emotion words, pay special attention not only to what the speakers say, but to how they say it.

This section contains three such questions. Can you spot them now, before you listen?

____

Sometimes it's not what they say but how they say it!

1. a. They're at a crowded restaurant.
   b. He's waiting for someone to come back.
   c. Every seat in the place is already occupied.

2. a. The boss has decided to give her a raise.
   b. She had another rough day at work.
   c. She did something that impressed the boss.

3. a. He already has plans for the evening.
   b. He's planning to get married soon.
   c. He doesn't want to go out with her.

4. a. She has not yet received his résumé.
   b. She's amused at how he sent his résumé.
   c. She was holding his résumé when he called.

5. a. He's just had a tooth pulled.
   b. He has a horrible toothache.
   c. His pain medication isn't working.

6. a. The recital was the best they've ever been to.
   b. The young musician showed great promise.
   c. She didn't expect to hear a piece she knew.

7. a. His alarm clock stopped unexpectedly.
   b. He forgot to set his alarm clock again.
   c. The batteries in his alarm clock went dead.

8. a. She's living with her parents at the moment.
   b. Finding a place to live is time-consuming.
   c. She's can't afford the apartment she saw.

9. a. He thinks flying is extremely risky.
   b. He' d like her to get to know him better.
   c. He always arranges things in advance.

10. a. He thinks what happened is funny.
    b. He can't wait till his son comes home.
    c. He's infuriated at what his son did.

11. a. They intend to finish in a few hours.
    b. She'll take a rest before she continues.
    c. There's no hope of their finishing on time.

12. a. He's lost an important document.
    b. His application is almost complete.
    c. His old boss has always been forgetful.

13. a. They're considering a major purchase.
    b. Her suggestion doesn't appeal to him.
    c. The couple has trouble making ends meet.

14. a. He likes the social aspect of it.
    b. It's the health benefits that motivate him.
    c. It's more of a bargain than he thought.

15. a. He likes her suggestion.
    b. He's indifferent to her suggestion.
    c. He thinks they order in too often.

16. a. The woman makes her feel inferior.
    b. She hates how the woman stares at her.
    c. She thinks the woman is jealous of her.

17. a. She thought Eve's reaction was strange.
    b. She and Eve argued about the film.
    c. The film disappointed her.

Part II

In this part, you will hear a question. From the three answer choices given, choose the one which best answers the question.

For problems 18 through 35, mark your answers on the separate answer sheet. No problems can be repeated. Please listen carefully. Do you have any questions?

Expect a number of questions to contain what the experts call **elisions**. These are words that we join together when we speak: e.g,. "Whatcha gonna do?" (What are you going to do?"), "How'd'ja like it?" (How would/did you like it?), and "Dya like him?" (Do you like him?). To answer correctly, you often need to identify the time frame the speaker is referring to and then choose your answer accordingly.

18. **a.** I'm sorry you feel that way.
b. I was referring to his incompetence.
c. I said it. You didn't.

19. **a.** I take the express train.
b. I was only a few blocks away when I called.
c. Sorry, I can't come later.

20. **a.** It's not me. It's the boss.
b. I always take my time.
c. If it were urgent, I'd tell you.

21. **a.** Sorry, you've got the wrong number.
b. A likely excuse.
c. Was it Adam's party?

22. **a.** You'd better not.
b. Maybe even better.
c. The sooner, the better.

23. **a.** That's what I'd do.
b. Provided you tell me.
c. I'm sure we can work something out.

24. **a.** None whatsoever. You'd better call.
b. I see no reason for it.
c. I think so, but you'd better check.

25. **a.** Tom had a new kitchen installed last week.
b. I haven't played tennis in a while.
c. It's awful, isn't it?

26. **a.** I'll pass, thanks.
b. A salad would be lovely.
c. I'm not in the habit of skipping meals.

27. **a.** You're right. There's nothing he can do.
b. There's no use, but maybe we can find one.
c. He used to, but not anymore.

28. **a.** I had no idea.
b. It couldn't have been.
c. A person with a very twisted sense of humor.

29. **a.** Stunning, isn't it?
b. Maybe another time.
c. Yes, I would.

30. **a.** Once, when I was a child.
b. I'd love to go there.
c. That's a hard one. There are so many!

31. **a.** What's taking so long?
b. Why am I not surprised?
c. Do you think you'll like it?

32. **a.** Mike and I saw a great movie.
b. I thought I'd go hiking. Care to join me?
c. I usually have lunch with Tim.

33. **a.** No, what did you have in mind?
b. Is it too late to back out?
c. Yes, I'd love to.

34. **a.** I never thought you'd ask.
b. I'd say you were wonderful!
c. I liked it a lot.

35. **a.** Yes, but it did no good.
b. He doesn't have a reason.
c. I suppose he could.

It's natural to want to panic if you hear unknown words as you listen to a long listening passage. If you feel yourself losing your cool, fight back the panic and try to stay focused so you concentrate on getting the basic message. See the tip at the bottom of the next page for advice on how to do this!

Part III

In this part, you will hear three short segments from a radio program. The program is called "Learning from the Experts." You will hear what three different radio guests have to say about three different topics.

Each talk lasts about two minutes. As you listen, you may want to take some notes to help you remember information given in the talk. Write your notes in the test booklet.

After each talk, you will be asked some questions about what was said. From the three answer choices given, you should choose the one that best answers the question according to the information you heard.

Remember, no problems can be repeated. For problems 36 through 50, mark all your answers on the separate answer sheet. Do you have any questions?

SEGMENT 1

36. What is the underlying purpose behind the Solar Decathlon?
- **a.** to show how aesthetically pleasing solar homes can be
- **b.** to demonstrate what solar homes can achieve
- **c.** to prove that solar homes are easily affordable

37. Who provides the largest amount of funding for a team's project?
- **a.** the students themselves
- **b.** the U.S. Energy Department
- **c.** wealthy graduates and corporations

38. Why is the term "decathlon" used to describe the competition?
- **a.** because the houses must be taken apart and transported in separate pieces
- **b.** because the houses are assessed in ten different categories
- **c.** because the houses must comply with set rules for living off the grid

39. In addition to being completely self-powered, what other "green" element did all of the entries incorporate?
- **a.** the use of recycled, reclaimed, or sustainably grown materials
- **b.** the sacrifices that people must make when they live "off-the-grid"
- **c.** the benefits of using solar power to recharge electric cars

40. What impressed the speaker about the interior of the University of Darmstadt entry?
- **a.** the design of its solar panels
- **b.** its cleverly designed oven
- **c.** the energy-efficient elevator

SEGMENT 2

41. How many Californian condors remained when experts decided to take drastic measures to save them?
- **a.** 3
- **b.** 22
- **c.** 300

42. According to Ethel Miller, what is currently the main obstacle to the condor's survival?
- **a.** the condor's unwillingness to breed in captivity
- **b.** hunters who regard the birds as pests
- **c.** lead bullet fragments found in dead game animals

43. What measure was finally taken in California in 2007 to protect the endangered bird?
- **a.** Legislators decided to shorten the hunting season.
- **b.** A law was passed banning hunters from using lead bullets.
- **c.** More game wardens were hired to enforce the new law.

(Segment 2 continues at top of next page)

44. What did William Cornatzer and a radiologist find when they conducted CAT scans on packages of ground deer meat?
   a. that just under 60% of the packages were contaminated with lead
   b. that the amount of lead they detected could pose no threat to humans
   c. that each package contained more fragments than experts had predicted

45. What final thought does Ethel Miller leave her listeners with?
   a. Even small amounts of lead can be lethal in humans.
   b. People needn't be alarmed by the presence of lead in small amounts.
   c. The danger of lead poisoning is real and must be addressed.

SEGMENT 3

46. According to Tim Reynolds, what is true of wildfires and building fires?
   a. Wildfires are easier to investigate than building fires.
   b. Both types are started more often by arsonists than by Mother Nature.
   c. Investigators use similar techniques to determine their origin.

47. Which of the following is NOT a predictable characteristic of wildfires?
   a. the exact path they will take once they get started
   b. the way they spread outward in a V- or U-shaped pattern
   c. the fact that they spread more quickly when moving uphill

48. Where would you expect experts to begin their investigation?
   a. the fire's point of origin
   b. the widest part of the V- or U-shaped burn
   c. any place that the wind changed the fire's burn path

49. Which of the following indicates to investigators that they are getting closer to a fire's point of origin?
   a. trees that have been damaged on one side
   b. fallen blades of grass with burned tips
   c. unburned tree limbs on burned ground

50. What point does Tim Reynolds make about finding the fire's point of origin?
   a. It does not always mean that the investigation is over.
   b. It means experts will soon have the evidence they need.
   c. It allows experts to determine the identity of the arsonist

Remember:

✓ Listen for the nouns and noun phrases that the speakers naturally emphasize. That's where the key content is.

✓ If you hear a technical term that you're unfamiliar with, don't give up! Chances are good that the term will be explained shortly before or after the speaker mentions it. If you're panicking, you may miss the explanation!

✓ Don't be thrown by descriptive verbs, adjectives, and adverbs that you may not have heard before. Most of the time these are window dressing and have little or no impact on the narrator's questions.

✓ The questions follow the order of information in the passage, so use them to organize your listening and help you stay focused on what's important. (See box at bottom of page 10.)

Don't panic! You don't have to understand every word!

Grammar – Cloze – Vocabulary – Reading 75 minutes

This section of the examination contains 120 problems, numbered 51 through 170. There are 40 grammar, 20 cloze, 40 vocabulary, and 20 reading comprehension problems. If you do not understand how to do the problems, raise your hand, and a proctor will explain the examples to you. None of the actual test problems can be explained.

Each problem has only one correct answer. Do not spend too much time on any one problem. If you do not know the answer to a problem, you may guess. Work quickly but carefully. You have one hour and 15 minutes (75 minutes) to answer all 120 problems. If you finish before the time is over, you may check your answers within the GCVR section only. Do not go back to the Listening section of the exam.

GRAMMAR

51. The new legislation will go into effect _____ the first of the year.
- **a.** as if
- **b.** as of
- **c.** as though
- **d.** as for

52. They didn't enjoy the movie the first time, so _____ it again is very slim.
- **a.** the likelihood of their seeing
- **b.** it's unlikely they'll see
- **c.** they probably won't see
- **d.** the likelihood of them to see

53. _____ so concerned about him if he had called you while he was away?
- **a.** Had you been
- **b.** Would you have been
- **c.** Were you
- **d.** Why were you

54. Ridership on city buses has fallen _____ dramatically since the 25% fare increase.
- **a.** out
- **b.** off
- **c.** down
- **d.** away

55. It's too early to say if he's finally found his dream job, but, as he puts it, "_____ ."
- **a.** So long
- **b.** So to speak
- **c.** So far, so good
- **d.** So be it

56. It was wrong of him _____ for what he did to you and your family.
- **a.** not having to apologize
- **b.** not to have apologized
- **c.** not apologizing
- **d.** that he hadn't apologized

57. She's just bought three new dresses, _____ her if she gains weight.
- **a.** none of them will fit
- **b.** that won't fit
- **c.** but none of them fit
- **d.** none of which will fit

58. He winked at me and gave me one of his _____ looks.
- **a.** known
- **b.** acknowledged
- **c.** knowing
- **d.** knowledgeable

59. _____ a new job until he was offered a substantial raise and promotion.
- **a.** His intention to find
- **b.** He's intent on finding
- **c.** He'd been intending to find
- **d.** His intention of finding

60. How dare you _____ your father's car without first asking his permission!
- **a.** have taken
- **b.** to take
- **c.** take
- **d.** taking

61. He said he didn't think the relationship would last, and _____ it didn't.
- **a.** to be sure that
- **b.** for sure
- **c.** sure enough
- **d.** as surely as

62. The child pleaded ignorance _____ the vase was broken.
- **a.** when asked him how
- **b.** when was he asked if
- **c.** when they asked him that
- **d.** when asked how

63. You'll save money if you buy the large, _____ size of that shampoo.
 a. economical
 b. economy
 c. economic
 d. economized

64. We slowed down our pace _____ let the children keep up with us.
 a. so
 b. so as to
 c. as if to
 d. in order that

65. The e-mail clearly says that the meeting _____ on the second floor at 3 p.m.
 a. holds
 b. will hold
 c. is to be held
 d. will be holding

66. The bigger and heavier the car, the more gas _____ to run it.
 a. it needs you
 b. you will need
 c. will need
 d. will need you

67. Of all the candidates we interviewed, _____ the necessary qualifications and experience.
 a. only one of them has
 b. only one of whom has
 c. there is the only one who has
 d. the only one who has

68. John's idea for the ad campaign is _____ the best that has been proposed.
 a. as far as
 b. few and far
 c. far away
 d. by far

69. Children _____ college-educated parents tend to read more than other children.
 a. whose
 b. who
 c. of
 d. by

70. There is no doubt in my mind that Marge was let go _____ to follow directions.
 a. in spite of her being unable
 b. of not being able
 c. on account of her inability
 d. in the event of not being able

Every ECPE grammar question tests one or more specific grammar topics. You can often get clues about what is being tested by studying the choices.

71. The Wilsons have recently purchased a _____ cottage on the outskirts of town.
 a. 19th-century, charming, stone
 b. charming, 19th-century, stone
 c. stone, 19th-century, charming
 d. charming, stone, 19th-century

72. The misunderstanding occurred because of your son _____ the message to you.
 a. didn't pass on
 b. not to pass on
 c. not passing on
 d. hadn't passed on

73. The employee assured his manager _____ a better job in the future.
 a. he would do
 b. that he did
 c. he is to do
 d. about having done

74. Unemployment is on the rise again, which means that good jobs are _____ .
 a. far and away
 b. far from it
 c. few and far between
 d. as far as they go

75. Not having seen the ad on TV, he _____ why everyone at the office was talking about it.
 a. lost himself to explain
 b. felt lost explaining
 c. was at a loss to explain
 d. got lost explaining

76. I hate to admit it, but I was _____ wrong about him. He's a charming young man.
 a. dead
 b. deathly
 c. deadly
 d. dying

77. _____ to pass the test is something that surprised everyone who knows him.
    a. How did he manage
    b. That he managed
    c. He managed
    d. Having managed

78. His grades are excellent, _____ he didn't get into the college of his choice.
    a. so
    b. still
    c. as
    d. yet

79. When she wants to, Maria _____ very sociable, but she has to be in the mood.
    a. may be
    b. might have been
    c. can be
    d. must be

80. If you want my honest opinion about her dress, I think it makes _____ heavy.
    a. her look
    b. her to look
    c. her looking
    d. that she looks

81. A problem seems _____ developing at the office, but I can't quite figure out why.
    a. that it is
    b. as though
    c. to be
    d. like

82. He already has a great job offer, so he _____ about his last-semester grades.
    a. is not concerning
    b. has not concerns
    c. does not concern
    d. is not concerned

83. _____ from me to tell you how you should run your life.
    a. So be it
    b. Far be it
    c. Let it be
    d. Be it not

84. _____ you can be reimbursed, your manager must give his approval.
    a. After
    b. Before
    c. Because
    d. Provided

85. As a result of an accident on the bridge, _____ to take a detour.
    a. the police asked that we
    b. we were asked
    c. the police asked to us
    d. we asked by the police

86. The new computer program is very user-friendly, so I'm sure you'll learn it _____ .
    a. for the time being
    b. in no time at all
    c. in due time
    d. on time

87. Without experience, she's got _____ to come for an interview.
    a. little chance of being asked
    b. little chance for asking
    c. a little chance to ask
    d. a little chance in asking

88. The main idea _____ in her essay is that we could be doing more to save the environment.
    a. is discussed
    b. discusses
    c. discussed
    d. discussing

89. The price they quoted us for the car was _____ of all taxes.
    a. included
    b. including
    c. inclusion
    d. inclusive

90. I'm inclined to agree _____ odd about the way she's been behaving.
    a. that there's something
    b. with something that's
    c. to what's
    d. on something

Cloze items often test your ability to follow the writer's train of thought (e.g., items 94 and 99). Before answering, widen your focus and consider several sentences before and after each blank.

Item 100 also tests train of thought. Note the word "in" before the blank. All of the choices collocate with "in," but which is the answer? Go back several sentences and consider each "in" phrase in context.

CLOZE

Passage 1 is about elephants.

Imagine a family of elephants, rumbling, trumpeting, their chorused voices deafening in the wilderness. To casual observers, the sight is pure animal theatrics, but biologist Joyce Poole knows there's a lot more happening than meets the ear. She knows that elephants not only trumpet their calls __(91)__ also squeal, cry, scream, roar, snort, rumble, and groan. Some sounds are so low-pitched that they aren't even __(92)__ to human ears.

Scientists say elephants have an elaborate __(93)__ of communication to maintain a complex social structure based on strong family ties. One of the __(94)__ identified so __(95)__ is what Poole describes as the "let's go" rumble, used to suggest "I want to go in this direction – let's go together." A drawn-out rumbling, it lasts about five to six seconds and is usually repeated every 80 seconds or so __(96)__ the caller gets results. __(97)__ is the "contact call." An elephant calling for a distant family member __(98)__ a powerful reverberating sound and then lifts its head and spreads its ears while listening for an __(99)__. If it receives one, it responds with an explosive sound, signifying "We're in __(100)__."

91. **a.** and **b.** can **c.** but **d.** they

92. **a.** dispensable **b.** audible **c.** sensible **d.** eligible

93. **a.** system **b.** way **c.** network **d.** technology

94. **a.** elephants **b.** relationships **c.** structures **d.** calls

95. **a.** long **b.** much **c.** far **d.** that

96. **a.** until **b.** because **c.** that **d.** provided

97. **a.** This **b.** There **c.** Another **d.** Rumbling

98. **a.** does **b.** emits **c.** exhales **d.** has

99. **a.** elephant **b.** enemy **c.** instant **d.** answer

100. **a.** touch **b.** danger **c.** love **d.** motion

Passage 2 is about sleep apnea.

At least half of all chronic snorers suffer from the disorder known as obstructive sleep apnea, in which breathing actually stops for as __(101)__ as 90 seconds, often hundreds of times a night. Each time the oxygen level drops, the snorer begins to waken __(102)__, with a loud snort, gasps for air. __(103)__ the heart must work harder during these episodes, sleep apnea __(104)__ the entire cardiovascular system and may eventually __(105)__ high blood pressure and enlargement of the heart. It may also __(106)__ the risk of stroke.

Apnea sufferers are __(107)__ chronically sleep deprived. __(108)__ their bodies must struggle constantly to keep the throat muscles tense enough to __(109)__ open airways, they __(110)__ slip into the deep sleep needed to wake up feeling rested.

101. **a.** far **b.** long **c.** soon **d.** little

102. **a.** up **b.** and **c.** but **d.** so

103. **a.** Since **b.** However **c.** Then **d.** Although

104. **a.** awakens **b.** destroys **c.** strains **d.** strengthens

105. **a.** lead **b.** cause **c.** raise **d.** suffer

106. **a.** endanger **b.** diminish **c.** increase **d.** promote

107. **a.** also **b.** not **c.** among **d.** more

108. **a.** Although **b.** Unless **c.** With **d.** Because

109. **a.** restrict **b.** close **c.** maintain **d.** block

110. **a.** rarely **b.** should **c.** gradually **d.** can

VOCABULARY

Take time to underline all key words in the question stem so you have the context firmly in mind before finalizing your answer. Doing so may save you from making careless mistakes on questions that are well within your range.

111. He realized that a generous pay raise would _____ the workers' morale.
- **a.** promote
- **b.** boost
- **c.** generate
- **d.** flourish

112. Don't let the iron get too hot, or you'll _____ that pretty silk blouse.
- **a.** shrink
- **b.** stain
- **c.** scorch
- **d.** rip

113. The landlord threatened to _____ him if he didn't pay his rent by the end of the month.
- **a.** exile
- **b.** repel
- **c.** evict
- **d.** deport

114. I've had enough of your _____ stories! Why don't you try telling the truth for a change?
- **a.** fabricated
- **b.** constructive
- **c.** manufactured
- **d.** assembled

115. The international community is now painfully aware of the _____ of rapid industrialization.
- **a.** coincidences
- **b.** constraints
- **c.** conclusions
- **d.** consequences

116. The children were _____ after the long hike in the woods.
- **a.** ravenous
- **b.** consumed
- **c.** ravaged
- **d.** devoured

117. He was desperate for money, so he sold his car at a _____ of its original cost.
- **a.** fraction
- **b.** fracture
- **c.** infraction
- **d.** fragment

118. Don't forget to _____ the envelope before you mail it.
- **a.** enclose
- **b.** weld
- **c.** seal
- **d.** inscribe

119. She fought bravely, but finally _____ to the devastating disease.
- **a.** perished
- **b.** surrendered
- **c.** expired
- **d.** succumbed

120. There's not much one can say about her, other than that she's quiet, plain, and rather _____ .
- **a.** infamous
- **b.** unconscious
- **c.** nondescript
- **d.** incomparable

121. To access your e-mail, you need to _____ with your user ID and password.
- **a.** boot up
- **b.** log on
- **c.** sign up
- **d.** check in

122. The police need _____ evidence before an arrest can be made; suspicion isn't enough.
- **a.** inevitable
- **b.** inaccessible
- **c.** tangible
- **d.** negligible

123. He was _____ embarrassed when the boss criticized him in front of the entire staff.
- **a.** indefinitely
- **b.** laudably
- **c.** rigorously
- **d.** acutely

124. He's hardly an Einstein yet. He's in his first year of physics and is still learning the _____ .
- **a.** outlines
- **b.** equations
- **c.** fundamentals
- **d.** grounds

Remember: ECPE reading questions are usually not in the same order as the facts presented in the text.

READING

Passage 1 is about string.

As with many household objects, a mundane ball of string can tell a complicated story. In Amazonian cultures, it is mostly the men who make natural string. They first strip the thin outer layer from the middle rib of a young palm leaf, then soak it for pliability. The strips are then dried and spun together, end over end. Hand-spun palm fiber string is so strong that it is used by the Tukano to weave hammocks and purses, to make bowstrings, and to tie feathers to headdresses, among a myriad of other uses. For anthropologists, this kind of string is a cultural marker, something that separates South American forest peoples from their neighbors on the open plains to the south. The more southerly cultures make their string from animal sinew, but forest dwellers prefer palm and other vegetation because it is abundant and serviceable. String made by people living at higher altitudes also incorporates alpaca and vicuna hair and sometimes human hair.

The making and use of plant-fiber string is, of course, not restricted to Amazonia. The Chinese have used macramé cord since antiquity to fasten and wrap things and also to record events. The Eskimos were enthusiastic practitioners of string games like cat's cradle, while the Polynesians used string maps for navigating. People have been making string for a very long time. From fiber impressions on fired clay, archaeologists have discovered evidence of string and rope-making technology in Europe dating back 28,000 years. And since string is highly perishable, the archaeological record can only hint at its wide range of uses. Our ancestors may have spun string long before our earliest record of it.

In the West, string is fading into memory. In most households, at least one ball of twine survives in the junk drawer, but when was the last time you needed it? In that sense, string (or the lack of it) in Western culture is also a cultural statement. We no longer have time to sit and weave. Nor do we receive bundles of mail tied up in twine; instead, e-mail comes in bundles of bytes that need no tying. And so, stringless, we too are set apart from forest people.

151. According to the passage, what is true about the making of plant-fiber string?
- **a.** It is a relatively recent phenomenon.
- **b.** It is a mundane yet necessary enterprise.
- **c.** It was unheard of in ancient China.
- **d.** It was widespread in ancient times.

152. What is true of string made by South American forest peoples?
- **a.** It has an extremely limited, though practical range of uses.
- **b.** It is not as strong as string made by open-plains dwellers.
- **c.** It is made from materials that are plentiful in the environment.
- **d.** It is more pliable and versatile than string from other cultures.

153. What is true about string in Western society?
- **a.** It is difficult to find in stores nowadays.
- **b.** We no longer have much need for it.
- **c.** It no longer makes a cultural statement.
- **d.** Few people remember what it was used for.

154. Why don't archaeologists know much about how early peoples used plant-fiber string?
- **a.** They were not interested in string until fairly recently.
- **b.** Ancient plant fibers have not survived the passage of time.
- **c.** String-making did not really appear until 28,000 years ago.
- **d.** The ancients burned string in clay pots, destroying the evidence.

155. What does the writer imply in the last paragraph?
- **a.** Technological societies have virtually outgrown their need for string.
- **b.** The lack of string in our society makes us superior to forest people.
- **c.** The lack of string in our society puts us at a distinct disadvantage.
- **d.** E-mail and computers have generally reduced the quality of our lives.

Passage 2 is about types of cells.

Within the human body there are cells that live rather like protozoans. Certain white blood cells, for example, are part of the immune system and flow as free individual cells within the blood; when they detect bacterial infections, however, they exit the circulatory system and enter affected tissues, where they crawl around to catch and eat the invaders. Like amoebas, they simply engulf the bacteria and digest them.

One specialized member of the immune system is called the "natural killer cell." Millions of them roam the body, searching for other cells that have turned cancerous. Once the killer cell finds its prey, it presses close and exudes a substance that kills the cell. Some researchers suspect cells frequently turn cancerous but are usually killed before they can proliferate into tumors. One reason tumors arise, then, may be defective killer cells, so some researchers are looking for ways to cure cancer by boosting the number of killer cells in the body.

Still other kinds of amoebalike cells inhabit bone tissue. When bones are growing, or healing after a fracture, these cells crawl through the hollow spaces, something like a snail that leaves a slime trail. The bone cell's slime, however, is a substance that hardens into the mineral part of bone, gradually building the bone's thickness. Other mobile bone cells do the opposite, taking up previously deposited bone by dissolving it in their path. Like sculptors, the two kinds of cells work in concert, removing bone here and adding bone there, to remodel the tiny bones of a baby into the big ones of an adult. When bones break, these cells receive a special signal that spurs them to knit the fragments together. Even if the bone fragments grow together in a crooked form, the bone sculptors will continue reshaping the affected area until it becomes normal again.

Skin cells also become mobile to heal wounds. Imagine a cut finger or a scraped knee. Special proto-skin cells crawl from the bottom layer of the epidermis and onto the exposed wound surface, where they multiply rapidly and distribute themselves in a thin layer over the entire damaged area. Once the cells have formed a complete layer, they begin dividing with a new result: the daughter cells change form and rebuild the skin's normally multi-layered structure.

156. What is true of skin cells that heal wounds?
- **a.** They begin their healing work at the deepest part of the wound.
- **b.** They begin their work by spreading over the outside of the wound.
- **c.** They are primitive so they multiply more slowly than other cells.
- **d.** They begin to heal all the layers of the skin simultaneously.

157. What do certain white blood cells and "natural killer cells" have in common?
- **a.** They kill their prey in exactly the same way.
- **b.** They both help the body fight against bacteria.
- **c.** They are both part of the body's immune system.
- **d.** They rarely venture outside the circulatory system.

158. Which cells secrete a substance that aids in the growth and repair of a certain tissue?
- **a.** specialized bone cells
- **b.** natural killer cells
- **c.** skin cells
- **d.** white blood cells

159. What may be true of "natural killer cells"?
- **a.** They cause cancerous tumors throughout the body.
- **b.** They pose a health risk only when they are defective.
- **c.** Lessening them may be the key to curing some cancers.
- **d.** They destroy malignant cells before they grow into tumors.

160. What is the main idea of the passage?
- **a.** Some cells bear a striking physical resemblance to protozoans and amoebas.
- **b.** Like primitive life forms, some cells are capable of motion and independent activity.
- **c.** The body is made up of millions of cells, each of which has a different function.
- **d.** Some cells are beneficial and constructive; others are harmful and destructive.

Passage 3 is about technology and evolution.

Contemporary crises – from nuclear overarmament to the degradation of the biosphere – highlight the potentially absurd character of cosmic evolution. The essence of this drama can be described in three phases: nature generates complexity; complexity generates efficiency; efficiency threatens the future of complexity.

Human beings possess prodigious intellectual faculties. They have split atoms, explored the solar system, and probed the first instants of the universe. The task they now face is incomparably more difficult: how to utilize the planet's finite resources to serve a projected population of 10 billion individuals. Our ancestors were never confronted with this problem. The Romans poured their waste waters into the Mediterranean Sea, but there were few Romans. The onus is on our generation and on those that follow to face and resolve this awesome challenge ... or else disappear. Nature makes no concessions. No species is sacred. Those that fail to establish a harmonious relationship with the biosphere are destined to die out rapidly.

The marvelous achievements of modern technology have grown in the context of biological evolution. Living creatures have developed behavioral patterns to survive in a hostile environment. The advent of the human species has raised these techniques to a formidable and problematic degree of complexity and efficiency. The various crises faced by humans through the recent decades call into question the very viability of this complexity and raise a fundamental issue: Is complexity not doomed to destroy itself upon reaching a certain level – which may, in fact, be the level it has reached today?

The significance of the possible failure of our complexity bears implications of cosmic dimensions. If life exists on other planets and living creatures have evolved and adapted, it is highly likely that intelligence and technology have developed as on Earth. Under these circumstances, crises analogous to ours have or will occur. A galactic voyage would reveal one of two distinct realities: living green planets harboring beings that have resolved the crises, or dead planets covered with toxic or radioactive debris where they have not. It is from this perspective that the evolution of life on earth takes on a truly cosmic significance.

161. According to the passage, what is the most difficult challenge that humanity has ever confronted?

- **a.** splitting the atom
- **b.** exploring the solar system
- **c.** meeting the needs of 10 billion people
- **d.** figuring out the origins of the universe

162. In the writer's opinion, what is the only thing humanity can do to save the planet from extinction?

- **a.** return to a more inefficient level of technology
- **b.** become much more efficient than it is now
- **c.** develop ways to survive in a hostile environment
- **d.** learn how to live harmoniously with the environment

163. Which of the following best sums up the paradox the author describes in the first paragraph?

- **a.** There has always been something absurd about the achievements of humanity.
- **b.** Contemporary humanity has deliberately put itself on a course of self-destruction.
- **c.** The more complex and efficient our achievements, the more we endanger our future.
- **d.** It is tragic that humanity has managed to endanger the environment with nuclear weapons.

164. According to the passage, which phrase best describes the accomplishments of modern technology?

- **a.** signs of our unsuccessful attempt to adapt
- **b.** a natural by-product of biological evolution
- **c.** proof that we are not as smart as we think
- **d.** doomed to bring about the end of civilization

165. Which statement best sums up the "cosmic significance" of the crisis that humanity now faces?

- **a.** It likely reflects the experience of intelligent societies on other planets, if they exist.
- **b.** If we are unable to resolve the crisis at hand, we will wind up with a dead planet.
- **c.** Living green planets are better than dead planets choked by toxic waste.
- **d.** If we succeed, intelligent life elsewhere in the universe may learn from us.

Passage 4 is about close relationships.

In Greek legend, a brash young sculptor named Pygmalion found the women of Cyprus so impossibly flawed that he resolved to carve a statue of his ideal woman. For months, he labored with all his prodigious skill (and also with a strange compulsion), rounding here, smoothing there, until he had fashioned the most exquisite figure ever conceived by art. So exquisite was his creation that Pygmalion fell passionately in love with it, and could be seen in his studio kissing its marble lips, fingering its marble hands, dressing and grooming the figure as if caring for a doll. But soon Pygmalion was desperately unhappy, for the lifeless statue could not return the warmth of his love. He had set out to shape his perfect woman, but had succeeded only in creating his own frustration and despair.

In our closest relationships, we all behave like Pygmalion to some extent. Many of us seem attracted at first to creatures quite different from ourselves, and we seem to take pleasure in the contrast. But as we start to vie for control of our relationships, we begin to see these differences as flaws and we set about to transform our loved ones according to our own values or agendas. Like Pygmalion, in short, we take up the project of sculpting them little by little to suit ourselves. And like Pygmalion, we are inevitably frustrated, since our well-intentioned efforts to make over our mates bring us little more than disappointment and conflict. Our Pygmalion projects must fail: either our loved ones fight back, and our relationships become battlegrounds; or they give in to us and become as lifeless as Pygmalion's statue. In this paradoxical game, we lose even if we win.

In the legend, Venus took pity on Pygmalion and brought his statue to life, and he and Galatea, as he named her, blushed, embraced, and married with the blessing of the goddess. The rest of us, however, cannot rely on such miraculous intervention. Living in the real world, we ourselves are responsible for the success of our relationships, and this means we must strive to abandon our Pygmalion projects. For only by respecting the right of our loved ones to be different can we begin to bring the beauty of our own relationships alive.

166. What is meant by the phrase "Pygmalion project"?
- **a.** a paradoxical game which no one wins and which everyone loses
- **b.** our vain attempt to change our loved ones to suit our own desires
- **c.** an artist's attempt to achieve perfection in whatever is created
- **d.** our attempt to regain and maintain control over our lives

167. What caused Pygmalion's frustration and despair?
- **a.** The women of Cyprus did not approve of what he had done.
- **b.** The statue the artist had sculpted was artistically flawed.
- **c.** He was ashamed of having fallen in love with a marble statue.
- **d.** The statue, though perfect, was incapable of returning his love.

168. What does the writer predict will happen if we continue our Pygmalion projects?
- **a.** Our loved ones will recognize our good intentions.
- **b.** Our loved ones will inevitably fight back and cause conflict.
- **c.** We are sure to bring more happiness into our lives.
- **d.** We will always be disappointed and frustrated.

169. Which is **not** true according to the text?
- **a.** Pygmalion's story ended happily, despite his original frustration.
- **b.** Most of us are attracted to people who are exactly like ourselves.
- **c.** It is counterproductive to try to change someone you love.
- **d.** Our Pygmalion projects are destined not to succeed.

170. In the writer's opinion, what should his readers do?
- **a.** stop worrying about their relationships
- **b.** pray for a miracle and don't give up hope
- **c.** honor the right of their loved ones to be different
- **d.** give up, because relationships are never perfect

Vocabulary Enhancement

Let There Be Light

In the opening lines of the Bible's Book of Genesis, the Lord says, "Let there be light" and there was light. But what kind of light was it? Did the Sun suddenly ***flare*** *into existence and begin to* ***radiate*** *a harsh* ***glare*** *... or did it slowly* ***illuminate*** *the sky with a gentle, rosy* ***glow****? And what if we were to take the galactic voyage suggested in Reading Passage 3? Would we find living green planets* ***glowing*** *with life and energy or balls of "radioactive debris" dimly* ***phosphorescing*** *in the distance? Let's take a closer look at these and other "light" words.*

A Shedding Light on "Light" Words – Study the explanations and examples, and then complete the sentences below.

Send out a steady stream of light: Shine means "give off light" – e.g., the sun **shines** brightly; eyes **shine** with joy. If something **beams**, it sends out light and warmth, often in rays (or **beams**) – e.g., the sun **beams** down, a flashlight emits a **beam** of light. **Beam** is also used figuratively to mean "smile broadly" – e.g., a person **beams** with joy. **Radiate** means "send out rays of light or heat"; it is also used figuratively – e.g., a person can **radiate** love, confidence, or health. Softer than these is **glow**, meaning "shine with a soft, steady, warm light" – e.g., coals **glow** in a fire, a person **glows** with health. Even softer is **phosphoresce**, "glow faintly, coolly." Finally, **illuminate** means "shine light on something, or light something up" – e.g., a single, bare light bulb **illuminates** the room. **Illuminate** can also be used figuratively – e.g., I learned a lot from the professor's **illuminating** discussion.

Shine suddenly and briefly: **Flash** means "give off a sudden, brief, bright light" – e.g., lightning **flashed**, then the sky went dark. **Flare** means "burst into sudden bright light that soon dims" – e.g., a match **flares** in the dark then goes out. **Glint** means "give off a short, bright reflection of light" – e.g., a knife blade **glints** in the sun.

Shine brightly with reflected light: If something with a smooth, clean surface reflects light steadily and brightly, it **gleams** – e.g., a clean car **gleams** in the sun, as do clean, white teeth. If things **sparkle** or **glitter**, they shine with short, bright flashes of light – e.g., a diamond **sparkles/glitters**. When light reflects off a wet surface, we use **glisten** – e.g., wet grass **glistens** in the sun.

Shine softly and unsteadily: **Twinkle** means "shine with a light that changes constantly from bright to faint" – e.g., lights **twinkle** in the distance and stars **twinkle** in the sky. Slightly more gentle are **glimmer** and **shimmer**, which mean "shine with a faint, unsteady light" – e.g., a lake **glimmers/shimmers** in the moonlight. **Shimmer** can also mean "appear to shake slightly" – e.g., a sidewalk may **shimmer** in the hot summer heat (but it does **not** glimmer). Finally, **flicker** means "shine on and off, weakly and unsteadily" – e.g., a candle **flickers** in the wind, lights **flicker** before a black-out.

Shine with a light that is hard to look at: When things shine so brightly that it is hard for us to see, we use **dazzle** – e.g., the car headlights **dazzled** us. Figuratively, you can also **be dazzled** (or deeply impressed) by someone's skill or beauty. When things shine with a harsh, unpleasant light, we use **glare** – e.g., the desert sun **glared** in the sky.

1. The shiny, new car **flickered** / **gleamed** / **phosphoresced** in the sun.
2. She remembers how her grandfather's eyes **glared** / **flickered** / **twinkled** when he smiled.
3. The sides of the horse **sparkled** / **glistened** / **radiated** with sweat.
4. Most skiers wear sunglasses to protect their eyes from the harsh **glare** / **glint** / **sparkle** of the sun.
5. The child asked his parents to buy him a watch that **twinkled** / **flared** / **glowed** in the dark.
6. As the old saying goes, "All that **glitters** / **sparkles** / **flashes** is not gold."
7. The rays of the setting sun **twinkled** / **beamed** / **flickered** through the clouds.
8. When the boss **glares** / **shimmers** / **dazzles** at you like that, be careful. It usually means that nasty temper of his is about to **flicker** / **flash** / **flare up**.

B An Illuminating Lightbox – Write the "light" word(s) suggested by each photo. Many answers are possible, so be ready to explain your thoughts.

1 ____________

2 ____________

3 ____________

4 ____________

5 ____________

6 ____________

7 ____________

8 ____________

C Enlighten Me, Please – Explain the differences between the words and phrases below.

1. **elucidate a poem / illustrate a poem -** ____________
2. **highlight a point / illustrate a point -** ____________
3. **highlighted hair / lustrous hair / luminous hair -** ____________
4. **an illustrated book / an illustrious book / an illuminating book / a lucid book -** ____________

D "Light" Idioms - Match the bold phrases in sentences 1-8 with their meanings (a-h).

1. ______ Their newborn child **is the light of their life**.
2. ______ I'm so tired that I'm sure I'll **go out like a light** as soon as my head hits the pillow.
3. ______ The boss has decided to **give the green light to** your proposal.
4. ______ We**'re** still **light years away** from solving the world's problems.
5. ______ When the facts **come to light**, she will have to resign.
6. ______ We're finishing the project next week. It feels good to **see light at the end of the tunnel**.
7. ______ I warned her not to marry him. Now I think she's finally starting to **see the light**.
8. ______ For their anniversary, they've decided to **trip the light fantastic** at a really fancy nightclub!

a. be a very long way from something
b. become known, be made public
c. be (somebody's) most special person
d. fall asleep immediately
e. feel relief that something is about to end
f. give permission for something to begin
g. go dancing in high style
h. understand the truth

Vocabulary Consolidation

VEXING VERBS

A Common Collocations – Complete each phrase with a word from the box.

accentuate *check in with* *reminisce* *shuffle* *snap* *thrive* *trickle* *twinkle*

1. eyes ______________ with delight
2. tears ______________ down your face
3. parents ______________ a baby-sitter
4. soldiers ______________ to attention
5. optimists ______________ the positive
6. dealers ______________ a deck of cards
7. plants ______________ on sunshine
8. good friends ______________ about old times

B Fine-Tuning Your Knowledge – The numbers below refer to questions in the Vocabulary section of Practice Test 3. After reviewing the words, fill in each blank with the correct form of the appropriate verb.

125. **flee** **spew** **stem** **trickle**	**a.** Have you got any idea what her bad mood ______________ from? **b.** No wonder you ______________ the company! The boss has a temper like a volcano! I've never heard anyone ______________ insults the way he does. **c.** Police are doing their best to ______________ the recent wave of burglaries. **d.** A few complaints have ______________ in, but by and large the public's reaction to the program is overwhelmingly positive.
128. **giggle** **squeak** **twinkle** **wince**	**a.** How can you sit there ______________ when I'm ______________ in pain? **b.** If you live in a big city, you can forget about watching the stars ______________ . **c.** Her hair is so clean that it ______________ when you touch it. **d.** Did you see how he ______________ when they mentioned his ex-wife? He's obviously still upset about the divorce.
131. **accentuate** **formulate** **pronounce** **renounce**	**a.** The ambulance came quickly, but the victim was ______________ dead on arrival. **b.** I love the way your new hairstyle ______________ your high cheekbones. **c.** People will be shocked if the prince decides to ______________ his right to the throne. **d.** It took them a month to ______________ their ideas for the new sales campaign.
139. **drum** **point** **snap** **tap**	**a.** I found myself ______________ my foot in time to the catchy tune. **b.** Lower your voice! How dare you ______________ at me like that! **c.** Nobody's been arrested, but all the evidence ______________ to the victim's wife. **d.** Would you please stop ______________ your fingers on the table? You're driving me crazy!
144. **arrive** **come** **draw** **reach**	**a.** The boss needs more time. He hasn't ______________ at a decision yet. **b.** What conclusions can you ______________ from your observations? **c.** When you ______________ a decision, please let me know. **d.** Has the committee ______________ to a decision yet?
147. **collaborate** **commiserate** **identify** **reminisce**	**a.** He quit the club when he realized he did not ______________ with its goals. **b.** Not wanting to do the project alone, he's decided to ______________ with a colleague. **c.** We spent the evening ______________ about old times. **d.** I had an awful day! I need someone to ______________ with. Can I come over?

NOTORIOUS NOUNS

A **Amusing Associations** – Find the phrase in the box that is suggested by each prompt.

all fours *an upset* *edge* *equations* *fundamentals* *subordinates* *the minority* *the rocks*

1. ______________ – If you can solve these, you've probably got a good head for math.
2. ______________ – If you're in this, your vote doesn't count for very much.
3. ______________ – Before you learned how to walk, you crawled around on these.
4. ______________ – You'd better learn these before you try anything more advanced.
5. ______________ – If your best friend refuses to talk to you, your relationship is probably on these.
6. ______________ – You don't have these if you're at the very bottom of the corporate ladder.
7. ______________ – If you're waiting for important news, you're probably on this.
8. ______________ – If you've just experienced one of these, you won't be in the mood for celebrating.

B **Fine-Tuning Your Knowledge** – The numbers below refer to questions in the Vocabulary section of Practice Test 3. After reviewing the words, fill in each blank with the appropriate word.

124. **equation** **fundamentals** **grounds** **outline**	**a.** $E = mc^2$ is a(n) ______________ that almost all people recognize. **b.** Many writers start with a(n) ______________ of their ideas before they begin to write. **c.** The company had plenty of ______________ for dismissing the new assistant. For starters, she was totally unfamiliar with the ______________ of office procedure.
130. **executives** **peers** **subordinates** **superiors**	**a.** In the corporate world, middle managers are considered junior ______________ . **b.** All managers have one or more ______________, whom they report to, and one or more ______________ , who report to them. **c.** The child was ill last year and now finds it hard to keep up with his ______________ .
132. **all fours** **edge** **firm ground** **the rocks**	**a.** Did they call yet? I'll be on ______________ until we know they're safe. **b.** The economy was strong a few years ago, but lately it's been on ______________ . **c.** When we arrived, Mom was down on ______________ , scrubbing the kitchen floor. **d.** She's done her research, so she'll be on ______________ when she speaks to the boss.
136. **memorabilia** **memorials** **reminders** **reminiscences**	**a.** The Washington Mall is the site of several ______________ to fallen soldiers. **b.** He intends to put his ______________ into a memoir; they'll make interesting reading. **c.** He's proud of having been in the Olympics. Have you seen all his ______________ ? **d.** The refrigerator in our house also functions as a family bulletin board. Mother is always taping ______________ to it so we don't forget things.
145. **uprising** **upset** **upstart** **upsurge**	**a.** If the ______________ spreads, the dictator will have a civil war on his hands. **b.** We all thought Joe would win, so Mike's victory was a real ______________ . **c.** I hate to admit it, but that young ______________ the boss hired knows what he's doing! Since he came on board, there's been a terrific ______________ in sales.
146. **account** **balance** **deposit** **statement**	**a.** According to her latest bank ______________ , she has plenty of money in her ______________ . Her ______________ is currently $5,000. With today's ______________ of $500, that will bring it up to $5,500. **b.** Witnesses are usually asked to fill out a sworn ______________ in which they write down an ______________ of what they saw.

AUDACIOUS ADJECTIVES

A Common Collocations – Complete each phrase with a word from the box.

acute *chubby* *deficient* *husky* *indigenous* *inevitable* *rigorous* *unfounded*

1. a(n) ______________ voice
2. a(n) ______________ baby
3. a(n) ______________ species
4. an iron-______________ diet
5. a(n) ______________ pain
6. a(n) ______________ outcome
7. a(n) ______________ accusation
8. a(n) ______________ examination

B Fine-Tuning Your Knowledge – The numbers below refer to questions in the Vocabulary section of Practice Test 3. After reviewing the words, fill in each blank with the appropriate word.

122. inaccessible **inevitable** **negligible** **tangible**	**a.** DNA testing is amazing. Even a single hair can be used as ______________ proof that someone has committed a crime. **b.** Once winter sets in, the remote mountain village is ______________ till spring. **c.** It was ______________ that he failed. He hadn't studied all semester. **d.** The doctors are concerned that the patient has made only ______________ progress.
127. hand-picked **offhand** **second-hand** **underhanded**	**a.** Many newly-weds furnish their first apartment with ______________ furniture. **b.** It was just a(n) ______________ remark. He didn't mean to offend you. **c.** A leader's ______________ choices do not always work out. Remember the finance wizard the boss brought in from his previous company? He turned out to be a(n) ______________ embezzler who stole $1,000,000!
133. dislocated **disoriented** **displaced** **disposed**	**a.** The refugee camp is operating at full capacity, providing shelter and food for more than 5,000 ______________ persons. **b.** The director hasn't given the project the green light yet, but she definitely seems favorably ______________ towards the idea. **c.** The driver suffered a ______________ shoulder and was slightly ______________ for a few hours after the crash, but he's expected to make a full recovery.
134. chubby **husky** **puffy** **wispy**	**a.** The sky was blue, with a few ______________ clouds here and there. **b.** The medication makes her retain water, which is why her ankles are ______________ . **c.** He's a bit overweight, but he's built too solidly to be called ______________ ; stout or ______________ would be a better way to describe him. **d.** The poor baby. People are always pinching her ______________ cheeks and tousling her fine, ______________ hair.
141. deficient **efficient** **proficient** **sufficient**	**a.** It's easier to become ______________ in English if you learn the language while living in an English-speaking country. **b.** He was fired because his performance was ______________ over the past year. **c.** A few hours should be ______________ time for you to finish the task. **d.** Air-conditioners are far from what you'd call energy-______________ .
149. incongruous **inconspicuous** **incredulous** **indigenous**	**a.** The Maori are an ______________ people of New Zealand. **b.** How ______________ to find someone still using an old manual typewriter in an office full of state-of-the-art computers. **c.** Did you really think you'd be ______________ in that outrageous outfit? Everyone's staring at you, and they've got the most ______________ looks on their faces!

PRICKLY PREPOSITIONS AND PARTICLES

The following extracts are taken from passages that you have encountered in Practice Test 3. Read each one quickly, and then fill in the gaps with an appropriate preposition or particle.

1. Scientists say elephants have an elaborate system ________ communication because they need it to maintain a complex social structure based ________ strong family relationships. One ________ the calls identified so far is what Poole describes ________ the "let's go" rumble, which is used to suggest "I want to go ________ this direction – let's go together." A drawn-out rumbling, it lasts about five ________ six seconds and is usually repeated every 80 seconds or so until the caller gets results.

2. People have been making string ________ a very long time. ________ fiber impressions ________ fired clay, archaeologists have discovered evidence ________ string and rope-making technology ________ Europe dating back 28,000 years. And since string is highly perishable, the archaeological record can only hint ________ its wide range ________ uses. Our ancestors may have spun string long ________ our earliest record ________ it. ________ the West string is fading ________ memory. ________ most households, ________ least one ball ________ twine survives ________ the junk drawer, but when was the last time you needed it? ________ that sense, string (or the lack ________ it) ________ Western culture is also a cultural statement. We no longer have time to sit and weave. Nor do we receive bundles ________ mail tied ________ twine; instead, e-mail comes ________ bundles ________ bytes that need no tying. And so, stringless, we too are set apart ________ forest people.

3. Still other kinds ________ amoebalike cells inhabit bone tissue. When bones are growing, or healing ________ a fracture, these cells crawl ________ the hollow spaces, something ________ a snail that leaves a slime trail. The bone cell's slime, however, is a substance that hardens ________ the mineral part of bone, gradually building the bone's thickness. Other mobile bone cells do the opposite, taking ________ previously deposited bone ________ dissolving it in their path. ________ sculptors, the two kinds ________ cells work ________ concert, removing bone here and adding bone there, to remodel the tiny bones ________ a baby ________ the big ones ________ an adult.

4. ________ our closest relationships, we all behave like Pygmalion ________ some extent. Many ________ us seem attracted ________ first ________ creatures quite different ________ ourselves, and we seem to take pleasure ________ the contrast. But as we start to vie ________ control ________ our relationships, we begin to see these differences ________ flaws and we set ________ to transform our loved ones according ________ our own values or agendas. Like Pygmalion, ________ short, we take ________ the project ________ sculpting them little ________ little to suit ourselves. And like Pygmalion, we are inevitably frustrated, since our well-intentioned efforts to make ________ our mates bring us little more than disappointment and conflict. Our Pygmalion projects must fail: either our loved ones fight ________, and our relationships become battlegrounds; or they give ________ ________ us and become ________ lifeless ________ Pygmalion's statue.

5. ________ the legend, Venus took pity ________ Pygmalion and brought his statue ________ life, and he and Galatea, as he named her, blushed, embraced, and married ________ the blessing ________ the goddess. The rest ________ us, however, cannot rely ________ such miraculous intervention. Living ________ the real world, we ourselves are responsible ________ the success ________ our relationships, and this means we must strive to abandon our Pygmalion projects.

4 Practice Test 4

Writing 30 minutes

- You may write in pen or pencil.
- You will have 30 minutes to write on one of the two topics. If you do not write on one of these topics, your paper will not be scored. If you do not understand the topics, ask the examiner to explain them.
- You may make an outline if you wish, but your outline will not count toward your score.
- Write about one-and-a-half to two pages. Your essay will be marked down if it is extremely short.
- You will not be graded on the appearance of your paper, but your handwriting must be readable. You may change or correct your writing, but you should not recopy the whole essay.
- Your essay will be judged on clarity and overall effectiveness, as well as on topic development, organization, and the range, accuracy, and appropriateness of your grammar and vocabulary. Your essay will be graded at the University of Michigan.

TOPICS For help in writing these compositions, see *Writing Tutorial*, pages 207-208.

1. The rising levels of congestion and air pollution found in most of the world's cities are a direct result of the rapidly increasing number of private cars in use. In order to reverse this, many cities have taken measures to encourage people to use their cars less and public transportation more. How effective have these measures been in your country? What new measures do you think should be put into effect to improve the situation?

2. Some people feel that in many countries the educational system is obsolete and that as result, students in these countries will not be prepared to compete in the world economy. Assess the situation in your country. What are the major strengths and/or weaknesses of the educational system? What steps do you think need to be taken to ensure that future generations will be prepared to compete in the modern world?

Writing Tasks that Don't Quite Fit the Mold

It's possible that one or both of the essay topics you're presented with will not quite conform to the four standard essay types that are outlined in the chart on page 9. Topic 2, for example, makes a statement, and then asks you to assess the situation by answering two questions: (a) What are the strengths and/or weaknesses ... ? and (b) What steps do you think should be taken ... ?

When responding to topics like these, you can almost always get ideas for structuring the Main Body (or "Tell them" part) of your essay by reading the task carefully and identifying exactly what the topic asks you to do. If the topic presents you with two questions or tasks (as with both topics above), then devote one paragraph of the Main Body to each. If the topic presents you with only one question or task (e.g., Discuss the qualities that contribute to the success of a particular invention.), then consider discussing two qualities with a paragraph devoted to each.

When you're ready to begin, write your essay, using the "Tell Them" prototype below.

"TELL THEM" Prototype

Introduction → Tell them what you're going to tell them.

Main Body → Tell them.

Conclusion → Tell them what you told them.

Listening approx. 35-40 minutes

This section of the examination tests your understanding of spoken English. The listening section has three parts. There are 50 questions. Mark all your answers on the separate answer sheet. Do not make any stray marks on the answer sheet. If you change your mind about an answer, erase your first answer completely.

Part I

In this part, you will hear short conversations. From the three answer choices given, choose the answer which means about the same thing as what you hear, or that is true based upon what you hear.

For problems 1 through 17, mark your answers on the separate answer sheet. No problems can be repeated.

Please listen carefully. Do you have any questions?

Coping with Paraphrase Items

Another common item type requires you to recognize a paraphrase (or simple restatement) of something that one of the speakers has said. Typically, the dialogues will contain one or more phrasal verbs or idioms that are easily misinterpreted if you don't fully understand what has been said.

Previewing the answer choices won't help you predict which items fall into this category or what language you'll be asked to paraphrase. So what can you do? As you listen, try jotting down the idiom or phrasal verb you hear. Your brief note may be just enough to help you discriminate between the correct paraphrase and a cleverly worded distractor.

1. **a.** She thinks he should buy some new boots.
   b. She'll start up her computer to help him.
   c. She recently bought some boots online.

2. **a.** She tripped over someone at the flea market.
   b. She bought something that isn't worth much.
   c. She spent a lot of money on something.

3. **a.** He was afraid she wasn't coming.
   b. He wants her to stay seated.
   c. He doesn't believe she's stuck in traffic.

4. **a.** He's managed to clog up the sink.
   b. He offers to fix the sink for her.
   c. He promises not to put gum in the sink again.

5. **a.** She wants to borrow something from him.
   b. She wants him to hand her something.
   c. She wants him to read something.

6. **a.** He argued with Tommy.
   b. He believed what Tommy said.
   c. He owes Tommy money.

7. **a.** He's a security detective.
   b. He's a purse snatcher.
   c. He works in a supermarket.

8. **a.** The company has financial problems.
   b. They've just lost their jobs.
   c. The company will have to close.

9. **a.** The boss was very understanding.
   b. The boss was displeased with her.
   c. The boss apologized for being unreasonable.

10. **a.** The article seemed to be well researched.
    b. They thought the writer's ideas were valid.
    c. They disagreed with the writer's objections.

11. **a.** They both have two children in college.
    b. She thinks the next few years will be difficult.
    c. She can't wait for her children to finish college.

12. **a.** Doctors are sure the patient will recover.
    b. The patient's condition is worsening.
    c. The patient's condition is about the same.

13. **a.** Her children were disappointed.
    b. Her children frequently misbehave.
    c. Her children don't like sailing.

14. **a.** She's tempted to return the TV she bought.
    b. She can't justify buying a new TV yet.
    c. She doesn't intend to buy a flat-screen TV.

15. **a.** She's not sure how much the car will cost.
    b. She drives an old car.
    c. Her car is still in the showroom.

16. **a.** She didn't like his moustache.
    b. She hadn't notice he'd shaved.
    c. She wishes he would shave.

17. **a.** He's been hiding the truth from her.
    b. He forgot to mail Marta's card.
    c. She doesn't believe him.

Part II

In this part, you will hear a question. From the three answer choices given, choose the one which best answers the question.

For problems 18 through 35, mark your answers on the separate answer sheet. No problems can be repeated. Please listen carefully. Do you have any questions?

Stay alert, particularly at the start of each question! If you miss the interrogative word at the beginning of an item, you may find that the answer you choose is a cleverly written distractor that contains similar information but not exactly what the question asked for!

And remember! Not all questions start with interrogatives! If the question starts with a helping verb – e.g., a form of *be, have, do,* or a modal such as *can, could, will, would, shall/should,* or *may* - then you're dealing with a *yes/no* question that requires a direct or indirect *yes/no* answer, with or without further comment.

18. **a.** It's Mary's birthday.
b. All of her old school friends.
c. I know, but I'm not sure when.

19. **a.** I didn't. I thought it was awful.
b. I'd love to. What time does it start?
c. Yes, I did. It was beautifully done.

20. **a.** Yes, it did. About an hour ago.
b. The weatherman says we're in for snow.
c. Hold on. I'll have to check.

21. **a.** I think he said Paris.
b. I'm pretty sure it's work-related.
c. I've always wanted to.

22. **a.** The boss's, but as usual he forgot.
b. Sorry, it was my fault.
c. I've got some free time, so I can do it.

23. **a.** Do you think you could do it?
b. I'll do it!
c. Little Tommy did it.

24. **a.** To Berlin.
b. London, I think.
c. From Manchester.

25. **a.** We've still got time. Relax.
b. If we hadn't, we would have been late.
c. Yes, we did.

26. **a.** Of course, he needs it.
b. No, he doesn't.
c. Of course, I am. The meeting's at 3:00.

27. **a.** We'll have to wait and see.
b. I wish she had. I needed the help.
c. To be honest, I'm not really sure.

28. **a.** I hadn't planned on it, but I will.
b. Until this report is finished.
c. By 5:00. I have to leave early.

29. **a.** I thought I paid you back already.
b. You couldn't have. I was broke last week.
c. Sorry, I don't have any cash on me.

30. **a.** When he said he was with you.
b. I know. He's still in bed.
c. Yes, I'm sure of it.

31. **a.** Yes, he definitely wants to see you.
b. Now, if possible.
c. No, he told me yesterday.

32. **a.** I know. They never used to fight.
b. About 10 o'clock, I think.
c. Something big, that's for sure.

33. **a.** Yes, Gary's.
b. No, I didn't find them.
c. No, I'm still looking for them.

34. **a.** No, you don't have to.
b. Sorry, I'll turn it down.
c. Why, can't you hear it?

35. **a.** You did, but I changed my mind.
b. When did you decide?
c. I wish you would.

Part III

In this part, you will hear three short segments from a radio program. The program is called "Learning from the Experts." You will hear what three different radio guests have to say about three different topics.

Each talk lasts about two minutes. As you listen, you may want to take some notes to help you remember information given in the talk. Write your notes in the test booklet.

After each talk, you will be asked some questions about what was said. From the three answer choices given, you should choose the one that best answers the question according to the information you heard.

Remember, no problems can be repeated. For problems 36 through 50, mark all your answers on the separate answer sheet. Do you have any questions?

When notetaking is a must ...

When a set of answer choices contains three numbers or dates, listen carefully for those numbers or dates during the recording. Chances are you will hear information related to all three choices, so it's vital to jot down a quick note next to each. By doing so, you'll be much better prepared to answer the narrator's question without having to rely on your memory.

Try doing this for items 38 and 41. As you listen to the recording, jot down a quick note next to each choice.

SEGMENT 1

36. What term does Simon Richie use to describe the distance that food travels from farm to plate?
- **a.** food miles
- **b.** greenhouse gas emissions
- **c.** locavores

37. For what reason do some people attempt to maximize their consumption of locally grown foods?
- **a.** so they can quantify what impact the food industry has on climate change
- **b.** to ensure that all locavores have sufficient access to farmers' markets
- **c.** in order to curb global warming by reducing the distance food travels

38. Which percentage is associated with agricultural and industrial practices related to the growing and harvesting of food?
- **a.** 11% of a family's food emissions ____________________
- **b.** 83% of a family's food emissions ____________________
- **c.** 13.5% of a family's total emissions ____________________

39. According to Simon Richie, which of the following statements is true?
- **a.** Being a locavore is the most efficient way to reduce food-based greenhouse emissions.
- **b.** Our driving habits produce more greenhouse gas emissions than our food-related activities
- **c.** Carbon dioxide has less impact on global warming than methane and nitrous oxide.

40. In Simon Richie's view, what is the main strength of the Carnegie Mellon study?
- **a.** It includes a better analysis of the impact of food miles.
- **b.** It looks at many more aspects of the life cycle of food production
- **c.** It excludes $C0_2$ and focuses on the impact of methane and nitrous oxide.

SEGMENT 2

41. In what month of 2007 did park rangers discover that the lake had disappeared?
- **a.** March ____________________
- **b.** mid-May ____________________
- **c.** late May ____________________

42. Which of the following was NOT related to scientists' theory that an earthquake had caused the lake's disappearance?
- **a.** evidence that global warming was shrinking nearby glaciers
- **b.** the fact that a tremor had occurred the previous month
- **c.** the sizable crack they found in the dry lake bed

(Segment 2 continues at top of next page)

43. What technical term does Margaret Wentworth use to describe a natural dam made of ice, rock, and sediment?
  a. a fissure
  b. a moraine
  c. an avalanche

44. To what did scientists eventually attribute the lake's disappearance?
  a. water running out through the bottom of the lake
  b. rising water levels causing the moraine to collapse
  c. chunks of ice melting on the dry lake bed

45. Why does Margaret Wentworth mention the appearance of the lake at the end of the broadcast?
  a. to point out how strange it is that no one knows exactly when it occurred
  b. to underline that it's natural for lakes to appear and disappear in Chile
  c. to suggest that few people back then were talking about global warming

SEGMENT 3

46. According to Colin Lyons, for what reason were narwhals so valued in the old days?
  a. for their odd skin texture
  b. for their unique tusks
  c. for scientific purposes

47. Why are researchers so keen to learn about the narwhal's wintering territory?
  a. It plays a key role in regulating the climate of northern Europe.
  b. No one has ever measured water temperature there before.
  c. Narwhals have never been studied in their natural habitat before.

48. How do scientists plan on collecting data in this part of the ocean?
  a. by enlisting dozens of narwhals to do the research for them
  b. by sending oceanographers to track and observe the whales
  c. by using satellite data provided by a limited number of whales

49. According to Colin Lyons, why is tagging narwhals so challenging?
  a. The whales swim off when they see the researchers' orange suits.
  b. The whales do not react calmly to being netted and restrained.
  c. The water is so icy that it makes it difficult to net the whales.

50. What point does Colin Lyons make at the end of the program?
  a. The data will put oceanographers on equal footing with atmospheric scientists.
  b. This is the first time that satellite-tag research has been done on narwhals.
  c. Without the narwhals, scientists would have no way to access vital data.

Grammar – Cloze – Vocabulary – Reading 75 minutes

This section of the examination contains 120 problems, numbered 51 through 170. There are 40 grammar, 20 cloze, 40 vocabulary, and 20 reading comprehension problems. If you do not understand how to do the problems, raise your hand, and a proctor will explain the examples to you. None of the actual test problems can be explained.

Each problem has only one correct answer. Do not spend too much time on any one problem. If you do not know the answer to a problem, you may guess. Work quickly but carefully. You have one hour and 15 minutes (75 minutes) to answer all 120 problems. If you finish before the time is over, you may check your answers within the GCVR section only. Do not go back to the Listening section of the exam.

GRAMMAR

51. What steps _____ to install this new computer program?
- **a.** are taking
- **b.** to take
- **c.** must I take
- **d.** that I take

52. Without experience, the chances _____ the job are extremely slim.
- **a.** to get him
- **b.** that he gets
- **c.** of him getting
- **d.** for his getting

53. Amoebas are primitive one-celled organisms, _____ jellyfish are more complex.
- **a.** whereas
- **b.** therefore
- **c.** since
- **d.** likewise

54. Our host and hostess could not have been more _____ .
- **a.** obliged
- **b.** obliging
- **c.** obligated
- **d.** obligatory

55. William's car is bright red, so that white car over there is obviously _____ .
- **a.** belongs to somebody else
- **b.** of somebody else
- **c.** somebody else's
- **d.** owned by somebody's else

56. It seems _____ something is bothering him, but he refuses to talk about it.
- **a.** as if
- **b.** though
- **c.** to be
- **d.** that there's

57. The runner trained _____ she could to get in shape for the marathon.
- **a.** so hard that
- **b.** harder so
- **c.** harder than
- **d.** as hard as

58. Before the test began, the examiner told _____ to each other.
- **a.** that we didn't speak
- **b.** us don't speak
- **c.** to us not to speak
- **d.** us not to speak

59. I'm happy to report that our two-week vacation was _____ perfect!
- **a.** absolute
- **b.** very
- **c.** just
- **d.** only

60. Much to our disappointment, our trip to Rio de Janeiro _____ from what we had expected.
- **a.** was totally different
- **b.** was a total difference
- **c.** differed in total
- **d.** had been differing totally

61. I've been going to a dietician who is helping me figure out _____ eat.
- **a.** that I shouldn't
- **b.** what not to
- **c.** how I don't
- **d.** that I not

62. If you're not sure what time the game starts, you'd _____ check with the coach.
- **a.** ought to
- **b.** rather
- **c.** better
- **d.** prefer to

63. It's really depressing. _____ without a terrorist attack somewhere in the world.
    a. A day goes by hardly
    b. Hardly a day goes by
    c. A day goes hardly by
    d. Hardly goes a day by

64. _____ the firm was a shock to everyone, including her husband.
    a. Her decision of leaving
    b. Her deciding to leave
    c. She decided to leave
    d. She decided on leaving

65. As many college graduates are finding out, good entry-level jobs seem to be _____ .
    a. few and far between
    b. so far so good
    c. far and away
    d. far from it

66. Scientists are predicting that the area is due _____ a difficult hurricane season.
    a. for
    b. to
    c. by
    d. of

67. Everyone in the class has made _____ improvement in their speaking skills.
    a. appreciable
    b. appreciative
    c. appreciating
    d. appreciation

68. That was fun. _____ spending the day with you. Let's do it again next week.
    a. I've enjoyed
    b. I'll enjoy
    c. I loved to
    d. I'd love to

69. He looks like he's going to recover, but the doctor says it's _____ to tell.
    a. sooner than
    b. sooner
    c. too soon
    d. soon enough

70. The boss is making a mistake. Of the three assistants he's hired, _____ has any experience.
    a. who none of them
    b. not one of them
    c. neither of whom
    d. none of whom

For difficult items, allow yourself two run-throughs. On the first, rule out the choices you know are wrong. On the second, analyze the stem again, focusing on what you have and what might be missing. Study the remaining choices: How are they similar? How are they different? Which sounds better in the sentence? If you're still unsure, guess and move on.

71. The information _____ all of you, so please pay attention.
    a. concerns
    b. is concerned about
    c. is concerned by
    d. is of concern

72. She didn't like his last book, so it's unlikely _____ his new one.
    a. to buy
    b. of her buying
    c. that she'll buy
    d. her buying

73. The doctors had done their best, _____ able to save the patient.
    a. but hadn't been
    b. though not being
    c. while not to be
    d. but they couldn't have been

74. _____ on buying a car, but when they both got unexpected raises, they decided to.
    a. They'd planned
    b. They aren't planning
    c. They hadn't been planning
    d. They'd been planning

75. Carol's not here yet, which is _____ at her desk by now.
    a. unusual not to be always
    b. unusually for her not to be
    c. unusual as she's always
    d. what's usual is her not being

76. Our house was burgled last night, but the police have no idea _____ the burglars got in.
    a. that
    b. if
    c. even though
    d. how

77. If we leave now, we'll get to the airport with plenty of _____ .
   a. spared time
   b. spare time
   c. time to spare
   d. time that spares

78. The worst thing about traveling for so many weeks is not having _____ .
   a. home-cooking meals
   b. cooking meals at home
   c. meals cooking at home
   d. home-cooked meals

79. According to a recent report, the disease is rare, affecting _____ ten thousand adults.
   a. only one out of every
   b. every one from
   c. out of every one
   d. the only one of

80. The changes included in the new tax legislation are _____ all taxpayers.
   a. concerned about
   b. of concern to
   c. concerning
   d. concerned by

81. China's a long way away, so she's unlikely _____ there again.
   a. to go
   b. of going
   c. that she'll go
   d. that she goes

82. Although the doctors did their best to save her, _____ able to.
   a. but they couldn't
   b. but hadn't been
   c. they weren't
   d. they couldn't be

83. We doubt she'll be hired for the position since she's inexperienced, _____ extremely shy.
   a. in addition
   b. as well
   c. let it alone
   d. not to mention

84. Her parents were very strict with her. She _____ to date until she was 18.
   a. didn't allow
   b. didn't let
   c. wasn't allowed
   d. wasn't let

85. I'm angry at him for the simple reason that I've told him repeatedly _____ my computer.
   a. never to use
   b. that never he is to use
   c. should he ever use
   d. that he is never using

86. The travel company was forced to cancel the cruise because _____ in it.
   a. of a lack of interest
   b. lack of interest
   c. there lacked interest
   d. interest lacked

87. A house with windows _____ unlocked is an open invitation to burglars.
   a. that left
   b. leaving
   c. that leave
   d. left

88. This section of the test _____ four parts: grammar, cloze, vocabulary, and reading.
   a. consists
   b. consists of
   c. is consisted of
   d. is consisting of

89. Realizing she wasn't cut out _____ a doctor, she decided to drop out of medical school.
   a. as
   b. for
   c. being
   d. to be

90. _____ he'd try to have the report finished by later today, didn't he?
   a. Did he say
   b. He did say
   c. It was said
   d. Didn't he say

Before choosing an answer, make sure that:

(a) it makes sense with the text that comes several sentences before and after the blank, and

(b) it fits in with the grammar of the surrounding text (e.g., subject-verb agreement, pronouns, dependent prepositions).

CLOZE

Passage 1 is about hybrid animals.

When it comes to mating, species don't always stick to their own kind. Take Kekaimalu the "wholphin," as she's known, the hybrid __(91)__ of a false killer whale and a bottlenose dolphin, who lives at Sea Life Park in Hawaii. Then __(92)__ the "liger," a hybrid of a female tiger and male lion – __(93)__ called a "tigon," if the mother is the lion. Ligers and tigons have manes like a lion, the sleek bodies and __(94)__ of a tiger, and the 900-pound heft of a lion.

But the list doesn't stop there. To create work animals with greater strength and agility, people have __(95)__ mules (sterile combinations of horses and donkeys) and zorses (a cross between a zebra and a horse). And not long ago, Russians __(96)__ with breeding combinations of jackals and husky dogs to form a hybrid with elite bomb-sniffing abilities.

Are hybrids like these __(97)__ ? Some __(98)__ that interspecies mating has long played a role in evolution. Others maintain __(99)__ hybrids are the result of unhealthy human interference and, if unleashed in the wild, can __(100)__ the integrity of existing species. Whether or not this is true, hybrids continue to appear, both in controlled settings, such as zoos and farms, and in the wild.

91. **a.** mate **b.** offspring **c.** sibling **d.** ancestor

92. **a.** is **b.** there's **c.** comes **d.** goes

93. **a.** successively **b.** subsequently **c.** alternatively **d.** unfortunately

94. **a.** stripes **b.** spots **c.** bands **d.** streaks

95. **a.** ridden **b.** grown **c.** bred **d.** saddled

96. **a.** associated **b.** considered **c.** collaborated **d.** experimented

97. **a.** natural **b.** physical **c.** physiological **d.** legal

98. **a.** quarrel **b.** recommend **c.** decide **d.** argue

99. **a.** whether **b.** that **c.** although **d.** because

100. **a.** improve **b.** conserve **c.** threaten **d.** ignore

Passage 2 is about being a parent.

Why do people keep having kids? Conventional wisdom dictates that people become parents because children bring joy. But do they really? A recent study that __(101)__ into the relationship between parenting and happiness levels in adult identical twins – some of whom are parents and some who aren't – may be getting to the __(102)__ of the issue.

The study found that people with children are, in fact, happier than those without children, but that a second or third child doesn't add to parental happiness at __(103)__. In fact, additional children seem to make mothers __(104)__ happy than mothers with __(105)__ one child – though still happier than women with __(106)__ children.

"If you want to maximize your subjective well-being," says the lead researcher, "you probably __(107)__ stop at one child. __(108)__ seems to happen over time is that you look forward to __(109)__ another child. Then you have it and find it really difficult, and your happiness dips." Overall, the lesson seems to be that just having __(110)__ at least once might be the crucial aspect that provides the happiness gain.

101. **a.** looked **b.** came **c.** explored **d.** researched

102. **a.** subject **b.** top **c.** point **d.** bottom

103. **a.** random **b.** most **c.** all **d.** last

104. **a.** less **b.** so **c.** are **d.** not

105. **a.** the **b.** over **c.** only **d.** barely

106. **a.** two **b.** no **c.** additional **d.** any

107. **a.** should **b.** don't **c.** may **d.** must

108. **a.** It **b.** Much **c.** What **d.** Something

109. **a.** bringing **b.** having **c.** making **d.** doing

110. **a.** married **b.** parents **c.** reproduced **d.** born

VOCABULARY

111. The company's plans for expansion are _____ on this year's sales.
 a. contingent
 b. contagious
 c. conspicuous
 d. conceivable

112. After several losing seasons, the team is hoping to make a strong _____ this year.
 a. setback
 b. backdrop
 c. comeback
 d. downfall

113. The dog is suffering in this heat; he's been _____ for hours.
 a. chuckling
 b. panting
 c. sobbing
 d. exaggerating

114. Continued unrest in the area has given _____ to higher fuel costs around the world.
 a. voice
 b. pause
 c. way
 d. rise

115. Students are infamous for coming up with _____ excuses for not doing their homework.
 a. devastated
 b. elaborate
 c. oppressive
 d. eminent

116. The new legislation will take _____ in June of next year.
 a. hold
 b. effect
 c. root
 d. notice

117. He is thrilled that his latest book has received such a positive _____ from critics.
 a. sensation
 b. publicity
 c. spectacle
 d. reception

118. I recommend reading the books _____ , starting with the very first.
 a. by accident
 b. at random
 c. in sequence
 d. on impact

> Always use process of elimination. The more choices you can rule out, the more you increase your chance of answering correctly – even if the word you finally choose is a word you've never seen before!

119. The police ordered the crowd to _____ so the ambulance could get to the victims.
 a. stand clear
 b. stand still
 c. stand corrected
 d. stand their ground

120. The article reported on the scandal without casting _____ on anyone.
 a. aspersions
 b. doubts
 c. a pall
 d. a spell

121. I'd like to thank everyone for helping me. Your support has been _____ .
 a. unfaltering
 b. uneasy
 c. unfathomable
 d. unattended

122. She carefully _____ the ingredients she would need to make the cake.
 a. carried out
 b. measured out
 c. spelled out
 d. spoke out

123. The injury left her without _____ in her left leg, but doctors say the damage is not permanent.
 a. sight
 b. composure
 c. temperament
 d. sensation

124. We feel sorry for the old woman. Her son visits her _____ , but usually she's all alone.
 a. sporadically
 b. adequately
 c. eloquently
 d. extravagantly

125. The company was taken to court and fined for not _____ with local environmental regulations.
- **a.** complying
- **b.** wrestling
- **c.** experimenting
- **d.** collaborating

126. The bakery is famous for its wonderful _____ . The cakes are simply fabulous.
- **a.** contraptions
- **b.** conventions
- **c.** confections
- **d.** confessions

127. The meeting will _____ promptly at 10 a.m. Please make sure you are on time.
- **a.** convene
- **b.** apportion
- **c.** donate
- **d.** distribute

128. Police have set up _____ on all roads leading out of town. The bank robbers must be caught.
- **a.** detours
- **b.** standstills
- **c.** roadblocks
- **d.** bottlenecks

129. I'm worried about Ed's performance. He's _____ coming in late and missing deadlines.
- **a.** taken in
- **b.** taken to
- **c.** taken up
- **d.** taken on

130. The smog is terrible today. A layer of hot, _____ air is trapped over the city.
- **a.** stagnant
- **b.** oppressive
- **c.** discernible
- **d.** muggy

131. The election results would make it clear which of the parties had _____ .
- **a.** changed hands
- **b.** lived hand to mouth
- **c.** had its hands full
- **d.** gained the upper hand

132. Have you heard? Mom's finally decided to _____ for a computer class. It's about time!
- **a.** sign up
- **b.** log on
- **c.** boot up
- **d.** check in

133. I'll be the dealer, but can you _____ the deck for me? I've never learned how to do it!
- **a.** fumble
- **b.** flourish
- **c.** shuffle
- **d.** disseminate

134. The twins do everything together. They're as close as two peas in a _____ .
- **a.** shell
- **b.** hull
- **c.** husk
- **d.** pod

135. The lecture contained so much jargon that most of the audience found it totally _____ .
- **a.** incoherent
- **b.** disadvantaged
- **c.** misshapen
- **d.** unfounded

136. It was clear from her _____ abdomen that her baby would soon be here.
- **a.** lingering
- **b.** overwhelming
- **c.** bulging
- **d.** thriving

137. Doubting his client's innocence, the lawyer has decided to _____ .
- **a.** lend him a hand
- **b.** wash his hands of him
- **c.** hand it to him
- **d.** put his life in his hands

138. We've checked the report _____ . I feel confident that the data is 100% correct.
- **a.** rigorously
- **b.** indefinitely
- **c.** laudably
- **d.** acutely

139. I wish I knew what to do about my future. I'm really in a _____ .
- **a.** transition
- **b.** quandary
- **c.** violation
- **d.** minority

140. I can give you a close _____ , but I won't know the exact cost till later next week.
- **a.** call
- **b.** collaboration
- **c.** estimate
- **d.** proximity

141. His leg injury turned out to be a _____ , not a sprain as the doctor first suspected.
  a. fraction
  b. fracture
  c. infraction
  d. fragment

142. If the military revolts, there's a good chance that the government will be _____ .
  a. overpowered
  b. overcome
  c. overthrown
  d. overtaken

143. Nothing ever upsets her. She's the kind of person who _____ .
  a. takes it upon herself
  b. takes it for granted
  c. takes everything to heart
  d. takes everything in her stride

144. Having a child puts a lot of _____ on a parent's free time.
  a. coincidences
  b. conclusions
  c. consequences
  d. constraints

145. The soldiers seemed _____ as they prepared for the battle.
  a. unappreciative
  b. ubiquitous
  c. undaunted
  d. unanimous

146. When does the new owner take _____ of the company?
  a. advantage
  b. precedence
  c. control
  d. place

147. Don't forget to _____ a check in the envelope when you pay your phone bill.
  a. inscribe
  b. seal
  c. enclose
  d. weld

148. The army fought bravely, but in the end they were forced to _____ .
  a. surrender
  b. perish
  c. expire
  d. succumb

149. The material is so sturdy that it is almost impossible to _____ .
  a. stain
  b. rip
  c. scorch
  d. shrink

150. She was _____ with guilt when she realized that the accident had been her fault.
  a. consumed
  b. ravaged
  c. devoured
  d. dazzled

When answering questions about main idea (e.g., 151), start by identifying the topic sentence in each paragraph. Next, consider all four choices. Rule out the ones that apply to the main idea in only one paragraph. The answer you choose should apply generally to each paragraph.

READING

Passage 1 is about art supplies.

Vincent van Gogh was a brilliant painter. He also went mad, cut off his ear, and committed suicide at the age of 37. Historians may never know what caused his long illness, but some attribute it to the toxic substances in the materials he used. And art can still be a dangerous business. While professional artists and children face the most serious health risks, even adult dabblers should choose and use their tools wisely.

Under the 1988 Labeling of Hazardous Art Materials Act, all art supplies must carry a warning if they contain substances known to be chronic health hazards. But the system is not foolproof. Some health advocacy groups charge that the review and labeling process is compromised by industry influence. Another common set of labels – the AP (Approved Product) and CP (Certified Product) seals – are industry-issued and do not require product testing. With labeling at best incomplete, it's important to do your own research and buy products with clearly listed ingredients.

Any art materials containing lead, a known hazard to the nervous system and brain, should be avoided, although certain paints, pottery glazes, printmaking inks, and stained-glass materials are exempt from consumer lead laws. The Art and Creative Materials Institute, a manufacturer's association, claims that lead is "essential to providing a high-quality, safe glaze." It similarly justifies the use of lead in paints because paintings are "archival" and meant to last centuries. The danger posed by lead, however, lasts just as long.

Among the most hazardous of other ingredients are solvents, found in many pens, inks, and paints. Xylene, a petroleum by-product used in some permanent markers, can cause dizziness or respiratory irritation, and, with repeated exposure, damage to the liver and kidneys. Some rubber cements contain hexane, which can cause nerve or skin damage if inhaled. Any products containing solvents should be used in a well-ventilated area and discarded at a household-hazardous-waste collection point. If poured down the sink or storm drain, solvents can kill off helpful bacteria at water treatment plants or harm aquatic life once they reach the waterways.

151. What is the main idea of the passage?
- **a.** toxic substances in the art of Vincent Van Gogh
- **b.** the hidden health risks associated with art supplies
- **c.** the health hazards faced by professional artists
- **d.** the inadequacy of the Labeling of Hazardous Art Materials Act

152. What does the writer imply about art products bearing the AP or CP seal?
- **a.** They are the only products that consumers should use.
- **b.** They are improperly labeled and should not be used.
- **c.** They may not be quite as safe as the seals suggest.
- **d.** They are in clear violation of the 1988 labeling law.

153. What health warning would you expect to find on products containing xylene and hexane?
- **a.** Wear gloves to avoid skin contact.
- **b.** Warning: Dangerous if breathed in.
- **c.** Keep windows closed when using.
- **d.** Toxic: Pour down sink after use.

154. What is the Art and Creative Materials Institute in favor of?
- **a.** allowing the manufacture of certain lead-based glazes and paints
- **b.** using art materials that are certified as being 100% lead free
- **c.** passing laws that limit the lead content of paints and glaze
- **d.** putting a ban on lead in high-quality glazes, inks, and paints

155. Who is the article intended for?
- **a.** green-minded amateur artists
- **b.** top-quality professional artists
- **c.** parents of artistically gifted children
- **d.** anyone who uses or buys art materials

Passage 2 is about athletes and scholarship money.

For decades, foreign athletes have come to the U.S. to train and bolster American university teams, boosting the level of competition and bringing American athletes shoulder to shoulder with multiculturalism. But now, with nearly $1 billion to spend in scholarship money and growing pressure to field winning teams, schools are increasingly filling their rosters with foreign athletes. The trend is fueling a debate about whether taxpayer-funded collegiate programs are developing international talent at the expense of aspiring American athletes, not to mention America's Olympic hopes. At last year's National Collegiate Athletic Association (NCAA) Division I swimming championships, for example, foreign athletes with scholarships at U.S. schools constituted 40 percent of the field. But it's not just swimming that's affected. Nearly one third of NCAA ice hockey and tennis athletes last season were not American. In other sports, the percentage of foreigners is lower, but they're concentrated at the top. Of the 20 "All-American" finalists in a recent NCAA skiing championship, for example, only six were American.

Zachary Violett, a cross-country skier who didn't make that half-dozen, would like to think he'd have pocketed at least three NCAA championships by now if it weren't for European skiers. Last year he finished fourth behind three Norwegians. Is that frustrating? "Well, I like to complain about it, but it's great having people to chase," says Violett, who emphasizes how much he's improved by skiing head to head with the Europeans. Not to be defeated, he reverse-engineered the process: he went to a ski academy in Gielo, Norway, where he trained "nonstop" and worked nights in restaurants to make ends meet. Now a senior with a full scholarship at the University of Alaska, Violett lives with Norwegian and German teammates.

Many coaches admit that putting a cap on the amount of scholarship money for foreign students is a reasonable approach, but few are willing to say so publicly for fear of putting themselves at odds with their athletic departments. As one puts it, "My job is to field the best team I can. Whether that means recruiting a kid from Arizona or Australia, it really doesn't matter."

156. What trend does the article discuss?

- **a.** the decrease in the number of U.S. athletes who are winning U.S. competitions
- **b.** the decline in the amount of scholarship money available for athletes
- **c.** the increase in pressure on American colleges to put together winning teams
- **d.** the rise in the number of athletic scholarships being given to foreign athletes

157. Which best describes the view of those who are against this trend?

- **a.** Taxpayers' dollars should not be used to fund sports programs.
- **b.** American scholarship money should not go to athletes from abroad.
- **c.** Foreign athletes should not be allowed to compete on American teams.
- **d.** Foreign athletes are taking medals away from American athletes.

158. Why don't more coaches support placing a limit on athletic scholarships for foreigners?

- **a.** They feel foreigners have just as much right to the money as Americans.
- **b.** They believe that teams with foreign athletes have a distinct advantage.
- **c.** They realize they might need foreigners to put together the best team possible.
- **d.** They know their departments would rather support Americans than foreigners.

159. What is Zachary Violett's attitude toward European skiers on U.S. college ski teams?

- **a.** He admits that he has benefited from his exposure to them.
- **b.** He resents the additional competition they pose for him.
- **c.** He feels that they have an unfair advantage over U.S. skiers.
- **d.** He thinks they should not be allowed to compete on U.S. teams.

160. Which NCAA sport has the highest percentage of foreign athletes on scholarship?

- **a.** skiing
- **b.** ice hockey
- **c.** tennis
- **d.** swimming

Passage 3 is about a common bacterium and heart disease.

Chlamydia pneumoniae is less famous than its sexually transmitted cousin, *Chlamydia trachomatis*, but it is far more widespread and may be far more dangerous. We all encounter the bacterium sooner or later, most of us more than once. It spreads through coughs and sneezes, causing a flulike respiratory condition that sometimes progresses to pneumonia. But this may be only the beginning of the mischief it causes. Scientists now have good reason to believe that *C. pneumoniae* may contribute to atherosclerosis, an inflammatory disease of the blood vessels.

The hypothesis goes like this: when immune cells called macrophages clear *C. pneumoniae* from the respiratory system, they sometimes become active carriers of the bug. The trouble starts when the immune system mobilizes itself to remove irritants from blood vessel walls. When an infected macrophage burrows into an artery wall to gobble up irritants such as fat or cholesterol, it may transfer *C. pneumoniae* to neighboring arterial cells. The infected tissue then attracts more macrophages, which deliver more bacteria, starting a vicious cycle of irritation and scarring. The result is a scabby lesion, or plaque, that narrows the blood vessel and impedes circulation. When pieces of plaque break loose, they can start blood clots that may cause a heart attack or stroke.

The evidence is impressive so far. Rabbits don't normally get atherosclerosis, even when fed high-fat diets, yet researchers have shown that some rabbits develop arterial plaque within weeks of being infected by *C. pneumoniae.* If new studies show antibiotics can stall plaque growth, it will be clear what triggered them.

The hope is that antibiotics will prove as useful for clearing arteries as they are for healing ulcers. Heart attack mortality has already dropped by half since the mid-1960s. The decline is due partly to changes in lifestyle and improvements in medical care, but it also coincides with the introduction of drugs like tetracycline and erythromycin. Researchers have begun to test these remedies. In one study, heart attack survivors were treated with the antibiotic azithromycin. After six months, they produced fewer inflammatory proteins than a control group who did not receive the drug. If researchers can show that this translates into improved survival, cardiology is in for a revolution.

161. What is *Chlamydia pneumoniae*?
- **a.** a sexually transmitted disease
- **b.** a common respiratory ailment
- **c.** a type of bacterium
- **d.** an extremely rare virus

162. What is suggested in the passage?
- **a.** *C. pneumoniae* may someday be used to cure atherosclerosis.
- **b.** The use of antibiotics could possibly revolutionize cardiology.
- **c.** Heart disease may someday be easier to cure than ulcers.
- **d.** Antibiotics may someday result in a dramatic rise in heart attack mortality.

163. How does the immune system normally aid in the prevention of atherosclerosis?
- **a.** It deploys macrophages to remove harmful substances from blood vessel walls.
- **b.** It sends *C. pneumoniae* to blood vessels to build up a protective layer of plaque.
- **c.** It ensures that otherwise healthy macrophages are infected by *C. pneumoniae*.
- **d.** It usually does not play any role whatsoever in preventing the common condition.

164. If scientists are correct, what happens when macrophages carrying *C. pneumoniae* enter the wall of an artery?
- **a.** A heart attack or stroke may follow within a very short time.
- **b.** Cholesterol and other dangerous irritants are quickly removed.
- **c.** Irritation and scarring occur, which lead to plaque formation.
- **d.** The blood vessel instantly contracts and blocks the flow of blood.

165. How do scientists plan to further test their hypothesis about atherosclerosis?
- **a.** by feeding rabbits high-fat diets
- **b.** by infecting more and more animals with *C. pneumoniae*
- **c.** by seeing if antibiotics contribute to the growth of plaque
- **d.** by showing that plaque growth can be slowed by antibiotics

Passage 4 is about a novel use for bacteria.

While most microbiologists focus on ways to manipulate bacterial genes or combat disease, several innovative researchers at the South Dakota School of Mines and Technology have found a somewhat more concrete use for bacteria. They are using them to make cement.

Many common types of bacteria use urea, the main component of urine, as their source of nitrogen. They break down urea, creating carbon dioxide and ammonia. The ammonia reacts with water to form ammonium hydroxide, which makes any nearby calcium precipitate out as calcium carbonate crystals, or limestone. "It's a very slow process in nature," say the researchers, "so we tried to speed things up a little."

The researchers separately mixed two ordinary soil bacteria, *Bacillus pasteurii* and *Sporosarcina ureae*, with sand and placed each into a syringe. Into the syringes they slowly dripped a urea-based nutrient broth that also contained calcium chloride. As the bacteria went to work metabolizing the urea, calcium carbonate crystals began to form around the bacteria, filling in the gaps between each grain of sand. Within a few days, the top half inch of sand in the syringes had solidified, stopping the flow of the broth. When the nutrients ran out, the bacteria died off, leaving limestone behind.

Unlike conventional sealing agents, the bacteria fill up fissures in cement from the inside out, completely meshing with the existing material. The research team hopes their bacterial builders can be used to seal up cracks and fissures in concrete buildings and other structures. So far they've used the bacteria to fix cracks in concrete blocks in the lab, and they're working on scaling up the process by encasing thousands of bacteria in separate gel beads for easy application.

Researchers now have their eyes on nearby Mount Rushmore* as a potential recipient of a bacterial facial. "The wind and weather wreak havoc on Mount Rushmore year after year," says the team leader. "The cracks constantly have to be filled in with silicone sealer, sand, and all sorts of things."

* *Mount Rushmore* – a memorial made up of four giant heads/faces of former U.S. presidents carved into a mountain.

166. What is true of urea?
- **a.** It is an important component of limestone.
- **b.** It is found in carbon dioxide and ammonia.
- **c.** It is used by bacteria as a source of nitrogen.
- **d.** If mixed with water, it forms calcium carbonate.

167. Under what conditions will limestone form?
- **a.** when the carbon dioxide in urea reacts with water
- **b.** when bacteria digest urea
- **c.** when ammonium hydroxide reacts with calcium
- **d.** when calcium carbonate crystals form limestone

168. Why must the urea-based nutrient broth contain calcium chloride as well?
- **a.** Without it, limestone formation would not occur.
- **b.** The bacteria depend on it to break down urea.
- **c.** The bacteria could not survive without it.
- **d.** It is necessary to help kill off the bacteria.

169. What are researchers hoping to use bacteria for?
- **a.** to seal off the surface of cracked concrete structures
- **b.** to repair cracks in concrete and stone from the inside out
- **c.** to manufacture gel beads that will repair concrete
- **d.** to treat concrete to prevent it from ever cracking

170. What advantage do the "bacterial builders" have over conventional sealing agents?
- **a.** They work much more quickly and are much easier to control.
- **b.** They are able to be used on a much wider range of materials.
- **c.** They are Mount Rushmore's only hope of enduring the forces of nature.
- **d.** They produce a substance that bonds better with cracked material.

4 Vocabulary Enhancement

Impish *Imp-* words

English is full of adjectives beginning with "imp-." Some of them – like ones we've seen in this test (e.g., ***imperfect, impatient, impossible****) – contain the prefix "im-", which you'll undoubtedly recognize as a variant of the prefix "in-", meaning "not." But not all "imp-" adjectives follow this pattern, which means they may cause you problems the first time you encounter them. Hence, the word "impish" in the title. An imp is a small magical creature that causes trouble in a playful way;* ***impish****, then, means "like an imp" – i.e., naughty, mischievous, or playfully troublesome. A perfect example of an "impish "imp-" word is* ***impertinent****, which looks like it should mean "not pertinent, unrelated, irrelevant," but in fact is a synonym of* ***rude*** *and* ***impolite****! Let's take a closer look at this and several other "imp-" adjectives that are worth knowing.*

A **Get the Picture?** – Language experts say you can learn new words more easily if you can associate them with a vivid mental image. To get you started, study photos A-E, and then match them to the sentences and short texts below.

A

B

C

D

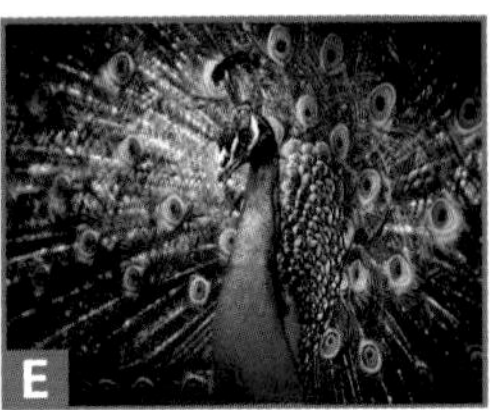
E

1. ________ A peacock's plumage is one of Mother Nature's most **imposing** creations!

2. ________ "Help! My company's sinking and I'm going down, too," cried the entrepreneur in a desperate, **imploring** voice.

3. ________ This photo is one of my all-time favorites. Totally unplanned, it was taken in one of those **impromptu** moments that photographers love. I felt sorry for the taxi driver, but the monkeys had nasty tempers so it would have been **imprudent** of me to try to help. At one point they began to screech fiercely at whoever approached, prompting an onlooker to remark, "They're rather **impertinent** little beasts, don't you think?"

4. ________ It takes a special kind of person to do this man's job. Amazingly, he seems **impervious** to the danger. If I were his wife, I'd feel a sense of **impending** doom every time the phone rang!

5. ________ Now here's a rather **implausible** sight! You'd have to be pretty **impressionable** to believe that this is a photo of something that really happened. It's obviously the work of some graphic artist who has an **impeccable** command of techniques for altering digital photographs.

B **Using Context Clues to Predict Meaning** – Now look at each text and corresponding photo in A again, and then match the bold *imp-* adjectives with their definitions below.

a. ________________ – rude, disrespectful

b. ________________ – unconvincing, unlikely to be real or true

c. ________________ – unwise and reckless, unconcerned about negative consequences

d. ________________ – about to happen, imminent

e. ________________ – (predicate adjective with *to*) unaffected or uninfluenced, resistant

f. ________________ – excellent, without flaw

g. ________________ – begging, pleading

h. ________________ – impressive in appearance

i. ________________ – easily influenced, naïve, gullible

j. ________________ – spontaneous, done without planning

Double Exposures

And while we're on the subject of photography, let's consider phrases that might be called "double exposures" – that is, phrases with repeating elements. For example, in Reading Passage 2, we read about American athletes "brought ***shoulder to shoulder*** *(i.e., working/standing together in a cooperative effort) with multiculturalism." We also saw Zachary Violett improve his skills by "skiing* ***head to head*** *with the Europeans" (i.e., in direct competition with them). These phrases are just two examples of English expressions that are formed by "doubling up" on a body noun. You're probably already familiar with* ***an eye for an eye, a tooth for a tooth****. Here are similar phrases that may prove useful. Most are used figuratively, but if you try to imagine them literally, you'll find the meanings virtually self-explanatory.*

C **Imagine This!** – Read the sentences carefully and try to visualize the actions that are described. Then fill in the blanks with one of the expressions in the box.

arm in arm	*cheek to cheek*	*ear to ear*	*eye to eye*	*hand in hand*	*hand-to-hand*
head to head	*heart-to-heart*	*mouth-to-mouth*	*neck and neck*	*shoulder to shoulder*	

Adverbial Phrases

1. They make a lovely couple, don't they? Just look at them **dancing** __________________ .
2. Something nice must have happened. You don't usually **grin from** __________________ like that.
3. What a race! The two front runners crossed the finish line __________________ . The judges are looking at the video now to see if they can determine the winner.
4. The twins not only look alike, but they have virtually the same world view. They **see** __________________ on almost everything you can think of.
5. Did you know Tom and Mary were dating? I saw them walking __________________ (OR __________________) down by the harbor on Saturday.
6. The two teams will **go** __________________ tonight in the final round of the championship.
7. I need your help. We need to stick together and meet this challenge __________________ .

Compound-Adjective + Noun Collocations

8. I would have died if the lifeguard hadn't been trained to give __________________ **resuscitation**.
9. Ninjas are masters of __________________ **combat**.
10. Adam and Annie are always fighting. I suggested they have a __________________ **conversation** to try and get their relationship back on track.

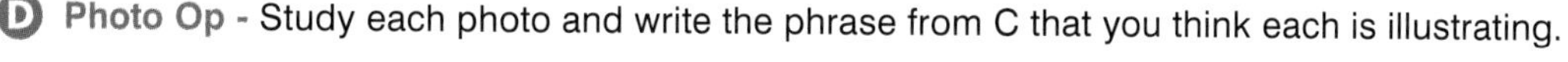

D **Photo Op** - Study each photo and write the phrase from C that you think each is illustrating.

1 __________________

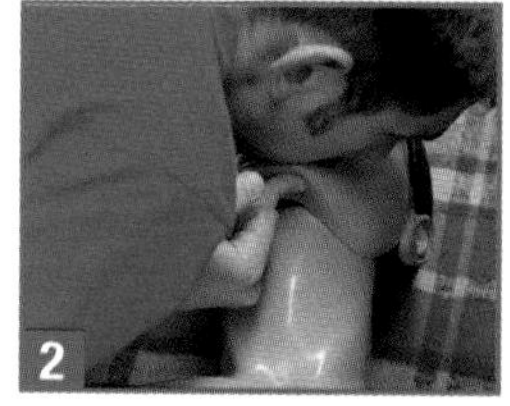
2 __________________

3 __________________

4 __________________

5 __________________

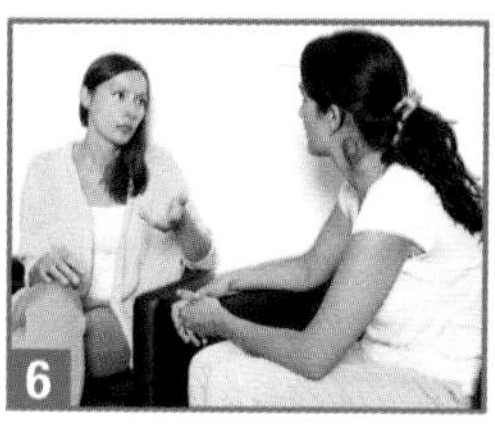
6 __________________

7 __________________

8 __________________

9 __________________

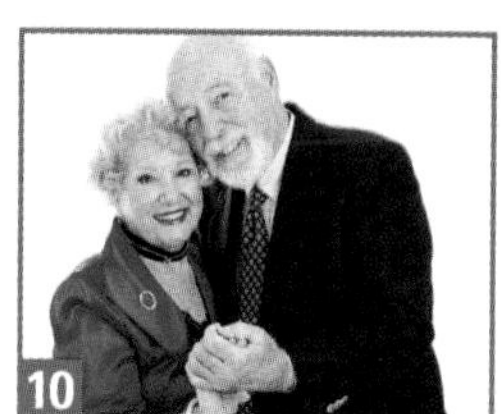
10 __________________

Vocabulary Consolidation

PASSAGES IN REVIEW

This section reviews a sampling of words you have met in the Cloze and Reading passages in Practice Tests 1-4. For each group, fill in the blanks with the appropriate words. For verbs, remember to use the correct form.

A Notorious Nouns

circulation *debate* *degradation* *emissions* *hibernation* *implication* *toll* *vegetation*

1. There has been much _______________ in the local press as to why trees and other _______________ in this area are beginning to wither and die. One theory is that air and soil pollution have finally taken their _______________ and resulted in the _______________ of the environment.
2. I haven't seen you all winter! I was beginning to think you'd gone into _______________ ! You've certainly taken yourself out of _______________ . Have you been away?
3. Tina's aspiration is to become a politician who fights to bring about a drastic reduction in greenhouse gas _______________ . In the meantime, she's concerned about the _______________ of the current government's failure to act.

B Vexing Verbs

chuckle *enhance* *fuel* *hover* *plummet* *probe* *resolve* *soak*

1. I can't believe how the temperature _______________ overnight. Yesterday I wore a short-sleeved shirt. Today I need a heavy sweater! I can't wait to get home and _______________ in a nice hot bath!
2. I hate the way the boss _______________ over my desk all day. What's worse is that she _______________ everything I do as if she's just waiting for me to make a mistake so she can fire me. I've _______________ to look for another job as there is little or nothing I can do to _______________ my chances of getting a promotion here.
3. What _______________ my anger was the sarcastic way he _______________ when I tried to apologize.

C Addling Adjectives

adjacent *controversial* *defective* *dwindling* *exempt* *scrupulous*

1. With all the talk about _______________ oil reserves, how can you even think about buying that gas-guzzler?
2. If the monitor is _______________, just bring it back and the store will give you a replacement.
3. John is a perfectionist who is known for paying _______________ attention to detail.
4. My dad is talking about buying the land that is _______________ to our house.
5. The government's plan to eliminate taxes for large corporations is highly _______________ . If you ask me, poor people should be _______________ from paying taxes, not big business!

D Audacious Adverbs

casually *desperately* *fittingly* *profoundly* *simultaneously*

1. If you're thinking about wearing jeans and a T-shirt, you won't be _______________ dressed for the wedding.
2. "By the way," he said _______________ , "did I mention that I'm getting married on Sunday?"
3. "Someone help me," shouted the young woman _______________ . "I can't find my little boy!"
4. She finds the recent escalation of gun violence in the USA _______________ disturbing.
5. Most states now have laws against driving and talking on your cell phone _______________ .

COMIC RELIEF

This section reviews words you have met in Vocabulary Enhancements 1-3.

A Amusing Associations – For each group, find the word or phrase in the box that is suggested by each prompt.

acid rain *avalanche* *dam* *exhaust* *famine* *humidity* *iceberg* *volcano*

1. ____________ – If your car always looks tired, it's probably producing too much of this.
2. ____________ – The new manager is as cold as one of these. If Helen of Troy had a face that launched a thousand ships, hers could sink the *Titanic*!
3. ____________ – Last month, we were so busy that everyone complained. This month, it's just the opposite. Guess the saying is true: it's either feast or one of these.
4. ____________ – Ed is so snowed under at work that he says his desk has been hit by one of these.
5. ____________ – Ann seems nice and calm, but watch out! If you push her, she erupts like one of these!
6. ____________ – Mike says the holes in his umbrella are a result of too much of this!
7. ____________ – There's so much of this in the air right now that you don't need to water your plants.
8. ____________ – If you spell this man-made feature backwards, you get a synonym of *angry*, which is how you might feel if the government decided to build one in your backyard.

go out like a light *hit the snooze button* *let sleeping dogs lie* *nod off* *sleep like a log* *sleep on it*

1. ____________ – If you do this, you may not hear a burglar break into your house.
2. ____________ – Most people do this when they can't face getting up in the morning.
3. ____________ – If you can't decide between two different plans, it's sometimes best to do this.
4. ____________ – If you do this at an important meeting, don't expect your boss to be pleased.
5. ____________ – If you think someone might get angry, it's sometimes best to do this.
6. ____________ – Some people do this if they drink a glass of warm milk and honey before bedtime.

B What's so "punny"? – Match the captions **(1-4)** to the drawings **(A-D)**. Then discuss the sentences with your classmates to see if you can identify the pun (or play on words) that is built into each situation.

A

____

B

____

C

____

D

____

1. When I asked you to enlighten me about your plans for decorating the tree, this is not what I had in mind!
2. When the couple said they were going out to trip the light fantastic, they hadn't planned on this!
3. People who want to "see the light" should start by paying their electric bills on time.
4. Here's what might happen if you asked an illustrious illustrator to illustrate a point!

PRICKLY PREPOSITIONS AND PARTICLES

The following extracts are taken from passages that you have encountered in Practice Test 4. Read each one quickly, and then fill in each blank with an appropriate preposition or particle.

1. Vincent van Gogh was a brilliant painter. He also went mad, cut _________ his ear, and committed suicide _________ the age _________ 37. Historians may never know what caused his long illness, but some attribute it _________ the toxic substances _________ the materials he used. ... Any art materials containing lead, a known hazard _________ the nervous system and brain, should be avoided, even though certain paints, pottery glazes, printmaking inks, and stained-glass materials are exempt _________ consumer lead laws. The Art and Creative Materials Institute, a manufacturer's association, claims that lead is "essential _________ providing a high-quality, safe glaze." It similarly justifies the use _________ lead _________ paints because paintings are "archival" and meant to last centuries. The danger posed _________ lead, however, lasts just _________ long.

2. The hope is that antibiotics will prove as useful _________ clearing arteries as they are _________ healing ulcers. Heart attack mortality has already dropped _________ half since the mid-1960s. The decline is due partly _________ changes _________ lifestyle and improvements _________ medical care, but it also coincides _________ the introduction _________ drugs _________ tetracycline and erythromycin. Researchers have begun to test these remedies. _________ one study, heart-attack survivors were treated _________ the antibiotic azithromycin. After six months they produced fewer inflammatory proteins than a control group who did not receive the drug. If researchers can show that this translates _________ improved survival, cardiology is _________ _________ a revolution.

3. _________decades, foreign athletes have come _________ the U.S. to train and bolster American university teams, boosting the level _________ competition and bringing American athletes shoulder _________ shoulder ... _________ multiculturalism. But now, _________ nearly $1 billion to spend _________ scholarship money and growing pressure to field winning teams, schools are increasingly filling their rosters _________ foreign athletes. The trend is fueling a debate _________ whether taxpayer-funded collegiate programs are developing international talent _________ the expense _________ aspiring American athletes, not to mention America's Olympic hopes. ... Many coaches admit that putting a cap _________ the amount _________ scholarship money _________ foreign students is a reasonable approach, but few are willing to say so publicly _________ fear _________ putting themselves _________ odds _________ their athletic departments.

4. So far researchers have used the bacteria to fix cracks _________ concrete blocks in _________ lab, and they're working _________ scaling _________ the process _________ encasing thousands _________ bacteria _________ separate gel beads _________ easy application. They now have their eyes _________ nearby Mount Rushmore _________ a potential recipient _________ a bacterial facial. "The wind and weather wreak havoc _________ Mount Rushmore year _________ year," says the team leader. "The cracks constantly have to be filled _________ _________ silicone sealer, sand, and all sorts _________ things."

PUZZLE TIME

The crossword is based on words you encountered in the Cloze and Reading passages of Tests 1-4. Use the words in the box and the Across and Down clues to help you solve the puzzle. The photos on the right should help you form a mental image of some of the answers. Write the words under the pictures to help you remember them for future use.

altitude brash brittle debate dimensions drought emerge exquisite factor fragment humble materials nutrient remote retrieve spur strive tumor twine vicious vie

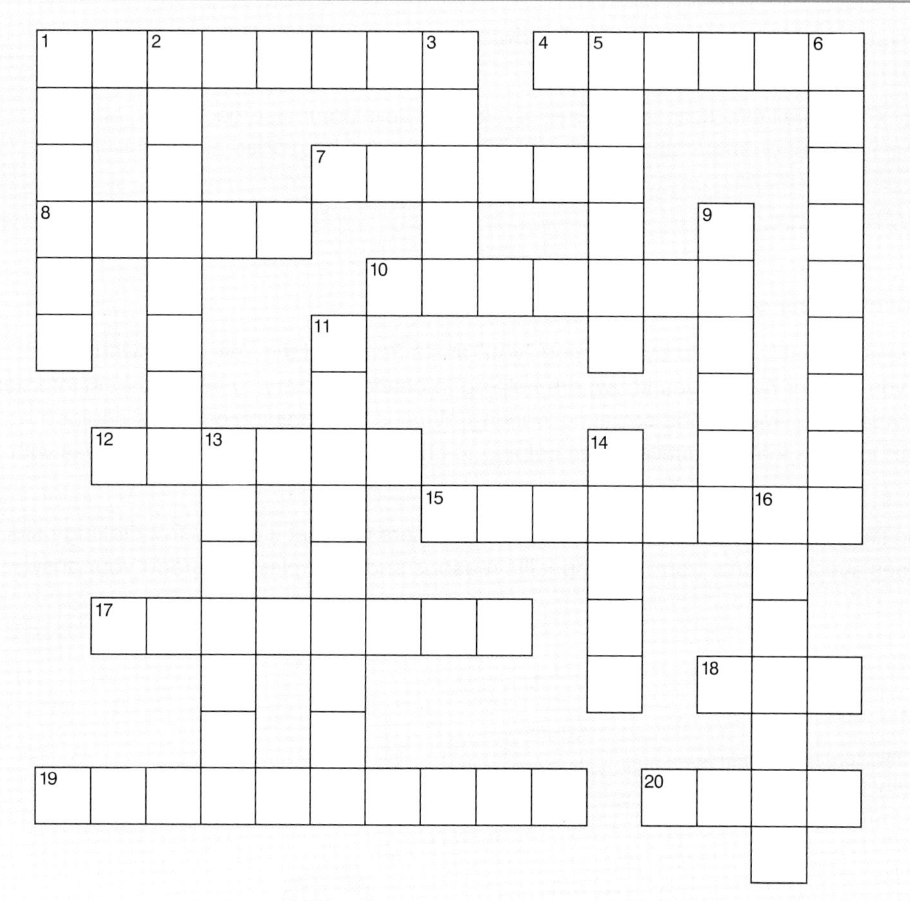

A

B

C

D

E

F

ACROSS

1. small broken-off piece
4. far away, hard to get to
7. ordinary, simple
8. a ball of ________
10. long period without rain
12. heated public discussion
15. dogs can be trained to do this
17. e.g., vitamin, protein, carbohydrate
18. compete
19. e.g., height, length, and width
20. encourage to develop

DOWN

1. something that influences a result
2. height above sea level
3. a malignant ________
5. come out into the open
6. very beautiful
9. try hard
11. e.g., glass, paper, and plastic
13. hard and dry (e.g., ancient papyrus)
14. overly confident, pushy (e.g., Pygmalion)
16. ________ cycle

NOTE: Highlighted numbers denote clues with related picture clues.

Practice Test 5

Writing 30 minutes

- You may write in pen or pencil.
- You will have 30 minutes to write on one of the two topics. If you do not write on one of these topics, your paper will not be scored. If you do not understand the topics, ask the examiner to explain them.
- You may make an outline if you wish, but your outline will not count toward your score.
- Write about one-and-a-half to two pages. Your essay will be marked down if it is extremely short.
- You will not be graded on the appearance of your paper, but your handwriting must be readable. You may change or correct your writing, but you should not recopy the whole essay.
- Your essay will be judged on clarity and overall effectiveness, as well as on topic development, organization, and the range, accuracy, and appropriateness of your grammar and vocabulary. Your essay will be graded at the University of Michigan.

TOPICS For help in writing these compositions, see *Writing Tutorial*, pages 209-210.

1. In December of 2006, *Time Magazine* surprised the world by selecting "you" as its Person of the Year. The award was made in recognition of the fact that you (and/or people you know) are helping to change society by taking part in Internet activities such as blogging, sharing videos and music, and social networking. What is your opinion of *Time*'s choice? Do you feel that people who take part in these Internet activities are helping to change society? Support your ideas with reasons and examples.

2. Some people believe that success in life is the result of careful planning, while others feel that it comes from taking risks or chances. In your opinion, what does success come from? Use specific reasons and examples to support your answer.

As you plan your essay, remember that examiners will be looking for evidence of your ability to organize and develop your ideas in a series of clear, well-structured paragraphs. You can't possibly explore every aspect of a topic in 30 minutes, but what you can do is lay out your argument so that it has a clear beginning, middle, and end and then use basic principles of rhetoric to develop each paragraph in a logical manner.

Refer back to the "Composition Checklist" at the bottom of page 8, commit it to memory, ... and then call it to mind every time you are asked to write an essay

Listening approx. 35-40 minutes

This section of the examination tests your understanding of spoken English. The listening section has three parts. There are 50 questions. Mark all your answers on the separate answer sheet. Do not make any stray marks on the answer sheet. If you change your mind about an answer, erase your first answer completely.

Part I

In this part, you will hear short conversations. From the three answer choices given, choose the answer which means about the same thing as what you hear, or that is true based upon what you hear.

For problems 1 through 17, mark your answers on the separate answer sheet. No problems can be repeated.

Please listen carefully. Do you have any questions?

Idioms are a common feature of conversational English and, as such, you can expect a number of questions in Part I and Part II to hinge on high-frequency idioms. If luck is on your side, you'll know at least some of the ones that come up on the day of the exam. If not, the best tactic is to stay calm and use the gist of the conversation to help you predict the idiom's meaning and narrow down the choices. With only three choices to choose, the odds are very much on your side. Ruling out even one choice means you have a 50-50 chance of guessing correctly!

1. **a.** He needs directions to the local dairy.
b. He's run out of fruit and vegetables.
c. He's shopping in a supermarket.

2. **a.** He needs to go to a doctor.
b. He's suffering from jet lag.
c. He was recently in a traffic accident.

3. **a.** The children are growing quickly.
b. She thinks the children are spoiled.
c. At first she didn't like the children.

4. **a.** He'd rather not talk about his problem.
b. He's worried about the pain in his chest.
c. She thinks he's hiding something from her.

5. **a.** He accidentally told Mary about the party.
b. Mary was surprised he gave her a cat.
c. They suspect Mary knew about the party.

6. **a.** Eddie's expected to arrive soon.
b. Eddie's grades aren't very good.
c. They haven't seen Eddie's report card yet.

7. **a.** He finds the discussion tiring.
b. He wants to think about it more.
c. He thinks her idea is better.

8. **a.** He feels sorry for John.
b. He's going to refuse John's request.
c. He expects John to repay him soon.

9. **a.** Her friend told her to expect bad weather.
b. Her friend is a weather expert.
c. Her friend tends to give lengthy answers.

10. **a.** Her friend expected the break-up.
b. Her friend was shocked by the break-up.
c. Her friend is furious at her ex-fiancé.

11. **a.** The boss is often late for meetings.
b. They're expected to show up on time.
c. They were late for the last meeting.

12. **a.** She enjoyed seeing Gene, as always.
b. She was too busy to see Gene.
c. She didn't know Gene was coming.

13. **a.** Bill thinks his firm is in danger.
b. Bill's optimism was refreshing.
c. Bill has a rather negative disposition.

14. **a.** They're in a taxicab.
b. They're stuck in traffic at the airport.
c. They're trying to get to the port.

15. **a.** Frank will be disappointed if she fails.
b. She'll be lucky if she succeeds.
c. She hopes someone answers her ad.

16. **a.** She's giving serious thought to the offer.
b. No one has made her an offer yet.
c. Her guess is they won't ask her.

17. **a.** Their friends didn't know they were coming.
b. Their friends were rude not to wait for them.
c. They should have made reservations earlier.

Part II

In this part, you will hear a question. From the three answer choices given, choose the one which best answers the question.

For problems 18 through 35, mark your answers on the separate answer sheet. No problems can be repeated. Please listen carefully. Do you have any questions?

Like idioms, phrasal verbs are a common feature of informal conversational English, so expect a healthy sprinkling of them to appear in (and influence the meaning of) both the questions you hear and the choices in your test booklet.

Hopefully, you've been keeping track of the phrasal verbs you've met in your studies. If so, use the months before the exam to review your notes often and keep your knowledge fresh. If you haven't, it's not too late to start. Take a few hours one weekend to go back over the materials you've used in the course of your ECPE preparation, and make a list of the phrasal verbs you find. Review the list often, and try using them in your everyday speech whenever you can.

18. **a.** They're not sure.
b. That doesn't seem to be an option.
c. He did, but she didn't.

19. **a.** It's not like him to break a promise.
b. Probably not before dinner.
c. He didn't say.

20. **a.** Why? Do you think it's gone off?
b. It's too soon to tell.
c. Not long enough.

21. **a.** Maybe Walter took it.
b. I thought it was your idea.
c. To be honest, I'm starting to regret it.

22. **a.** No, but I asked Ed and he figured it out.
b. All day, with no success.
c. Yes, you know I like working out.

23. **a.** Don't ask. He turned up two hours late.
b. Great. The auditorium was packed!
c. You should have told me earlier.

24. **a.** Not at all. Enjoy yourself.
b. Of course I didn't object.
c. I used to, but I don't anymore.

25. **a.** He's right on time.
b. It's hard to say.
c. You're right. He hasn't.

26. **a.** Believe me, I've tried.
b. Yes, they moved in last week.
c. I wouldn't if I were you.

27. **a.** He struck me hard. Can you believe it?
b. Nothing that I can put my finger on.
c. The odds are slim, I know.

28. **a.** I think I'll give it a miss.
b. Not that I know of.
c. It's not for sale yet.

29. **a.** I think he'll do a great job.
b. It's hard to say, but I'm betting it's the economy.
c. No, I think that will come later.

30. **a.** At today's meeting, in front of the whole staff.
b. He was raised in Chicago, wasn't he?
c. To make sure everyone was aware of it.

31. **a.** I don't want you to be disappointed.
b. I knew you'd be upset.
c. You didn't know, that's why.

32. **a.** I was at the game last night.
b. I have gained some weight, but not much.
c. I'd like that. Ask me later.

33. **a.** He refused to say.
b. It's not for you to judge him.
c. My guess is that it will.

34. **a.** No, I'm sure they'll turn up eventually.
b. Yes, I shouldn't have trusted him with it.
c. Not that I know of. Have you?

35. **a.** Ever since I moved.
b. Not for ages.
c. The sooner the better.

Part III

In this part, you will hear three short segments from a radio program. The program is called "Learning from the Experts." You will hear what three different radio guests have to say about three different topics.

Each talk lasts about two minutes. As you listen, you may want to take some notes to help you remember information given in the talk. Write your notes in the test booklet.

After each talk, you will be asked some questions about what was said. From the three answer choices given, you should choose the one that best answers the question according to the information you heard.

Remember, no problems can be repeated. For problems 36 through 50, mark all your answers on the separate answer sheet. Do you have any questions?

Don't sweat the fine detail!

No matter how difficult a passage seems, you are only going to be asked five questions about it. This means that there is not much chance of your being asked about a lot of specific detail. The questions usually focus on the broad outline of the program: e.g., its main idea and four supporting details. You should do fine if you use key phrases in the questions and in the answer choices to organize your listening and then do your best to focus on the main flow of the passage.

SEGMENT 1

36. What astonished Marcia Trent when she began to read *The Unnatural History of the Sea*?
- **a.** how little we still understand about the sea
- **b.** how plentiful sea life used to be
- **c.** how difficult it is to be a fisherman now

37. Which factor has NOT contributed to the dramatic rise in the global demand for fish?
- **a.** increased prosperity in China
- **b.** global health trends
- **c.** the state of underwater ecosystems

38. Of the following, which does Marcia Trent say has provided the global fishing industry with the financial means to bring world fisheries to the brink of collapse?
- **a.** government subsidies
- **b.** inadequate stock management
- **c.** modern fishing technology

39. According to statistics mentioned in the passage, what percentage of fish stocks around the world are currently overfished?
- **a.** 17%
- **b.** 25%
- **c.** 50%

40. Which of the following best sums up the idea that Marcia Trent leaves with her listeners?
- **a.** Despite what scientists say, the riches of the seas are still inexhaustible.
- **b.** Technology has allowed us to fish areas we never dreamed possible.
- **c.** We have fished the seas to a point where fish stocks may never recover.

SEGMENT 2

41. What does William Anderson say about students who do NOT ride buses to school?
- **a.** They are less likely to suffer from childhood obesity.
- **b.** A large majority of them eat lunch at fast-food restaurants.
- **c.** No one monitors where they go before and after school.

42. What problematic trend does the University of Illinois document?
- **a.** that fast-food outlets in the USA continue to open at an alarming rate
- **b.** that over 33% of secondary schools are close to fast-food outlets
- **c.** that urban schools are seldom located near fast-food outlets

(Segment 2 continues at top of next page)

43. What sets the University of Illinois study apart from other recent studies?
- **a.** It showed that 78% of all schools in Chicago are near fast-food outlets.
- **b.** It showed that the problem existed in four separate communities in Atlanta.
- **c.** It showed that the trend existed for secondary schools all over the USA.

44. According to the study, what should schools focus their efforts on to ensure that healthy food options are available to students?
- **a.** enhancing the food environment both on and off school grounds
- **b.** improving school cafeterias and vending machine offerings
- **c.** raising student awareness of the dangers of childhood obesity

45. What do the researchers think could be done to address the problem at the community level?
- **a.** see that all secondary schools impose a "closed-campus" lunchtime policy
- **b.** revise planning and zoning policies so fast-food outlets are not built near schools
- **c.** keep track of all students' eating habits inside and outside of school

SEGMENT 3

46. According to Neil Reynolds, why are athletes who exercise outside significantly more at risk than sedentary people?
- **a.** They breathe more deeply and more frequently.
- **b.** They breathe in much higher levels of pollutants.
- **c.** They fail to check air-quality forecasts before exercising outside.

47. Of the following three health problems, which does Neil Reynolds consider the least serious?
- **a.** premature aging of the lungs caused by ground-level ozone
- **b.** irritation and inflammation caused by fine particulates
- **c.** damage to blood vessels caused by fine particulates

48. What is tPA?
- **a.** a form of fine particulate found in diesel exhaust
- **b.** a chemical that inhibits blood and oxygen from reaching muscles
- **c.** a naturally occurring protein that helps dissolve blood clots

49. According to one expert, which condition would pose more risk to a runner?
- **a.** repeated exposure to high levels of pollution over months or years
- **b.** a large dose on a single occasion
- **c.** smoking

50. What is the main gist of the message Neil Reynolds leaves with his listeners?
- **a.** Running and cycling are healthy activities only when practiced indoors.
- **b.** When caution is exercised, it's beneficial and safe for us to run and cycle.
- **c.** People who live in polluted areas should drastically limit their exercise.

Grammar – Cloze – Vocabulary – Reading 75 minutes

This section of the examination contains 120 problems, numbered 51 through 170. There are 40 grammar, 20 cloze, 40 vocabulary, and 20 reading comprehension problems. If you do not understand how to do the problems, raise your hand, and a proctor will explain the examples to you. None of the actual test problems can be explained.

Each problem has only one correct answer. Do not spend too much time on any one problem. If you do not know the answer to a problem, you may guess. Work quickly but carefully. You have one hour and 15 minutes (75 minutes) to answer all 120 problems. If you finish before the time is over, you may check your answers within the GCVR section only. Do not go back to the Listening section of the exam.

GRAMMAR

51. Last week's powerful earthquake resulted _____ .
- **a.** in being severely damaged
- **b.** in severe damage
- **c.** from being severely damaged
- **d.** from severe damages

52. Up until last year, she'd never been to Brazil, and _____ .
- **a.** I haven't either
- **b.** neither would I
- **c.** neither had I
- **d.** I didn't either

53. By this time next year, they hope _____ enough money to buy a new car.
- **a.** to have saved
- **b.** to be saved
- **c.** they would save
- **d.** they saved

54. She said she would be home somewhere _____ 6 and 7 o'clock.
- **a.** from
- **b.** about
- **c.** until
- **d.** between

55. We laughed when we realized that my retired art teacher and her grandfather were _____ .
- **a.** one and the same
- **b.** all the same
- **c.** more of the same
- **d.** just the same

56. _____ need help with your computer, don't hesitate to call me.
- **a.** Should you ever
- **b.** Whenever should you need
- **c.** You should ever
- **d.** If ever should you

57. He considers _____ fortunate to have gone to an excellent university.
- **a.** him that he is
- **b.** his being
- **c.** being
- **d.** himself

58. Your report should have been perfect. You had _____ time to check it over.
- **a.** much too much
- **b.** more than enough
- **c.** quite a few
- **d.** little enough

59. _____ , that's Al's teacher over there in the corner, isn't it?
- **a.** Making no mistake
- **b.** Having not been mistaken
- **c.** If I'm not mistaken
- **d.** If I don't make a mistake

60. I realize you _____ the meeting, but I'm glad you did as your advice was invaluable.
- **a.** must not have attended
- **b.** didn't have to attend
- **c.** shouldn't have to attend
- **d.** aren't intending to attend

61. In today's society, skilled computer technicians are _____ .
- **a.** highly demanding
- **b.** demanded highly
- **c.** high on demand
- **d.** in high demand

62. I'll leave you my phone number _____ you need to get in touch with me.
- **a.** in case
- **b.** provided
- **c.** if only
- **d.** as long as

63. A drill _____ holes in wood and other materials.
- **a.** used to make
- **b.** is used for making
- **c.** uses in making
- **d.** is used to making

64. She's feeling bad about their breakup, but she'll soon realize that _____ fish in the sea.
- **a.** there is plenty
- **b.** he's not only a
- **c.** there are other
- **d.** he's another

65. It rained last night, so it isn't _____ hot and muggy today.
- **a.** that
- **b.** quite
- **c.** so much
- **d.** such a

66. They plan on being in England _____ the 1st to the 10th of June.
- **a.** between
- **b.** by
- **c.** since
- **d.** from

67. Her excellent grades in college led _____ a high-paying job after graduation.
- **a.** to get her
- **b.** in getting her
- **c.** to her getting
- **d.** her getting

68. I'm having trouble with my advanced mathematics course. I wish _____ it.
- **a.** to have never taken
- **b.** to never take
- **c.** that I never took
- **d.** I'd never taken

69. The boss just sent me an e-mail saying that I _____ every single entry in the report.
- **a.** am checking
- **b.** have to be checked
- **c.** am to check
- **d.** will have checked

70. Since the landlord is raising your rent again, that's _____ reason for you to move.
- **a.** more and more
- **b.** all the more
- **c.** many more
- **d.** even more of the

Structure Alert! (see item 63)
- *used to do sth* → past habit
- *be/get used to sth* → be accustomed
- *be/get used to doing sth* → be accustomed
- *be used for sth* → (things) purpose
- *be used to do* → (things) purpose

71. He doesn't regret _____ to Rome with Ed. Now he has enough money for a new car.
- **a.** not to go
- **b.** to have gone
- **c.** not having gone
- **d.** that he doesn't go

72. Ask Ted if you need a second opinion. His comments are always _____ .
- **a.** constructed
- **b.** constructive
- **c.** construction
- **d.** constructing

73. That old banged-up car over there really needs _____ , doesn't it?
- **a.** to be washed
- **b.** to wash
- **c.** to washing
- **d.** that it is washed

74. Remind Al that the information is classified, so it's urgent that _____ anyone.
- **a.** he won't tell
- **b.** he isn't telling
- **c.** he didn't tell
- **d.** he not tell

75. I love you new car, but isn't it the _____ model that Tanya bought last month?
- **a.** exactly the same
- **b.** very same
- **c.** exact same as
- **d.** exactly same

76. Be sure _____ your tire pressure before going on a long road trip.
- **a.** you will check
- **b.** to check
- **c.** of checking
- **d.** that it's checked

77. _____ you were really sick today, you'll still have to take the test tomorrow.
   a. However
   b. Provided
   c. In case
   d. Even though

78. If tutoring is _____ , I'm sure Sarah would be glad to help you.
   a. what you need
   b. that you need
   c. what do you need
   d. needing

79. I'm not feeling well. I'd rather _____ to the party tonight, if that's OK with you.
   a. not to go
   b. not have gone
   c. not go
   d. I hadn't gone

80. I haven't seen Mark in weeks, so I assume that he _____ on vacation.
   a. should have gone
   b. had better have gone
   c. must have gone
   d. would have gone

81. If you move to the suburbs, I'm guessing you won't use your bike to get to work, _____ ?
   a. aren't I
   b. don't you
   c. will you
   d. do you

82. The catalytic converter was designed _____ toxic emissions.
   a. so it reduced
   b. that it reduces
   c. to reduce
   d. by reducing

83. Do you know _____ to fly from New York to Athens?
   a. how long does it take
   b. how long to take
   c. how long it takes
   d. how long that it takes

84. I really wish my neighbors _____ playing their music so loud. It's driving me crazy.
   a. should stop
   b. have stopped
   c. had stopped
   d. would stop

85. She's really upset with him, _____ she's decided to call off their engagement.
   a. so long as
   b. in so far as
   c. so much so that
   d. so much as

86. He says he won't be leaving the office _____ the report.
   a. by the time he is finishing
   b. until he has finished
   c. until he is finished
   d. since he finishes

87. Mary will drive us to the game if her father lets her _____ his car.
   a. borrows
   b. borrowing
   c. to borrow
   d. borrow

88. "What's that noise?"
"I must have a hole in my _____ pipe."
   a. exhaust
   b. exhausted
   c. exhaustive
   d. exhausting

89. _____ tiny woodland animal that defends itself by emitting a terrible smell.
   a. Skunks are
   b. The skunk is a
   c. A skunk, which is a
   d. Many a skunk is

90. As always, his presentation was well received, so the worrying he did _____ .
   a. it was for all or nothing
   b. that it was for nothing at all
   c. was all for nothing
   d. which was not for nothing

Before choosing a comparative word like *worse* or *better* (as in item 92), make sure the text requires a comparative. The presence of *than* is usually a good indicator but when there are two or more comparative options, which should you choose? Reread several sentences before and after the blank. Then choose the word that fits both the structure and meaning of the surrounding text.

CLOZE

Passage 1 is about babies and sign language.

Teaching an infant sign language may sound like an odd thing to do, but research has shown that it makes good sense. Babies have the cognitive capacity to understand language __(91)__ they can speak, and early on, they have __(92)__ control of their hands than their __(93)__ . If babies can learn signs for objects and concepts (milk, for example, or dirty), then they can __(94)__ their needs rather than simply cry.

Linda Acredolo, psychologist and co-author of *Baby Sign: How to Talk to Your Baby Before Your Baby Can Talk*, first investigated sign language with her infant daughter in 1985. __(95)__ up on her initial experiment with years of lab research, she found that most children can learn to sign at around one, __(96)__ a lot depends on a child's individual development. It usually takes several months of parental signing before a child will respond.

Parents often __(97)__ that signing will slow verbal development, but Acredolo's research shows that early signing may __(98)__ promote language learning. In one study of 140 pairs of parents, couples __(99)__ randomly asked to use either hand signals or verbal stimulation. The babies __(100)__ parents signed to them later scored higher on repeated tests of verbal ability. And at age 8, the children who had signed scored an average of 12 points higher on an intelligence (IQ) test.

91. a. so b. before c. and d. because

92. a. worse b. no c. some d. better

93. a. legs b. mouths c. fingers d. parents

94. a. increase b. verbalize c. communicate d. interpret

95. a. Growing b. Checking c. Following d. Giving

96. a. though b. because c. providing d. that

97. a. deny b. doubt c. worry d. hope

98. a. actually b. have c. be d. not

99. a. that b. had c. they d. were

100. a. of b. have c. and d. whose

Passage 2 is about a clever teenage inventor.

Kavita Shukla may be just 16, but she's been inventing stuff for years. In fourth grade, she came up with an egg slicer (decorated with a plastic chicken) that was activated by a marble. At 13, after her mother had lost three gas caps from her car, Kavita rigged up a temperature-sensitive system that __(101)__ when the cap was off. But her best invention so far – for __(102)__ she recently won a Lemelson-MIT High School Invention Apprenticeship – was __(103)__ while visiting her grandmother in Bhopal, India, where tap water teems with bacteria. One day, after Kavita __(104)__ some water while brushing her teeth, her grandmother gave her fenugreek – an herb used in Indian cooking and medicine. Kavita didn't get sick, and she began to __(105)__ whether the herb could really protect __(106)__ bacteria. Soon her family's refrigerator was full of berries, some rotting, others remaining remarkably __(107)__ . Now after two years of experimenting, Kavita has shown that paper treated with fenugreek does __(108)__ preserve fruits and vegetables for weeks.

No one knows the why or how of fenugreek's __(109)__ properties, but the apprenticeship should help her find out. It will __(110)__ her to continue her research in a well-equipped lab under the guidance of a leading scientist.

101. a. cooled b. gestured c. signaled d. stopped

102. a. whom b. that c. when d. which

103. a. inspired b. dreamed c. built d. founded

104. a. boiled b. swallowed c. spilled d. ran

105. a. doubt b. understand c. wonder d. deny

106. a. against b. of c. people d. harmful

107. a. cool b. fresh c. moldy d. organic

108. a. indeed b. not c. therefore d. hence

109. a. restorative b. healing c. destructive d. preservative

110. a. give b. let c. allow d. make

VOCABULARY

If you're faced with one or more choices that are unfamiliar and difficult-sounding, don't assume that one of them must be the answer. Sometimes the easy word is wanted, especially when the context involves an ordinary event like eating (or not eating) lunch! Item 111 is a good example.

111. He's on a tight deadline, so he's decided to _____ lunch.
- **a.** extend
- **b.** exclude
- **c.** skip
- **d.** revoke

112. As a result of a boating accident, they were _____ on a desert island for two weeks.
- **a.** quarantined
- **b.** swamped
- **c.** marooned
- **d.** abandoned

113. They make the best cappuccino here. It's really _____ .
- **a.** crunchy
- **b.** frothy
- **c.** chewy
- **d.** soggy

114. Here's a summary of the plan. If you need more detail, we'll be happy to _____ .
- **a.** magnify
- **b.** enhance
- **c.** inflate
- **d.** elaborate

115. Sadly, neither driver survived the accident. Both died on _____ .
- **a.** collision
- **b.** impulse
- **c.** impact
- **d.** contact

116. After not being watered for several weeks, her plants had all gone _____ .
- **a.** limp
- **b.** lame
- **c.** flabby
- **d.** willowy

117. The burglars knew what the risks were. Now they'll have to suffer the _____ .
- **a.** consequences
- **b.** losses
- **c.** music
- **d.** defeat

118. Your clothes are covered in cat hair. Old Whiskers must be _____ again.
- **a.** shriveling
- **b.** shredding
- **c.** shedding
- **d.** shrugging

119. If my _____ is correct, she'll soon be wearing his ring.
- **a.** fantasy
- **b.** hunch
- **c.** hint
- **d.** omen

120. The collapse of the peace talks was viewed as a _____ to war.
- **a.** foreground
- **b.** prelude
- **c.** debut
- **d.** matinée

121. Smaller companies are finding it hard to _____ with larger companies nowadays.
- **a.** make waves
- **b.** keep pace
- **c.** hold water
- **d.** stay afloat

122. Instead of _____ all your old clothes, why don't you donate them to charity?
- **a.** dispatching
- **b.** dispelling
- **c.** discarding
- **d.** dismantling

123. The judge is soft on first-time offenders. Usually, all he does is give them _____ .
- **a.** a slap on the wrist
- **b.** a pat on the back
- **c.** a pain in the neck
- **d.** a peck on the cheek

124. As a result of _____ circumstances, they were forced to cancel their trip.
- **a.** unsightly
- **b.** unseen
- **c.** unforeseen
- **d.** untold

125. The _____ in the witnesses' stories aroused the investigator's suspicions.
 a. misgivings
 b. inequalities
 c. discrepancies
 d. similarities

126. It's _____ in here. Would someone please open a window?
 a. misty
 b. stuffy
 c. sticky
 d. moist

127. Doctors feel that their only option is to treat the cancer _____ .
 a. graciously
 b. inadvertently
 c. vehemently
 d. aggressively

128. There's an _____ truce between the two nations. War could erupt at any time.
 a. uneasy
 b. unfounded
 c. unbounded
 d. ungainly

129. Johnny has really _____ up over the summer. Just look at how tall he is!
 a. sprouted
 b. stood
 c. shown
 d. measured

130. Sadly, they have reached a _____ . Neither side is willing to compromise.
 a. standoff
 b. stand-in
 c. standstill
 d. standpoint

131. The barefoot beggar stood out in _____ contrast to the luxurious setting.
 a. stark
 b. verdant
 c. cordial
 d. laudable

132. As soon as the receptionist finds another job, she'll ____ her notice.
 a. hand down
 b. hand in
 c. hand out
 d. hand over

133. He's been very full of himself since his promotion. Somebody needs to take him _____ .
 a. down a peg or two
 b. up on it
 c. for granted
 d. at his word

134. A police officer gave her a ticket for changing lanes without _____ .
 a. waving
 b. displaying
 c. signaling
 d. pointing

135. Carbon dioxide (CO_2) is a _____ of burning petroleum-based fuels.
 a. breakthrough
 b. by-product
 c. setback
 d. comeback

136. The water in that stream isn't safe to drink. It's _____ with toxins.
 a. tinted
 b. contaminated
 c. infested
 d. strewn

137. Doesn't this pie smell great? Have a _____ . It just came out of the oven.
 a. lick
 b. puff
 c. whiff
 d. sip

138. Despite her excellent qualifications, her application was _____ .
 a. rejected
 b. negated
 c. submitted
 d. considered

139. If you don't mind my _____ an opinion, I think you're making a terrible mistake.
 a. preferring
 b. offering
 c. withholding
 d. donating

140. The child was not only rude but _____ , too. The class was hard to control when he was present.
 a. distinctive
 b. dismissive
 c. diminutive
 d. disruptive

141. Splitting the nucleus of an atom _____ huge amounts of energy.

- **a.** wastes
- **b.** unleashes
- **c.** omits
- **d.** recovers

142. He had to find a solution fast as the future of the company was at _____ .

- **a.** danger
- **b.** jeopardy
- **c.** a loss
- **d.** stake

143. One look at the child's skeletal limbs and swollen belly told her he was severely _____ .

- **a.** malformed
- **b.** maladroit
- **c.** malignant
- **d.** malnourished

144. Having fought the blaze for hours, the firefighters' faces were black with _____ .

- **a.** fumes
- **b.** smog
- **c.** soot
- **d.** grease

145. _____ foods like meat and vegetables need to be refrigerated to prevent spoilage.

- **a.** Deceased
- **b.** Dwindling
- **c.** Perishable
- **d.** Vulnerable

146. She called the Health Department to complain about the _____ of the sewer.

- **a.** aroma
- **b.** waste
- **c.** stench
- **d.** residue

147. They used twigs and old newspaper to _____ the campfire.

- **a.** kindle
- **b.** generate
- **c.** induce
- **d.** incinerate

148. The artist took _____ in her work after the tragic death of her infant son.

- **a.** pity
- **b.** refuge
- **c.** shelter
- **d.** aim

149. The sink is _____ again. We'll have to call the plumber.

- **a.** crowded
- **b.** swarming
- **c.** clogged
- **d.** congested

150. The orphanage was renovated with the help of a generous contribution from an anonymous _____ .

- **a.** beneficiary
- **b.** benefit
- **c.** benefactor
- **d.** benevolence

READING

Passage 1 is about plants.

Using terminology more characteristic of a thermal engineer than a botanist, we can think of plants as mechanisms that must balance their heat budgets. A plant by day is staked out under the sun with no way of sheltering itself. All day long it absorbs heat. If it did not lose as much heat as it gained, then eventually it would die. Plants get rid of their heat by warming the air around them, by evaporating water, and by radiating heat to the atmosphere and the cold, black reaches of space. Each plant must balance its heat budget so that its temperature is tolerable for the processes of life.

Plants in the Arctic tundra lie close to the ground in the thin layer of still air that clings there. A foot or two above the ground are the winds of Arctic cold. Tundra plants absorb heat from the sun and tend to warm up; they probably balance most of their heat budgets by radiating heat to space, but also by warming the still air that is trapped among them. As long as Arctic plants are close to the ground, they can balance their heat budgets. But if they should stretch up, as a tree does, they would expose their working parts, their leaves, to the streaming Arctic winds. Then it is likely that the plants could not absorb enough heat from the sun to avoid being cooled below a critical temperature. Your heat budget does not balance if you stand tall in the Arctic.

A desert plant faces the opposite problem – the danger of overheating. It is short of water and so cannot cool itself by evaporation without dehydrating. The familiar stick-like shape of desert plants represents one of the solutions to this problem: the shape exposes the smallest possible surface to incoming solar radiation and provides the largest possible surface from which the plant can radiate heat. In tropical forests, by way of contrast, the scorching sun is not a problem for plants because there is sufficient water.

151. Which factor is most responsible for preventing plants from growing tall in the Arctic?

- **a.** the small amount of sunshine
- **b.** the cold, destructive winds
- **c.** the hard, frozen ground
- **d.** the thin, still air

152. Why is it important for a plant to lose as much heat as it gains?

- **a.** so it radiates heat into space
- **b.** so it doesn't absorb too much water
- **c.** so critical life processes can occur
- **d.** so water can evaporate into the air

153. Which of the following characteristics of plants does the passage generally discuss?

- **a.** their ability to grow well in all environments
- **b.** their effects on the earth's atmosphere
- **c.** their ability to store water for long periods
- **d.** their ability to balance heat intake and output

154. Why is the sun **not** a problem for plants in a tropical rain forest?

- **a.** It never gets excessively hot there.
- **b.** There is no shortage of water.
- **c.** They have an ideal sticklike shape.
- **d.** It is not mentioned in the passage.

155. What would probably happen to desert plants if they did **not** have a stick-like shape?

- **a.** They would perish from overheating and dehydration.
- **b.** They would be able to absorb considerably more water.
- **c.** They would be exposed to even less solar radiation.
- **d.** They would find other ways to adapt to the environment.

Passage 2 is about cancer.

A new approach in the fight against cancer is based on the simple yet critical observation that a tumor needs a blood supply to grow. A genetic mutation may prompt a normal cell to divide uncontrollably, but unless the resulting mass can spawn a network of blood vessels to deliver nutrients and oxygen, it will grow to the size of a pea and settle into a harmless, dormant state. Unfortunately, these little sleepers can wake up. After sitting idle for months or even years, a pea-size mass may suddenly provoke nearby blood vessels to send out new branches or capillaries. That vascular flowering, or angiogenesis, is supposed to occur only briefly during menstruation, pregnancy or wound healing. But when tumors set the process in motion, it enables them to grow uncontrollably, invading healthy tissues and seeding the bloodstream with malignant cells.

No one knows why small tumors suddenly go angiogenic, but researchers now know that healthy cells constantly regulate the growth of nearby blood vessels by generating chemical messengers known as inducers and inhibitors. The cells that line our vessels have receptors for both types of molecules. Normally the inhibitors predominate. But if a few cancer cells stop sending out their share of inhibitors, the inducers take over and the cells in nearby vessels start proliferating wildly to form new capillaries. The new capillaries have receptors that enable them to attach themselves to the tumor. They also bind readily with enzymes called MMPs, which serve roughly the function of drill bits. Armed with MMPs, the new vessels can bore into the tumor and set up a full-service link into the circulatory system.

Over the years researchers have developed several dozen angiogenesis inhibitors that can thwart this process at one stage or another, but most have side effects that limit their use. The most promising work is now being done with two naturally occurring protein molecules – endostatin and angiostatin – that scientists found lurking in tumors themselves. Initial experiments on mice suggest that the new treatments appear less toxic than chemotherapy and less prone to resistance. A growing body of experts are cautiously optimistic about the research, but they assume the new inhibitors will have to be used in combination with other forms of treatment. Almost no cancer has been cured by a single agent.

156. What is angiogenesis?
- **a.** a kind of cancer in which flower-like tumors grow from blood vessels
- **b.** a revolutionary new approach in scientists' fight against cancer
- **c.** the process by which blood vessels grow or extend themselves
- **d.** a genetic mutation that causes a normal cell to become cancerous

157. What is **not** true of inhibitors and inducers?
- **a.** Cells generate them to regulate the growth of nearby blood vessels.
- **b.** In healthy cells, inhibitors usually exert more influence than inducers.
- **c.** Angiogenesis cannot take place if there are inducers present.
- **d.** Cancerous cells produce fewer inhibitors than healthy cells.

158. What happens when cells become cancerous?
- **a.** Inducers cause nearby blood vessels to grow capillaries that attach to the tumor.
- **b.** The cells produce a higher level of inhibitors, which in turn triggers angiogenesis.
- **c.** The cells usually enter a resting state before beginning to divide uncontrollably.
- **d.** The cells produce their own capillaries that link up with nearby blood vessels.

159. According to the passage, what role do MMPs play in angiogenesis?
- **a.** They act as inducers to further encourage the growth of new capillaries.
- **b.** They regulate the inhibitors so that the inducers do not have to work as hard.
- **c.** They allow blood vessels to attach themselves to the outside of the tumor.
- **d.** They enable capillaries to enter the tumor and link it to the circulatory system.

160. What is **not** true about research into angiogenesis and cancer?
- **a.** The link between angiogenesis and cancer has only recently been discovered.
- **b.** Researchers have identified substances in tumors that may prove invaluable in cancer treatment.
- **c.** Previous efforts have uncovered substances that slow angiogenesis but have unwanted side effects.
- **d.** Researchers believe that treatment with inhibitors may need to be combined with other therapies.

Passage 3 is about the sun.

Like other stars, the sun is essentially a vast thermonuclear fusion reactor held together by gravity. Deep in its interior, some 600 million tons of hydrogen fuse into helium every second, producing energy that radiates from the incandescent outer layers as sunlight. The question is, how? In the past, astronomers had a tough time answering that, mainly because those same incandescent outer layers made it impossible to see what was going on below. Recently, however, they've been able to look right through the surface and map the inner dynamics of the sun with remarkable clarity, thanks to a technique known as "helioseismology."

Helioseismology allows scientists to study the sun by analyzing the sound waves traveling through it, explains John Leibacher, astronomer and director of the Global Oscillation Network Group (GONG). Much as the waves produced by earthquakes roll through the Earth, he says, sound waves pass through the sun's gaseous mass and set its surface pulsating like a drumhead. With six telescopes set up around the Earth collecting data every minute, GONG scientists can measure the pulsations and learn about the sun's structure, dynamics, and magnetic field. Analysis of the data has shown that theories about the structure of the sun need refining. For example, the convection zone – the area beneath the surface where pockets of hot matter rise quickly and mix violently with ambient material – is much larger than once thought.

New insight into the sun's core came recently when analysts announced they had discovered a solar "heartbeat." That is, they'd found that some layers of gas below the sun's surface speed up and slow down in a predictable pattern, about every 16 months. The pattern appears to be connected to the cycle of eruptions, or solar storms, on the sun's surface, which can cause significant disturbances in Earth's own magnetic field and wreak havoc with telecommunications and satellite systems. A major breakthrough in the ability to forecast these storms occurred when astrophysicists developed a technique to image explosive regions on the far side of the sun. Such images should provide early warnings of potentially disruptive solar storms before their effect is felt on Earth.

161. Scientists are beginning to understand more about the sun as a result of ...
- **a.** the improved capacity of telescopes to see through the its outer layers.
- **b.** a dramatic increase in seismographic activity in the sun's inner core.
- **c.** a new technique that analyzes sound waves moving through the sun.
- **d.** an increase in the amount of energy radiated by the sun's outer layers.

162. What situation made it difficult for scientists to study the sun in the past?
- **a.** The light from the surface made it impossible to see beneath the surface.
- **b.** Little or nothing was understood about thermonuclear fusion reactors.
- **c.** Maps which clearly showed the inner dynamics of the sun did not exist.
- **d.** They couldn't calculate how much hydrogen and helium were present.

163. What is GONG?
- **a.** a solar phenomenon detected by helioseismology
- **b.** a type of telescope that measures global oscillation
- **c.** an international network of helioseismology experts
- **d.** a group of seismologists who study earthquake activity

164. What has enabled scientists to predict solar storms?
- **a.** the discovery of a solar heartbeat below the surface
- **b.** a method that images certain areas on the far side of the sun
- **c.** the fact that many of these storms occur in cycles
- **d.** the advent of telecommunications and satellites

165. What have scientists recently learned about the sun's convection zone?
- **a.** It is much more massive that it used to be.
- **b.** It is hotter than researchers ever imagined.
- **c.** It is even more violent than it used to be.
- **d.** It is greater in area than previously assumed.

Passage 4 is about Permian times.

During Permian times, some 250 million years ago, Earth's landmasses formed a single supercontinent and an unbroken sea covered the rest of the planet. Today, water near the poles becomes so cold and dense that it sinks to the ocean bottom and flows around the world before surfacing again. But in late Permian times the climate was warmer and there was little flow in the deep at all. As dead organisms rained down from the surface into this nearly stagnant water, the decay of all that material gradually sucked the oxygen out of it. With few currents floating into the deep, there was no way to bring in fresh oxygen from the surface. It has long been thought that the Permian extinctions were a case of death by suffocation, triggered when anoxic (or oxygen-poor) deep water was somehow mixed into shallower regions, where most of the animals were. A new theory, however, indicates that the real culprit was more likely carbon dioxide (or CO_2), a by-product of organic decay.

As oxygen disappeared, CO_2 began to build up in the Permian deep and may have reached concentrations of 30 times its present-day level. The ocean became a disaster waiting to happen. What finally unleashed it was a cooling of the climate, caused in part by the build-up of CO_2 in the oceans and the subsequent reduction of CO_2 in the atmosphere. For the first time in tens of millions of years, polar glaciers appeared, chilling the neighboring surface water and sending it coursing through the deep. That circulation pushed noxious CO_2-laden water from the deep into shallow regions, and the extinctions began. The CO_2 not only killed marine life but also slowly returned to the atmosphere and heated the climate back up again. The polar ice melted, and the deep-ocean circulation in turn slowed down, creating a brief respite from mass extinction before the whole cycle repeated itself. While CO_2 poisoning decimated life in the sea, the rapid climate swings also made times rough for organisms on land. The extinctions wiped out 95 percent of all species on earth, compared to the process that eliminated the dinosaurs 65 million years ago, when an asteroid or comet slammed into the planet, taking out a mere 50 percent of all species.

166. According to new theory, what triggered the Permian extinctions?

- **a.** shifts in the ocean's currents
- **b.** an excess of oxygen in deep water
- **c.** a massive build-up of CO_2 in deep water
- **d.** an unexpected increase in organic decay

167. What did earlier theories hold to be the cause of these extinctions?

- **a.** an increase of cold, dense water near the poles
- **b.** a lack of oxygen near the surface of the ocean
- **c.** a sudden and extreme warming of the earth's climate
- **d.** the flow of oxygen-poor deep water into shallower areas

168. According to the text, how does our environment today compare with that of Permian times?

- **a.** Nowadays the climate is cooler and the ocean has stronger currents.
- **b.** Nowadays there is much less carbon dioxide in the atmosphere.
- **c.** Today there is less polar ice than there was during Permian times.
- **d.** There are fewer continents today than there were in Permian times.

169. Which of the statements about Permian times is not true?

- **a.** Life forms on land and in the sea were both drastically affected by climate changes.
- **b.** The depletion of CO_2 in the atmosphere gradually led to the formation of polar ice.
- **c.** The extinctions that occurred were milder than that which put an end to dinosaurs.
- **d.** The earth's climate underwent several swings: from warm to cool and back again.

170. What happened when polar glaciers restored circulation to the ocean?

- **a.** Marine life was unable to adapt in time to the freezing water.
- **b.** It brought a temporary halt to one of the waves of mass extinction.
- **c.** It caused a rapid warming of the climate, causing many species to perish.
- **d.** The CO_2-rich deep water flowed into shallower regions, killing marine life.

Vocabulary Enhancement

Watery States and Stages

A **Water Magic: Now You See It, Now You Don't** – *In the first paragraph of Reading Passage 1, we came across the concept of water* ***evaporating****, i.e., changing into* ***vapor*** *(or* ***steam****). Here's a look at this and other verbs associated with water in its various states.*

Study the definitions, and then choose the correct word in the examples below.

LIQUID TO GAS - When water **evaporates**, it changes from a liquid to a gas – i.e., it becomes **vapor** or **steam**. When we **steam** food, we cook it by exposing it to steam. When a boat **steams** somewhere, it moves with the aid of steam power. We can also use steam to **steam** things **open** (e.g., envelopes) or **steam** things **off** (e.g., stamps off an envelope). Metaphorically, when we **let off steam**, we release energy, relieve stress, or express strong emotion by behaving actively or noisily. When we **run out of steam**, it means we no longer have energy or enthusiasm.

GAS TO LIQUID - When steam touches a cold surface and becomes liquid again, we say it **condenses**.

LIQUID TO SOLID - If we expose water to very cold temperatures, it **freezes** (i.e., turns to ice or frost). When ice is exposed to heat, it **melts** or becomes liquid again. (We can also say it **liquefies**, but don't confuse this with **liquidate**, which means "close down a business and sell whatever is possible to pay off its debts"!) When we remove ice from the freezer compartment of a refrigerator, we **defrost** the freezer. When we allow frozen food to come back to room temperature, we **defrost** or **thaw** it. When winter turns to spring, snow **thaws**, as does frozen ground. **Thaw** is also used figuratively to describe what happens when an attitude or relationship becomes warmer and more friendly.

1. The two nations are age-old rivals, but recently diplomatic relations have begun to **melt / thaw / liquidate** .
2. It was so cold that a chill penetrated the house and the windows were wet with **steam / frost / condensation** .
3. They can't go ice-skating on the pond as the warm sun has begun to **liquidate / defrost / melt** the ice.
4. Experts say that that **steaming / evaporating / melting** food helps preserve its vitamin content.
5. She enjoys playing basketball with her friends as it helps her let off **evaporation / vapor / steam** .
6. By mid-morning, the puddles from the previous night's rain had **steamed / evaporated / condensed** and the sidewalks were dry.

B **Beware, Water Shortage** – *In Reading Passage 1, we also saw that desert plants are adapted to prevent* ***dehydration*** *– that is, the loss of large amounts of water. Here are other words that are associated with not having enough water.*

Study the definitions, and then choose the appropriate word in the examples below.

If plants or flowers do not get enough water, they will **wilt** or **droop** (i.e., bend downwards and appear weak). If they continue to be deprived of water, they will **shrivel** and die (i.e., they will become shrunken, dry, and wrinkled). Another word for this is **wither**. When we say something is **parched**, we mean it is dried out from the heat. During a **drought** (a long, dry period without rain), for example, the land becomes **parched** and may appear cracked. The word can also be used metaphorically to mean "very thirsty" (e.g., "I'm parched! Let's stop for a drink!"). When rains finally come and soak the earth, making the soil moist and healthy again, we say the earth is **slaked** (i.e., its thirst has been satisfied).

1. The shipwreck survivors were exhausted and **shriveled / dehydrated / wilted** but otherwise all right.
2. The soil was **withered / shriveled / parched** from the long dry spell.
3. By the time he arrived, the flowers he had bought for her had already **withered / slaked / wilted** .
4. It was a funny-looking dog with a sad face and long, **shriveled / wilted / droopy** ears.

C **Water from the Sky** – Water comes out of or hangs in the sky in different forms. Match the "water words" in the box with their meanings below.

blizzard	dew	drizzle	fog	hail	haze	mist	precipitation	sleet	smog

1. ______________ – light rain
2. ______________ – frozen rain
3. ______________ – thick, low cloud of water drops
4. ______________ – thinner, less dense version of (3)
5. ______________ – light, warm-weather form of (4)
6. ______________ – balls of ice that fall from the sky
7. ______________ – general term for rain, snow, etc.
8. ______________ – severe snowstorm
9. ______________ – polluted mix of smoke and fog
10. ______________ – drops appearing on grass at night

D **Common Adjective + Noun Collocations** – Pair up one word from A with another from B, and then write the combination under the appropriate photo. The first has been done as an example.

A	droopy	honey	melted	misty	morning	parched	shriveled	spring	~~steam~~	vegetable
B	cheese	dew	drizzler	expression	eyes	~~iron~~	landscape	skin	steamer	thaw

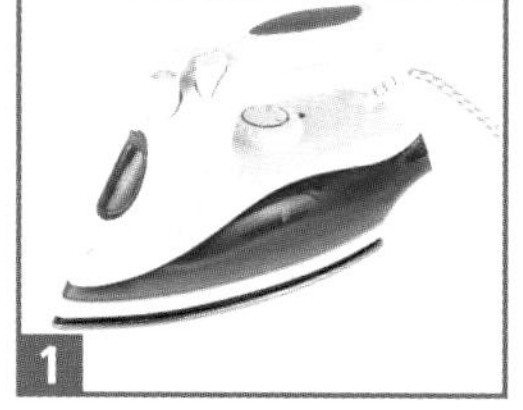
1 steam iron

2 ______________

3 ______________

4 ______________

5 ______________

6 ______________

7 ______________

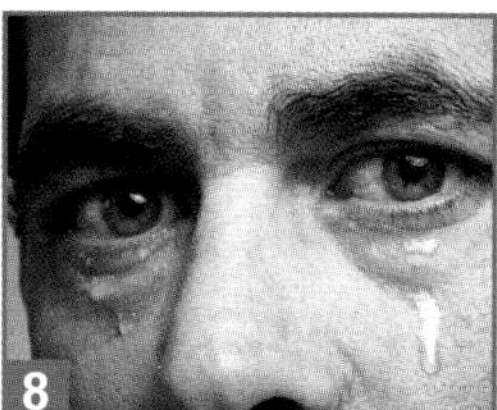
8 ______________

9 ______________

10 ______________

E **Instant Replay** – Now use the phrases you constructed in D to complete the following. (One phrase will not be used.)

1. If you're on the verge of crying, you probably have both of these: ______________
2. If you want to buy a housewarming gift for a friend, consider these: ______________
3. If you hate cold weather, you make your way through the winter hoping for this: ______________
4. If you're getting ready for a trip to the desert, be ready to see plenty of this. ______________
5. If you use moisturizers or face creams, you're probably hoping to avoid this: ______________
6. If you like to take walks at dawn, you're probably no stranger to this: ______________

Vocabulary Consolidation

VEXING VERBS

A Common Collocations – Complete each phrase with a word from the box.

abandon *dispel* *extend* *hand* *point* *quarantine* *revoke* *shrug*

1. ______________ a warm welcome to sb
2. ______________ a contagious patient
3. ______________ out a flaw in an argument
4. ______________ a sinking ship
5. ______________ a false rumor
6. ______________ sb's driver's license
7. ______________ your shoulders
8. ______________ in your resignation

B Fine-Tuning Your Knowledge – The numbers below refer to questions in the Vocabulary section of Practice Test 5. After reviewing the words, fill in each blank with the correct form of the appropriate verb.

111. exclude extend revoke skip	**a.** Your credit card privileges will be ______________ if you exceed the spending limit. **b.** Women are no longer ______________ from holding high-level corporate positions. **c.** The teacher told us to ______________ chapter 8 and go straight to chapter 9. **d.** The company has decided to ______________ the deadline by two weeks.
114. elaborate enhance inflate magnify	**a.** I'm not saying he's lying, but he does tend to ______________ the truth at times. **b.** A pump is used to ______________ tires. **c.** The computer program can ______________ photos by improving color contrast. **d.** The elderly woman reads with the help of a special lens that ______________ type.
118. shed shred shrivel shrug	**a.** Your plants will ______________ up and die if you don't water them more often. **b.** The boss instructed his assistant to ______________ the documents so no one else could read them. **c.** She's hoping to ______________ a few pounds by the end of the month. **d.** When I asked him where he was going, he just ______________ and left the room.
122. discard dismantle dispatch dispel	**a.** The boss called a meeting to ______________ fears that the firm would have to close. **b.** The country is under pressure to ______________ its nuclear power station. **c.** The courier service ______________ packages all over the world. **d.** Before you ______________ your old clothing, why don't you see if the church accepts donations?
138. consider negate reject submit	**a.** The President has just ______________ a new proposal to raise taxes. His supporters ______________ this a slap in the face as it ______________ his campaign promises. Everyone is hoping that the Congress will ______________ the plan outright. **b.** The villagers had no choice but to ______________ to the demands of the powerful invaders.
139. donate offer prefer withhold	**a.** John has ______________ to help repaint the main dining area of the orphanage. I think it's generous of him to ______________ his free time in this way. **b.** I'd ______________ it if you told me the whole story. It will do you no good to ______________ information that I'm bound to find out anyway.

NOTORIOUS NOUNS

A **Amusing Associations** – Find the word or phrase in the box that is suggested by each prompt.

a comeback *a matinée* *a sip* *a whiff* *the music* *setbacks* *waves* *your losses*

1. ______________ – You'll want to try to make one of these if your popularity has dipped.
2. ______________ – Try making these if you want the police to patrol your area more regularly.
3. ______________ – Avoid these if you want to keep on making good progress.
4. ______________ – Take one of these if you want to make sure your tea has enough sugar in it.
5. ______________ – Go to one of these if you don't want to pay full price for an evening performance.
6. ______________ – You'll have to face this if the police find you driving without your seatbelt fastened.
7. ______________ – Avoid taking one of these if there's an angry skunk lurking in the bushes.
8. ______________ – You'll want to cut these if the stock market takes a sudden dive.

B **Fine-Tuning Your Knowledge** – The numbers below refer to questions in the Vocabulary section of Practice Test 5. After reviewing the words, fill in each blank with the appropriate word.

117. **consequences** **defeat** **losses** **music**	**a.** Their ______________ in the semi-finals was a crushing blow. **b.** Suffering the ______________ of your mistakes is never easy, but it helps to face the ______________ and then get on with your life. **c.** Joe's financial advice is usually sound; if you don't follow it, you might suffer heavy ______________ and the ______________ for your retirement could be disastrous.
119. **fantasy** **hint** **hunch** **omen**	**a.** What if his ______________ of living in the White House were to come true? **b.** I have a ______________ that we haven't seen the last of him. **c.** In ancient times, a total eclipse of the sun was seen as a bad ______________ . **d.** A ______________ of sadness comes into his voice when he mentions his late wife.
120. **debut** **foreground** **matinée** **prelude**	**a.** Everyone fears that the breakdown of diplomacy is a ______________ to war. **b.** In London, we saw two shows a day: a ______________ and an evening performance. Yesterday, we even saw a British TV star make her ______________ in a West End play. **c.** Computer networking began in the early 1960s. It took more than 30 years for the concept to come into the ______________ .
130. **stand-in** **standoff** **standpoint** **standstill**	**a.** When I called you from the highway, traffic was at a total ______________ . **b.** Who will be your ______________ when you go on vacation next month? **c.** The negotiations have reached a ______________ . Neither side will compromise. From the union's ______________ , a strike is inevitable.
135. **breakthrough** **by-product** **setback** **comeback**	**a.** Divorce is frequently a ______________ of financial stress in a marriage. **b.** Over the past five years, the researchers have suffered one ______________ after another, but they feel they are finally on the verge of a major ______________ . **c.** At half-time, the team was down 2 goals to 1, but hopefully they will make a ______________ in the second half.
137. **lick** **puff** **sip** **whiff**	**a.** When she failed to get into medical school, her dream vanished like a ______________ of smoke. **b.** This ice cream cone is delicious. Would you like a ______________? **c.** Open the oven and take a ______________ . Mom's making cookies again. **d.** You'll need a ______________ or two of water to get those pills down.

AUDACIOUS ADJECTIVES

A **Common Collocations** – Complete each phrase with a word from the box.

disruptive *inadvertent* *infested* *misty* *moist* *strewn* *tinted* *verdant*

1. a car with _______________ windows
2. a beach _______________ with garbage
3. a house _______________ with termites
4. _______________ tropical islands
5. a class clown's _______________ behavior
6. _______________ errors
7. a cake with a(n) _______________ texture
8. eyes _______________ with tears

B **Fine-Tuning Your Knowledge** – The numbers below refer to questions in the Vocabulary section of Practice Test 5. After reviewing the words, fill in each blank with the appropriate word.

116. flabby **lame** **limp** **willowy**	**a.** He's been _______________ ever since his leg was broken in a car accident 10 years ago. **b.** To avoid getting _______________, get plenty of exercise and watch your diet. **c.** She felt herself go _______________ when she realized she had won the lottery jackpot. **d.** We all admired the grace with which the _______________ ballerina moved across the stage.
124. unforeseen **unseen** **unsightly** **untold**	**a.** In addition to creating an _______________ mess on beaches all the way up the coast, the massive oil spill has done _______________ damage to the marine habitat. **b.** Due to _______________ costs the project has been postponed indefinitely. **c.** By wearing a disguise, the actor managed to slip into the room _______________.
126. misty **moist** **sticky** **stuffy**	**a.** It was so _______________ today that you couldn't see the lighthouse in the harbor. **b.** Your hands are all _______________. Have you been eating honey? **c.** Please don't overcook the fish. I like it nice and _______________ inside. **d.** She found the five-star restaurant a bit too _______________ for her simple tastes.
128. unbounded **uneasy** **unfounded** **ungainly**	**a.** I keep telling you not to worry. Your fears are totally _______________. There's no need to feel _______________. **b.** Before she lost weight, she was always tired; now she has _______________ energy. **c.** Children's first steps are always _______________ until they find their "sea legs."
131. cordial **laudable** **stark** **verdant**	**a.** It's no accident that Ireland is known as the Emerald Isle. It's probably the most _______________ place I've ever visited. Its lush vegetation presents a _______________ contrast to the Sahara Desert, where I traveled last year. **b.** The mayor commended the firefighters for their _______________ job performance. **c.** We thanked our hosts for their _______________ hospitality.
140. diminutive **dismissive** **disruptive** **distinctive**	**a.** The 10-week strike has had a terribly _______________ effect on the economy. **b.** I'm sick and tired of your _______________ comments. You're always putting me down. **c.** The young opera star has a most _______________ voice. **d.** Jean is of average height but next to her husband, a professional basketball player, she seems positively _______________.

PRICKLY PREPOSITIONS AND PARTICLES

The following extracts are taken from passages that you have encountered in Practice Test 5. Read each one quickly, and then fill in each blank with an appropriate preposition or particle.

1. A desert plant faces the opposite problem – the danger _________ overheating. It is short _________ water and so cannot cool itself _________ evaporation _________ dehydrating. The familiar sticklike shape _________ desert plants represents one _________ the solutions _________ this problem: the shape exposes the smallest possible surface _________ incoming solar radiation and provides the largest possible surface _________ which the plant can radiate heat. _________ tropical forests, _________ way _________ contrast, the scorching sun is not a problem _________ plants because there is sufficient water.

2. A new approach _________ the fight _________ cancer is based _________ the simple yet critical observation that a tumor needs a blood supply to grow. ...The most promising work is now being done _________ two naturally occurring protein molecules – endostatin and angiostatin – that scientists found lurking _________ tumors themselves. Initial experiments _________ mice suggest that the new treatments appear less toxic than chemotherapy and less prone _________ resistance. A growing body _________ experts are cautiously optimistic _________ the research, but they assume the new inhibitors will have to be used _________ combination _________ other forms _________ treatment. Almost no cancer has been cured _________ a single agent.

3. New insight _________ the sun's core came recently when analysts announced they had discovered a solar "heartbeat." That is, they'd found that some layers _________ gas _________ the sun's surface speed _________ and slow _________ in a predictable pattern, _________ every 16 months. The pattern appears to be connected _________ the cycle _________ eruptions, or solar storms, _________ the sun's surface, which can cause significant disturbances _________ Earth's own magnetic field and wreak havoc _________ telecommunications and satellite systems. A major breakthrough _________ the ability to forecast these storms occurred when astrophysicists developed a technique to image explosive regions _________ the far side _________ the sun. Such images should provide early warnings _________ potentially disruptive solar storms before their effect is felt _________ Earth.

4. _________ late Permian times, the climate was warmer and there was little flow _________ the deep _________ all. As dead organisms rained down _________ the surface _________ this nearly stagnant water, the decay _________ all that material gradually sucked the oxygen out _________ it. _________ few currents floating _________ the deep, there was no way to bring _________ fresh oxygen _________ the surface. It has long been thought that the Permian extinctions were a case _________ death _________ suffocation, triggered when anoxic (or oxygen-poor) deep water was somehow mixed _________ shallower regions, where most _________ the animals were. A new theory, however, indicates that the real culprit was more likely carbon dioxide (or CO_2), a by-product of organic decay. ... While CO_2 poisoning decimated life _________ the sea, the rapid climate swings also made times rough _________ organisms _________ land. The extinctions wiped _________ 95 percent _________ all species _________ earth, compared _________ the process that eliminated the dinosaurs 65 million years ago, when an asteroid or comet slammed _________ the planet, taking _________ a mere 50 percent _________ all species.

6 Practice Test 6

Writing 30 minutes

- You may write in pen or pencil.
- You will have 30 minutes to write on one of the two topics. If you do not write on one of these topics, your paper will not be scored. If you do not understand the topics, ask the examiner to explain them.
- You may make an outline if you wish, but your outline will not count toward your score.
- Write about one-and-a-half to two pages. Your essay will be marked down if it is extremely short.
- You will not be graded on the appearance of your paper, but your handwriting must be readable. You may change or correct your writing, but you should not recopy the whole essay.
- Your essay will be judged on clarity and overall effectiveness, as well as on topic development, organization, and the range, accuracy, and appropriateness of your grammar and vocabulary. Your essay will be graded at the University of Michigan.

TOPICS For help in writing these compositions, see *Writing Tutorial*, pages 211-212.

1. An American humorist once said, "I must say I find television very educational. The minute somebody turns it on, I go to the library and read a good book." Over the years people have been very critical of television. Do you think that television is living up to its full potential as a form of mass media, or are there other, more beneficial ways that it could be used? Support your ideas with specific examples.

2. As the Rolling Stones acknowledged in their now classic song, "You can't always get what you want." There are times in all our lives when things don't work out the way we want them to: for example, losing a game, not doing well on an exam, or simply having to face the harsh reality that an important goal or dream cannot be achieved. No one enjoys these moments, but it's often been said that important lessons can be learned from them. Describe an incident in which things didn't work out for you. How did you cope with the experience, and what lessons did you learn that might benefit others?

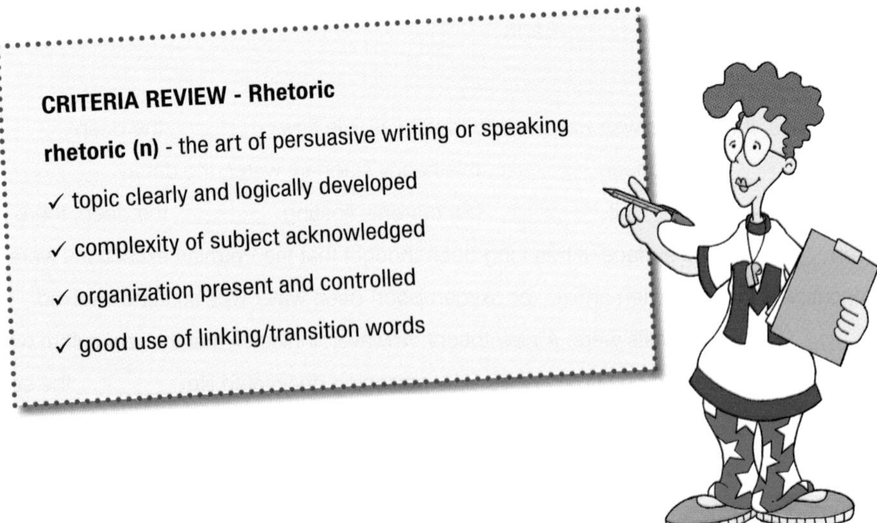

CRITERIA REVIEW - Rhetoric
rhetoric (n) - the art of persuasive writing or speaking
✓ topic clearly and logically developed
✓ complexity of subject acknowledged
✓ organization present and controlled
✓ good use of linking/transition words

Listening approx. 35-40 minutes

This section of the examination tests your understanding of spoken English. The listening section has three parts. There are 50 questions. Mark all your answers on the separate answer sheet. Do not make any stray marks on the answer sheet. If you change your mind about an answer, erase your first answer completely.

Part I

In this part, you will hear short conversations. From the three answer choices given, choose the answer which means about the same thing as what you hear, or that is true based upon what you hear.

For problems 1 through 17, mark your answers on the separate answer sheet. No problems can be repeated.

Please listen carefully. Do you have any questions?

Expect a number of questions to test your understanding of verb tenses, conditionals, modals, causative form, passive voice, and other structures that might lead to misunderstanding. Some items of this type are fairly easy to spot. As you preview the choices, be on the lookout for sets of answer choices that include similar language with a range of time frames (e.g., *He already did it. / He may do it later. / He should have done it, but he didn't.*) or a range of agents (e.g., *He did it. / He got someone else to do it./ Someone else will do it later*). This is your cue to listen carefully for verb structures, time markers, and other grammar clues that will help you narrow down the choices.

Five of the questions below clearly fall into this category. Can you identify them? ____________

1. **a.** She hasn't checked on the flight yet.
   b. She assumes the flight will be late.
   c. She'll check on the flight at the airport.

2. **a.** He's going to do the work himself.
   b. He's sure the twins will agree to do the work.
   c. The twins may agree to do the work.

3. **a.** She's afraid to talk to Tim.
   b. She thinks Tim won't take her advice.
   c. Tim is hard of hearing.

4. **a.** Sarah has already eaten the pie.
   b. Sarah will be hurt if he eats the pie.
   c. Sarah is not home from school yet.

5. **a.** Sam is currently away on business.
   b. Sam had to call off his business trip.
   c. Sam has come back to be with his mother.

6. **a.** Her résumé needs updating.
   b. Her company is about to close.
   c. She's looking for new employment.

7. **a.** He thinks they should get a new car first.
   b. He wants to wait till their car loan is paid off.
   c. He doesn't like her plan for the attic.

8. **a.** Mary will probably not help her cook.
   b. Mary said she could count on her help
   c. He thinks Mary is unreliable.

9. **a.** They may have a buyer for their house.
   b. They both like the house they just saw.
   c. He's against buying the house.

10. **a.** She doesn't remember turning the oven on.
    b. She thinks Ann may be in danger.
    c. She wants to play it safe and go back.

11. **a.** She's annoyed with Judy.
    b. He thinks Judy should lose weight.
    c. He'll make Judy do the dishes later.

12. **a.** Someone painted the garage for him.
    b. He's decided to paint the garage himself.
    c. Next time he'll paint the garage himself.

13. **a.** She just got off the phone with Larry.
    b. He didn't expect Larry to be away so long.
    c. He's surprised Larry is back in California.

14. **a.** She can't use her car to shop next week.
    b. He disapproves of her commuting style.
    c. He's surprised she's thinking of moving.

15. **a.** She thinks he's wasting his time.
    b. He's trying to call his bank.
    c. He wants to have something sent to him.

16. **a.** The accident was totally his fault.
    b. He should have been wearing his seat belt.
    c. She thinks things could have been worse.

17. **a.** She's had to rearrange her plans.
    b. Her friend forgot about Billy's appointment.
    c. The women will definitely meet tomorrow.

Part II

In this part, you will hear a question. From the three answer choices given, choose the one which best answers the question.

For problems 18 through 35, mark your answers on the separate answer sheet. No problems can be repeated. Please listen carefully. Do you have any questions?

Grammar considerations also play a role in Part II, but previewing the answer choices usually won't help you identify which questions are grammar-based. How should you cope? The best strategy is to listen carefully and focus on identifying the function of the question and the time frame it is asking about. Then look for a response which is logically connected.

Something to consider: It's perfectly natural for a question to be in one time frame and the answer to be in another. The trick is to pay attention to tenses, hypothetical language, time markers, and other grammatical elements in the question ... and then make sure the answer you choose is logically connected.

18. **a.** He called in sick.
b. Tomorrow, I think.
c. Not for a while.

19. **a.** As soon as she calls.
b. What's the use?
c. She will be when I tell her.

20. **a.** Harry did.
b. Apparently, Harry's.
c. I thought Harvey was.

21. **a.** They weren't sure.
b. Yes, I think they will.
c. It's highly unlikely.

22. **a.** I know, but I appreciate your asking.
b. Mary sent me a text message.
c. Don't worry. If it happens, I'll tell you.

23. **a.** How many cars were involved?
b. No, do you think there'll be another?
c. No, was it good?

24. **a.** Not if I can help it.
b. Yes, but I may need a few more days.
c. I'm doing everything in my power.

25. **a.** What's chance got to do with it?
b. I suppose I could have.
c. I might. Let me think about it.

26. **a.** No, there wasn't a seat in the house.
b. I have an extra ticket. Do you want it?
c. It must have been.

27. **a.** I could, but I was in Boston.
b. Yes, everyone needs to fill this in.
c. A number of changes have been made.

28. **a.** I was a day late, but the instructor accepted it.
b. I think so. When is it due?
c. Yes, but I left it in my room.

29. **a.** She will be if she gets in.
b. More than you can imagine.
c. Wait until she hears.

30. **a.** You should have seen their faces.
b. They were astounded.
c. I can only imagine their joy.

31. **a.** You're joking. Is that how it happened?
b. Of course, I wouldn't.
c. You're not accusing me, are you?

32. **a.** Sorry, only one per customer.
b. At the Motor Vehicle Bureau.
c. Whenever it's convenient.

33. **a.** I don't know. It was hard to see.
b. It was so thick I couldn't see a thing.
c. Not enough, from what I could see.

34. **a.** Yes, but that was the last time.
b. Often. It's where they met.
c. I'm sure the next time will be better.

35. **a.** I'll know it when I see it.
b. As long as you're driving, it's OK.
c. If traffic is light, figure two hours.

Part III

In this part, you will hear three short segments from a radio program. The program is called "Learning from the Experts." You will hear what three different radio guests have to say about three different topics.

Each talk lasts about two minutes. As you listen, you may want to take some notes to help you remember information given in the talk. Write your notes in the test booklet.

After each talk, you will be asked some questions about what was said. From the three answer choices given, you should choose the one that best answers the question according to the information you heard.

Remember, no problems can be repeated. For problems 36 through 50, mark all your answers on the separate answer sheet. Do you have any questions?

Sometimes the examiners like to include distractors known as "truth statements." These are choices that are true according to the information you hear but that are wrong as answers because they don't answer the narrator's questions. Be on the lookout for these, and be sure you don't fall right into the examiners' trap!

SEGMENT 1

36. Why are officials at the World Health Organization so excited about the Safer Surgical Checklist?
- **a.** It resembles the safety checklist used by airplane pilots.
- **b.** It is simple, effective, and costs little or nothing to implement.
- **c.** If it succeeds, it will make the stethoscope obsolete.

37. What point does Julia Framingham make when she cites statistics from studies done in the United Kingdom?
- **a.** The public health establishment needs to set new priorities.
- **b.** The situation in the United Kingdom is far from perfect.
- **c.** The problem is not just limited to developing nations.

38. On average, how many patients a year die in the United Kingdom due to treatment error?
- **a.** eight million
- **b.** one in eight
- **c.** two thousand

39. Statistically speaking, exactly how effective has the checklist been in reducing the number of deaths and complications in the eight health centers that piloted the program?
- **a.** It's too early to quantify the results.
- **b.** They've been reduced by at least 64 percent.
- **c.** The rate of errors has dropped significantly.

40. How far-reaching are the World Health Organization's plans for the checklist in the near future?
- **a.** They hope to reach hospitals servicing 75% of the world's total population.
- **b.** The plan is to start small, by starting with hospitals in five countries.
- **c.** They began by piloting the checklist in eight hospitals around the world.

SEGMENT 2

41. At the start of the program, what American institution does Ted David say has become endangered?
- **a.** the natural world
- **b.** the two-week family vacation
- **c.** the workplace

42. In the view of family psychologists that Ted David interviewed, what is it that helps brings families together?
- **a.** self-reliance
- **b.** their daily routine
- **c.** shared adventure

43. What is it that 137 countries have that the United States lacks?
- **a.** laws that guarantee minimum paid leave
- **b.** pensions and health plans
- **c.** a six-week vacation

(Segment 2 continues at top of next page)

44. From Ted David's perspective, why is it that Americans who do have paid-vacation benefits often choose not to take the full amount of time they are entitled to?
   a. They are incurable workaholics.
   b. They fear it will lead to their being fired.
   c. They think their colleagues will resent them.

45. Which of the following best sums up the point that Ted David makes in the closing portion of the program?
   a. More parents should support programs like No Child Left Inside.
   b. The economy will flourish if Americans start taking vacations again.
   c. We should not lose sight of the values that are important in life.

SEGMENT 3

46. According to Barry Rivers, who are the unsung heroes of the natural world?
   a. tigers and polar bears
   b. plants and invertebrates
   c. yew trees and rosy periwinkles

47. Which of the following was the inspiration for an energy-efficient fan that is now starting to be used in computers and air conditioners?
   a. the Namibian beetle
   b. the spiral design of mollusk shells
   c. super-sticky mussel proteins

48. What point does Barry Rivers make about extinctions?
   a. There is nothing at all natural about them.
   b. They are usually disastrous in the long term.
   c. They often have undesirable short-term consequences.

49. What impact has the collapse of the mussel population had in the Chesapeake Bay area?
   a. It has led to a major decline in the area's fresh- and salt-water habitats.
   b. Filtration plants in the bay area have been forced to shut down.
   c. Fisheries have started to thrive in ways that were not anticipated.

50. Which of the following best sums up Barry Rivers' view of the Endangered Species Act?
   a. It is flawed and should probably be repealed.
   b. It has failed to protect both mammals and invertebrates.
   c. It should be doing more to protect at-risk invertebrates.

Grammar – Cloze – Vocabulary – Reading 75 minutes

This section of the examination contains 120 problems, numbered 51 through 170. There are 40 grammar, 20 cloze, 40 vocabulary, and 20 reading comprehension problems. If you do not understand how to do the problems, raise your hand, and a proctor will explain the examples to you. None of the actual test problems can be explained.

Each problem has only one correct answer. Do not spend too much time on any one problem. If you do not know the answer to a problem, you may guess. Work quickly but carefully. You have one hour and 15 minutes (75 minutes) to answer all 120 problems. If you finish before the time is over, you may check your answers within the GCVR section only. Do not go back to the Listening section of the exam.

GRAMMAR

51. The worst had happened, and he had no idea what _____ next.
- **a.** was he to do
- **b.** he would do
- **c.** was to do
- **d.** would he have done

52. The magician's act was amazing. He _____ into thin air.
- **a.** had disappeared the rabbit
- **b.** made the rabbit to disappear
- **c.** had made the rabbit disappear
- **d.** had the rabbit disappearing

53. I admire Tina. _____ a good student; she's a nice person as well.
- **a.** She isn't just
- **b.** She just isn't
- **c.** Just is she not
- **d.** If she weren't just

54. Suddenly the couple were faced with the awesome responsibility _____ quadruplets.
- **a.** to have to raise
- **b.** to having raised
- **c.** of having to raise
- **d.** of having to be raised

55. It's been a while since Eleanor e-mailed me, _____ she's back or not.
- **a.** so no way of knowing if
- **b.** because I don't know that
- **c.** which is why I don't know whether
- **d.** due to my not knowing

56. The appointment of a new director, _____ next month, will mean big changes for the company.
- **a.** to be made
- **b.** having been made
- **c.** will be made
- **d.** that is to make

57. They did _____ they could to cope with a very difficult situation.
- **a.** their best
- **b.** the better
- **c.** better than
- **d.** the best

58. We walked back to where we had parked the car _____ it had been towed away.
- **a.** having found
- **b.** only to find
- **c.** not only did we find
- **d.** only just finding

59. Tom and Nick play even more basketball now _____ before.
- **a.** than never
- **b.** rather than
- **c.** than doing so
- **d.** than they did

60. On hearing the good news, she was so excited that she couldn't help _____ for joy.
- **a.** to jump
- **b.** it to jump
- **c.** herself from jumping
- **d.** jumping

61. According to the personnel director, there are more women in the firm than _____ .
- **a.** are men there
- **b.** are there men
- **c.** there are men
- **d.** men are there

62. Only when the phone woke them at 3 a.m. _____ that something was terribly wrong.
- **a.** did they realize
- **b.** they realized
- **c.** to realize
- **d.** having realized

63. The boss wants the report _____ and on his desk by the time he leaves tomorrow.
   a. to write
   b. you'll have written
   c. to be written
   d. you are writing

64. He really needs to consider going on vacation. He's been _____ lately.
   a. hardly working
   b. hard working
   c. working hardly
   d. working hard

65. Jonathan's cabin in the mountains is roughly _____ from the city.
   a. five-hour driving
   b. a five-hours drive
   c. a drive for five hours
   d. a five hours' drive

66. They've been in love _____ since their first year in college.
   a. with each other
   b. each another
   c. one another
   d. one to the other

67. We're expecting him to be here _____ . He said he'd be home early.
   a. about time
   b. any minute now
   c. sooner or later
   d. whenever

68. He's uneasy about renting the apartment he saw as he feels he has nothing _____ .
   a. compared to it
   b. to compare it to
   c. to be compared to
   d. to which he can compare

69. _____ to express her true feelings about the manager's suggestion, she remained silent.
   a. She was afraid
   b. Been afraid
   c. Afraid
   d. Because afraid

70. Did you know that several churches in this town _____ in the 18th century?
   a. constructed
   b. have constructed
   c. were constructed
   d. have been constructed

Expect a number of "killer questions" that test fine points of complex sentence structure and colloquial grammar that you may not have met before. How should you cope? Admit you don't know, guess, and move on! Spending extra time on items like this means you're using up time that is better spent on Cloze and Reading items.

71. She should have called yesterday, but by the time she left today she still _____ so.
   a. isn't doing
   b. hadn't done
   c. hasn't done
   d. doesn't do

72. Would you have gone to New York with him if he _____ you?
   a. were to ask
   b. would ask
   c. had asked
   d. has asked

73. I'd love to join you and Rachel for dinner tonight but, unfortunately, _____ .
   a. I'm otherwise engaged
   b. I'll engage otherwise
   c. otherwise I'm engaged
   d. I'm engaging otherwise

74. She's hoping _____ from Michael by the end of the week.
   a. she would hear
   b. that she heard
   c. to hear
   d. to hearing

75. He's intending to be home by 7:00, _____ to stay late again.
   a. provided his boss makes him
   b. unless his boss asks him
   c. except for his boss telling him
   d. despite his boss wanting

76. The problem with public transit nowadays is that the trains are _____ on time.
   a. frequently
   b. almost always
   c. rarely
   d. somewhat

77. The trip started disastrously. He forgot his ticket, _____ his passport as well.
   a. not to mention
   b. as much as
   c. as long as
   d. not only

78. From what I know, Tom's been working here longer than _____ .
   a. is Mike working
   b. Mike does
   c. Mike has
   d. Mike's working

79. I see he's bought a new car. It was a Ford he used to drive, _____?
   a. wouldn't he
   b. didn't he
   c. didn't it
   d. wasn't it

80. After graduation, he's planning to spend the summer in Europe, but _____ he has no idea.
   a. beyond that
   b. after there
   c. by then
   d. on that point

81. I didn't realize she's pregnant. When _____ the baby?
   a. did she have
   b. has she had
   c. is she having
   d. does she have

82. Elizabeth hasn't left the house yet, but apparently she is _____ .
   a. just about to do so
   b. ready to do now
   c. so going to do now
   d. only now to do so

83. The two sisters, both _____ are doctors, are working at different hospitals.
   a. they
   b. who
   c. of them
   d. of whom

84. It's amazing how much the Smith twins resemble _____ .
   a. to the other one
   b. each other
   c. one to the other
   d. one other

85. I had _____ work late last night, as the boss threatened to fire me if I didn't.
   a. the only choice to
   b. a choice not to
   c. not only a choice to
   d. no choice but to

86. _____ uses a manual typewriter nowadays. PCs have really caught on.
   a. Anyone rarely
   b. Hardly anyone
   c. Rarely does anyone
   d. Scarcely no one

87. Harvard is still regarded _____ one of the best universities in the United States.
   a. to being
   b. as it is
   c. as being
   d. that it is

88. He's a shy fellow who prefers _____ going to parties.
   a. that he stays at home than
   b. to stay at home to
   c. staying at home to
   d. that he'd rather stay at home than

89. From what I hear, he's planning to resign by the end of the year _____ .
   a. and later not
   b. if not later
   c. at the very latest
   d. and not very later

90. Despite _____ , the new research assistant is turning out to be an exceptional employee.
   a. she lacks experience
   b. that she's inexperienced
   c. of her inexperience
   d. her being inexperienced

Linking words (e.g., *because, while, although, and, but*) are often removed to test your understanding of the text's overall meaning. Items 93 and 96 are good examples. Before you answer, examine the context several sentences before and after the blank to see how the text flows from one sentence to the next and one clause to the next.

CLOZE

Passage 1 is about birds and tall buildings.

Many tall office buildings leave their lights on at night – a wasteful practice that has lethal consequences for migrating birds. Confused by the lit windows, millions of birds slam into tall buildings and die every year, says a conservation ecologist at the Chicago Field Museum. He and his colleagues quantified the losses by ___(91)___ the number of birds that hit McCormick Place, a 90-foot-tall glass convention center in Chicago. Over the last two years, 1,297 birds – mostly sparrows, warblers, and thrushes – perished after flying into ___(92)___ windows.

During the same period, only 192 died from hitting dark windows, ___(93)___ the windows were unlit nearly half the time during the study. The ___(94)___ place an additional strain on ___(95)___ species such as wood thrushes. "This is just another pressure that the birds don't need," says the ecologist. ___(96)___ most window collisions occur during the peak migratory times after midnight, he ___(97)___ that skyscrapers turn ___(98)___ their lights from 11 p.m. ___(99)___ dawn during the two migration seasons, from late March through May and from mid-August to Thanksgiving. A seasonal lights-out campaign would also ___(100)___ the buildings' electricity bills.

91. **a.** identifying **b.** burying **c.** tagging **d.** counting

92. **a.** illustrative **b.** illuminated **c.** illustrated **d.** illustrious

93. **a.** because **b.** although **c.** while **d.** whenever

94. **a.** windows **b.** facts **c.** deaths **d.** birds

95. **a.** declining **b.** extinct **c.** deadly **d.** threatening

96. **a.** Since **b.** After **c.** While **d.** Unless

97. **a.** admits **b.** implies **c.** suggests **d.** regrets

98. **a.** up **b.** over **c.** in **d.** out

99. **a.** and **b.** at **c.** every **d.** until

100. **a.** subtract **b.** reduce **c.** deduct **d.** downgrade

Passage 2 is about a paleobiologist's discovery.

Bugs have been eating plants for over 300 million years. But insects that actually reside within the plants they feed on are generally assumed to have emerged about 120 million years ago. A paleobiologist has found ___(101)___ of an insect larva[1] that apparently ___(102)___ within fern fronds in the swamp forests of Illinois some 300 million years ago. Modern insects like the sawfly deposit their eggs inside a plant's leaf or stem ___(103)___ that the larvae will have plant cells to feed on when they hatch. ___(104)___ the larvae begin to feed, the plant responds to injury by surrounding its wounds with protective cells that also ___(105)___ to be highly nutritious. The insects thus trick their host into ___(106)___ them with a choice meal.

Researchers recognized the hallmarks of a similar strategy ___(107)___ studying slices of the 300-million-year-old fossilized fern fronds. Some of the ferns bore scars left by grubs[2] of some kind ___(108)___ had tunneled through the fronds. The grubs had chewed their way out before the ferns fossilized, ___(109)___ they left behind waste matter, which was ___(110)___ to contain resin-filled cells identical to surrounding plant cells.

[1] **larva:** a young insect that emerges from its egg in the form of a short, fat worm that gradually metamorphoses into an adult. The plural is **larvae**.

[2] **grub:** same as **larva** (see previous note).

101. **a.** signals **b.** signs **c.** tracks **d.** symptoms

102. **a.** lived **b.** flew **c.** inhabited **d.** discovered

103. **a.** and **b.** proving **c.** hoping **d.** so

104. **a.** As **b.** Before **c.** Knowing **d.** Perhaps

105. **a.** have **b.** occur **c.** happen **d.** claim

106. **a.** deceiving **b.** providing **c.** making **d.** giving

107. **a.** of **b.** for **c.** were **d.** while

108. **a.** they **b.** that **c.** and **d.** after

109. **a.** because **b.** that **c.** but **d.** so

110. **a.** found **b.** supposed **c.** analyzed **d.** used

VOCABULARY

111. Once the writer begins a novel, she totally _____ herself in it until it is finished.
- **a.** devotes
- **b.** throws
- **c.** immerses
- **d.** pursues

112. The students felt less than _____ when presented with the difficult essay topic.
- **a.** buoyant
- **b.** overflowing
- **c.** irrepressible
- **d.** bottomless

113. You're the most _____ person I know. I'm sure you'll figure out a solution.
- **a.** resourceful
- **b.** pensive
- **c.** curious
- **d.** distinctive

114. The editors have spent months _____ material for a new poetry anthology.
- **a.** conjecturing
- **b.** deciphering
- **c.** deducing
- **d.** compiling

115. More and more people are becoming aware of the need for energy _____ .
- **a.** conservation
- **b.** diversity
- **c.** pollution
- **d.** ecology

116. Suddenly, the silence was shattered by a _____ scream.
- **a.** heartwarming
- **b.** back-breaking
- **c.** eye-catching
- **d.** blood-curdling

117. It's hard not to be influenced by his _____ . He's the most enthusiastic person I know.
- **a.** abundance
- **b.** exuberance
- **c.** quips
- **d.** quantity

118. Aren't you done yet? You've been _____ with that rusty old bike all day!
- **a.** dabbling
- **b.** speculating
- **c.** tinkering
- **d.** probing

> Watch for Vocabulary items that have a grammatical twist to them (e.g., 111 and 118). Always check to see if a particle or preposition follows the blank. If it does, do your best to find the word that goes with it. It's likely that at least one question will test phrasal verbs or words that collocate with dependent prepositions.

119. If the doctors don't stop the _____ soon, the crash victim will bleed to death.
- **a.** transfusion
- **b.** hemorrhage
- **c.** seizure
- **d.** laceration

120. It's an extremely difficult task, but we're determined to _____ .
- **a.** surmise
- **b.** unravel
- **c.** accumulate
- **d.** persevere

121. The _____ trees swayed gracefully in the soft tropical breeze.
- **a.** gangly
- **b.** stout
- **c.** slender
- **d.** plump

122. If the firm offered to double my salary, of course I'd stay. That's a _____ !
- **a.** presence of mind
- **b.** mind-boggler
- **c.** brain-teaser
- **d.** no-brainer

123. The famine has hit children the hardest. Many are _____ and may die if they aren't helped.
- **a.** trim
- **b.** corpulent
- **c.** malnourished
- **d.** flabby

124. A ferocious _____ tore down the slope of the mountain, crushing everything it encountered.
- **a.** volcano
- **b.** avalanche
- **c.** hurricane
- **d.** earthquake

125. One of the biggest problems we face is where to dispose of _____ waste.
- **a.** recycled
- **b.** emaciated
- **c.** toxic
- **d.** scrap

126. I've been _____ my brains all day. Do you remember when her birthday is?
- **a.** racking
- **b.** crossing
- **c.** picking
- **d.** bearing

127. The massive tidal wave _____ low-lying areas, washing away everything in its path.
- **a.** receded
- **b.** toppled
- **c.** inundated
- **d.** scorched

128. With such a _____ of cell phones on the market, it's hard to know which to choose.
- **a.** dearth
- **b.** profusion
- **c.** deficit
- **d.** deficiency

129. The boss is furious. You can see the anger _____ in her eyes.
- **a.** smoldering
- **b.** spewing
- **c.** billowing
- **d.** incinerating

130. An atom is composed of tiny _____ known as protons, electrons, and neutrons.
- **a.** contaminants
- **b.** vermin
- **c.** stacks
- **d.** particles

131. He's looking for a _____ that is both safe and economical.
- **a.** motorist
- **b.** collision
- **c.** passenger
- **d.** vehicle

132. History can be exciting but, sadly, most textbooks make it seem _____ .
- **a.** mundane
- **b.** translucent
- **c.** murky
- **d.** unruffled

133. Like fish, the bodies of reptiles such as snakes and lizards are covered in _____ .
- **a.** feathers
- **b.** antlers
- **c.** scales
- **d.** stingers

134. He'll be furious if you tell him. I'd let sleeping dogs _____ .
- **a.** lay
- **b.** nap
- **c.** hibernate
- **d.** lie

135. The new assistant is fast and hardly ever makes mistakes. He's very _____ .
- **a.** lucid
- **b.** efficient
- **c.** conscious
- **d.** risky

136. Our teacher is very patient, but she admits that sometimes we test her to the _____ .
- **a.** border
- **b.** line
- **c.** limit
- **d.** margin

137. Everyone looked up and waved when they saw the news helicopter _____ overhead.
- **a.** dissolving
- **b.** reflecting
- **c.** hovering
- **d.** plummeting

138. She's neither short nor tall. I guess you could say she's of _____ height.
- **a.** mediocre
- **b.** average
- **c.** characteristic
- **d.** compact

139. You've been _____ lately. Is everything going OK at work?
- **a.** within limits
- **b.** out of line
- **c.** on edge
- **d.** off limits

140. He's a captain in the Marines, so he really makes his children _____ .
- **a.** toe the line
- **b.** be on the line
- **c.** be out of line
- **d.** draw the line

141. The _____ of hostilities in the area has once again halted the peace talks.
- **a.** retention
- **b.** replacement
- **c.** resumption
- **d.** reduction

142. The poor child cried for hours; the babysitter could do nothing to _____ her.
- **a.** cater
- **b.** savor
- **c.** relieve
- **d.** console

143. The child's sketches made it evident that she was _____ with exceptional artistic talent.
- **a.** endowed
- **b.** confronted
- **c.** fraught
- **d.** afflicted

144. The principal threatened to _____ any student caught vandalizing school property.
- **a.** dispel
- **b.** expel
- **c.** repel
- **d.** compel

145. He finds that a long, hot shower helps to _____ his aching muscles after a long work-out.
- **a.** bask
- **b.** comfort
- **c.** soothe
- **d.** alleviate

146. The patient has been in a coma for weeks, with no _____ improvement in his condition.
- **a.** perceptive
- **b.** discriminating
- **c.** distinguished
- **d.** discernible

147. The committee has gone to great _____ to find a workable solution to the problem.
- **a.** expenses
- **b.** lengths
- **c.** troubles
- **d.** pain

148. The urgent note in his voice brought home to us the _____ of the situation.
- **a.** frivolity
- **b.** gravity
- **c.** vitality
- **d.** emergence

149. It is said that _____ parents run the risk of spoiling their children.
- **a.** indulgent
- **b.** pacific
- **c.** sedate
- **d.** comfortable

150. His dismissal was a direct _____ of his incompetent performance.
- **a.** accession
- **b.** consequence
- **c.** sequence
- **d.** succession

You'll probably be pressed for time on this section, so don't get hung up on any one item. If a question is difficult for you, guess, mark it in your test booklet, and move on. There may be easier items just ahead, and your task is to find them before time runs out. If you finish early, revisit the items you marked.

READING

Passage 1 is about a famous diamond.

People have long claimed that other diamonds were cut from the same stone as the Hope Diamond, the world's largest dark blue diamond. But now a gem expert with the aid of computer technology has put such claims to rest. The first recorded mention of the diamond that would become the Hope came more than 350 years ago when Indian merchants sold a beautiful, rough-cut, 115-carat stone to a French entrepreneur called Jean Baptiste Tavernier. In 1668, Tavernier sold the stone to King Louis XIV of France, whose jewelers cut it into the 67-carat French Blue. In 1792, however, the diamond was stolen during the French Revolution. It eventually fell into the hands of London jewelers, who cut the stone into its present form. By 1839, British banker Henry Philip Hope had acquired the now 45.52-carat diamond, and that's when it got its name. The stone changed hands several more times and was eventually bought by the New York jewelry firm of Harry Winston, who donated it to the Smithsonian museum in Washington in 1958.

All in all, some 69 carats had been trimmed from the original. That has left open the possibility that other diamonds were cut from the cast-off material. But Jeff Post, the gems and minerals expert who currently oversees the stone, has always doubted such claims. To prove his point, he collaborated with a gem cutter and a computer modeler. From historical drawings of the Hope's ancestors – the Tavernier and the French Blue – 3-D computer models were created of each stone. These were then used to carve facsimiles of the historic jewels out of cubic zirconia, which in turn were used to create plastic molds of each stone.

Placing the reproduction French Blue inside the mold of the Tavernier, Post then proceeded to fill in the leftover spaces with hot, liquid wax. When dry, the wax represented the material that had to have been cut away to make the French Blue. He then repeated the process with the facsimile of the Hope, placing it inside a mold of the French Blue. What he found was that there wasn't enough material left in either case to make diamonds of more than a carat or two; and even that wouldn't have been possible because the crude cutting tools in use before the 20th century would have reduced the excess material to dust.

151. How did the Hope Diamond wind up at the Smithsonian museum?
- **a.** It was sold to the museum by a jeweler named Harry Winston.
- **b.** It was donated to the museum by a firm that had bought it illegally.
- **c.** It was given to the museum by a famous New York jewelry firm.
- **d.** It was purchased by Harry Winston on behalf of the great museum.

152. According to the passage, what was true about the French Blue?
- **a.** It was more than twice the size and weight of the Hope.
- **b.** It was originally cut from a much larger rough-cut stone.
- **c.** It was eventually bought by a British banker who had it recut.
- **d.** It was cut under the direction of Jean Baptiste Tavernier.

153. What was it that Jeff Post had always believed?
- **a.** that the Hope Diamond had never been cut from the French Blue
- **b.** that other diamonds must have been cut from the Tavernier stone
- **c.** that the Tavernier had actually come from an even larger stone
- **d.** that no other diamonds had been cut from the Tavernier

154. What conclusion did Post come to?
- **a.** No other diamonds could have come from the leftover material.
- **b.** A few small diamonds might have been cut, but nothing of value.
- **c.** It's amazing that such crude tools were used with such great skill.
- **d.** He realized that his original assumptions now had to be revised.

155. Which of the following were **not** used by Post to help him prove his hypothesis?
- **a.** plastic molds of the Tavernier and French Blue
- **b.** sophisticated computer modeling techniques
- **c.** drawings of the Tavernier and French Blue
- **d.** jeweler's tools from the 1800s

Passage 2 is about a rare disease called moyamoya.

Moyamoya is a rare disease that creates blockages in arteries deep inside the skull, cutting off blood circulation to parts of the brain. The name is Japanese for "puff of smoke," which is what the disorder looks like on X-rays: a wispy cloud of fragile blood vessels that develop in the brain where normal vessels are blocked. It was first identified in Japan in 1959. Most patients with moyamoya are children from 5 to 15, or adults from 30 to 40, and nearly two-thirds are female. Some have strokes; others, in earlier stages, have temporary speech problems, headaches, seizures, or attacks of numbness or weakness in their limbs. The symptoms, though transient, can occur so often that people cannot function. Some adult patients also notice problems with thinking or memory. But sometimes the symptoms are mild, ignored by patients or misdiagnosed as coming from pinched nerves or migraines.

The arterial blockages in moyamoya are different from the arterial blockages caused by fatty deposits in atherosclerosis. In moyamoya, the inner surface of the arteries and the muscle in the artery walls grow thicker until the vessels actually close off. The shutdowns occur in a limited but vital area near the base of the brain, a loop of vessels about the size of a coin 2.5 cm in diameter, called the Circle of Willis. It looks a bit like a traffic circle – with branches that provide nearly all of the brain's circulation.

Over the years doctors tried giving moyamoya patients aspirin, blood thinners, and other stroke-preventing drugs. They also tried opening blocked vessels with balloons and severing nerves believed to be causing artery spasm. None of these treatments were effective. Surgery to restore blood flow is the only thing that works. The most common operation is a bypass of the pinched-off vessels. Because the disease seems to affect arteries at just a few specific points, surgeons can usually find healthy vessels to splice together, rerouting blood around the blockages. In children or other patients whose arteries are too small to sew together, surgeons use other techniques, like placing a scalp artery or other tissue containing blood vessels on the brain so that branches will grow into the oxygen-starved areas.

The bypass doesn't cure the disease, but it effectively treats it. The goal is to perform the operation before patients have the big stroke, the devastating one that changes their life forever. Amazingly, a huge majority of patients, 95 percent or more, have no further strokes or related problems after the surgery.

156. How are moyomoya and atherosclerosis similar?

- **a.** They're not; they have nothing in common.
- **b.** Both disorders involve arterial blockages.
- **c.** Both are caused by thickening of arterial muscle tissue.
- **d.** Both are caused by deposits of fat that can clog arteries.

157. What is true of the symptoms of moyomoya?

- **a.** They are sometimes so mild that the disease goes undetected.
- **b.** They are less noticeable in children and middle-aged females.
- **c.** Once symptoms appear, they almost never go away.
- **d.** Symptoms are almost always mild and they rarely reoccur.

158. What is so critical about the Circle of Willis?

- **a.** its size
- **b.** its shape
- **c.** its location
- **d.** its thickness

159. According to the passage, what accounts for the high surgical success rate?

- **a.** the insertion of a balloon into affected blood vessels
- **b.** the ability of doctors to sever nerves in affected arteries
- **c.** the technical skill of the doctor performing the surgery
- **d.** the fact that the disease affects only a few specific spots

160. What is the ultimate goal of bypass surgery?

- **a.** to cure 95 percent of patients suffering from strokes
- **b.** to slow down the thickening of affected arteries
- **c.** to allow new arteries to grow in affected areas
- **d.** to restore circulation to affected areas of the brain

Passage 3 is about Franklin Delano Roosevelt.

The Second World War found democracy fighting for its life. By 1941, there were only a dozen or so democratic states left on earth. But great leadership emerged in time to rally the democratic cause. Future historians, looking back at this most bloody of centuries, will very likely regard the 32nd president of the U.S., Franklin Delano Roosevelt (or FDR), as the leader most responsible for mobilizing democratic energies and faith against economic collapse and military terror.

FDR was the best loved and most hated American president of the 20th century. He was loved because, though patrician by birth, upbringing, and style, he believed in and fought for plain people – for the "forgotten man" (and woman), for the "third of the nation, ill-housed, ill-clad, ill-nourished." He was loved because he radiated charm, joy in his work, optimism for the future. Even Charles de Gaulle, who well knew Roosevelt's disdain for him, succumbed to the "glittering personality of that artist, that seducer," as he put it. "Meeting him was like uncorking a bottle of champagne."

But he was hated, too – hated because he called for change, and the changes he proposed reduced the power, status, income and self-esteem of those who profited most from the old order. Hatred is happily more fleeting than love. The men who sat in their clubs denouncing "that man in the White House," that "traitor to his class," have died off. Their children and grandchildren mostly find the New Deal reforms familiar, benign, and beneficial.

FDR was not a perfect man. In the service of his objectives, he could be, and often was, devious, guileful, manipulative, evasive, underhanded, even ruthless. But he had great strengths. He relished power and organized, or disorganized, his administration so that conflict among his subordinates would ensure that the big decisions would come to him. A politician to his fingertips, he rejoiced in party combat. "I'm an old campaigner, and I love a good fight," he would say, and "Judge me by the enemies I have made." An optimist who fought his own brave way back from polio, he brought confidence and hope to a scared and stricken nation.

161. What was Charles de Gaulle's opinion of Roosevelt?

- **a.** He disliked him for being a womanizer.
- **b.** He looked down on the U.S. president.
- **c.** He admired Roosevelt's artistic talents.
- **d.** He was enchanted by the American.

162. Who was Roosevelt most unpopular with?

- **a.** the poor people of the United States
- **b.** members of exclusive men's clubs
- **c.** politicians from his own political party
- **d.** wealthy people of his own social class

163. What can be inferred about the types of reform Roosevelt called for?

- **a.** They were largely economic and social.
- **b.** They were largely political and military.
- **c.** They were largely anti-terrorist.
- **d.** They were largely pro-democracy.

164. Which statement sums up Roosevelt's approach to making major decisions?

- **a.** He was comfortable with letting others make them.
- **b.** He enjoyed watching his subordinates argue about them.
- **c.** He ensured that he would have the final say.
- **d.** He was ruthless yet extremely disorganized.

165. What is **not** true of Roosevelt's time as president?

- **a.** The changes he brought about were not popular with everyone.
- **b.** His ruthless hunger for power made him an ineffective leader.
- **c.** He led the country out of a difficult period of economic crisis.
- **d.** He was an steadfast champion of America's lower classes.

Passage 4 is about disease in the New World.

In 1492, the Caribbean, Mexico, Central America, and Andean South America were among the most densely populated regions of the hemisphere. Yet, within a span of several generations, each experienced a cataclysmic population decline. The culprit, to a large extent, was microbial infection: European-brought diseases such as smallpox, pulmonary ailments, and gastrointestinal disorders, all of which had been unknown in the Americas during the period before Columbus discovered America. Native Americans were immunologically vulnerable to this invisible conqueror.

The destruction was especially visible in Latin America, where great masses of susceptible individuals were congregated in cities such as Tenochtitlān and Cuzco, not to mention the innumerable towns and villages of the countryside. As the indigenous population in the Caribbean plummeted, Spaniards resorted to slave raids on the mainland of what is now Florida to bolster the work force. When the time came that this, too, proved insufficient, they took to importing West Africans to work the cane fields and silver mines.

Those Native Americans who did survive were often assigned, as an entire village or community, to a planter or mine operator to whom they would owe all their services. The *encomienda* system, as it came to be known, amounted to virtual slavery. This too, broke the spirit and health of the indigenous peoples, making them all the more vulnerable to the diseases brought by the Europeans.

Death from microbial infection was probably not as extensive in the Canadian forest, where most of the indigenous peoples lived as migratory hunter-gatherers. Village farmers, such as the Huron north of Lake Ontario, did, however, suffer serious depopulation in waves of epidemics that may have been triggered by Jesuit priests and their lay assistants, who had established missions in the area.

166. What was the major cause of the decline in population among indigenous American people?
- **a.** the enslavement of local populations
- **b.** the psychological trauma of conquest
- **c.** the importing of slaves from West Africa
- **d.** diseases that were spread by Europeans

167. Who or what was the "invisible conqueror" referred to at the end of paragraph 1?
- **a.** Native Americans with weak immune systems
- **b.** Columbus and the Europeans who came after him
- **c.** a devastating outbreak of a mysterious disease
- **d.** illnesses previously unknown in the Americas

168. Why did the decline in population present a problem for the Europeans?
- **a.** It left the indigenous people with drastically weakened immune systems.
- **b.** In some areas there weren't enough people to work in the fields and mines.
- **c.** Without enough people to rule, their conquest had little or no significance.
- **d.** They were morally uncomfortable with the idea of having to import slaves.

169. Where were the consequences of the population decline least likely to have been felt?
- **a.** in areas where Jesuit priests set up missions
- **b.** in rural towns and villages of Latin America
- **c.** in the forests of Canada
- **d.** in cities like Cuzco and Tenochtitlān

170. What often happened to indigenous people who were not killed off in epidemics?
- **a.** They eventually built up resistance to many diseases and died of natural causes.
- **b.** They were obliged to work in fields or mines under conditions resembling slavery.
- **c.** They were sent to West Africa, where they worked in cane fields and silver mines.
- **d.** They were sent to the Florida mainland where they were forced to work as slaves.

6 Vocabulary Enhancement

The Matter at Hand

As we learned in Reading Passage 1, the French Blue was stolen during the French Revolution and eventually ***fell into the hands of*** *London jewelers, who reduced the stone to 45.52 carats and then sold it to Henry Philip Hope in 1839. After that the famous stone* ***changed hands*** *several more times. Let's take a closer look at expressions with* ***hand****.*

A **Setting the Scene** – Read the paragraph, and then use the bold phrases to complete the definitions. (With verb phrases, use the base form.)

Over the centuries a lot of interesting stories have been **handed down** about the famed stone that we now call the Hope Diamond, but let's **wash our hands of** the oft-told tales and **take matters into our own hands**. Connoisseurs of the legends will no doubt **wring their hands** and charge that the following flight of fancy **is out of hand**, but frankly the matter is **out of their hands**! This writer needs no excuse to **take** the facts **in hand** and bend them to meet pressing pedagogical needs. So, gentle readers, if you **have time on your hands**, read on and let's consider how the illustrious diamond might have **changed hands** after the Indian merchants **handed over** the enormous blue stone to the legendary Jean Baptiste Tavernier . . .

1. ______________________ – have spare time
2. ______________________ – pass on by tradition
3. ______________________ – take control of sth
4. ______________________ – change owners
5. ______________________ – take action by oneself (rather than letting others do so)
6. ______________________ – be/get out of control
7. ______________________ – be beyond sb's control
8. ______________________ – give sth up (to sb)
9. ______________________ – ignore, abandon
10. ______________________ – twist one's hands to show anxiety or despair

B **Once Upon a Time** – Use the words below to fill in the blanks. When you've finished, match the expressions in bold with their definitions below. (With verb phrases, use the base form.)

Nouns:	back	fist	hand	mouth	palm	putty
Verbs:	became	knew	live	made	played	sit

You have to hand it to Jean Baptiste Tavernier. Judging from the fact that he managed to sell the beautiful, 115-carat, dark-blue diamond to none other than Louis XIV, he must have been a shrewd businessman who __________ **money hand over** __________ . (Think about it: Anyone who deals directly with kings does not __________ **hand to** __________ .) But let's not digress. As we've said, the merchant was shrewd, and he __________ his king **like the** __________ **of his hand**. Never one to __________ **on his hands**, old Jean Baptiste – **with** gem **in** __________ , of course – went straight to the Palace of Versailles and demanded an audience with the king. Now Louis, of course, was a fancier of fine things. Upon seeing the enormous blue rock, he immediately __________ __________ **in** the merchant's **hands**. As the Sun King's eyes glazed over with greed, old Jean Baptiste knew the monarch had __________ **right into his hands**. The deal was all but done, and he had Louis right where he wanted him. Where, you ask? Where else, but **in the** __________ **of his hand**!

1. ______________ – with sth in one's possession
2. ______________ – do nothing
3. ______________________ – know sb well
4. ______________________ – sb deserves credit for sth
5. ______________________ – do exactly what sb hoped
6. ______________________ – barely make ends meet
7. ______________________ – be easily influenced
8. ______________________ – (have sb) completely in one's control

C A Handy Look at Hand Actions – For each group, fill in the blanks with the correct form of the words in the box. Then decide which word or bold phrase each photo represents.

GROUP 1

clench join knock pat point punch raise shake tickle

1. If you never ___________ your hand, you can't expect the teacher to call on you!
2. After signing the contract, the two men ___________ hands.
3. The angry customer ___________ her fist and banged it hard on the desk. What she really wanted to do was ___________ the wall, but she was afraid of hurting herself!
4. We gathered in a circle and all ___________ hands.
5. Someone's ___________ on the door. I wonder who it is.
6. Graduating college is a huge achievement. You should ___________ yourself on the back.
7. He's ___________ at something. Can you see what it is?
8. My mother just loved to ___________ me when I was a child, and from the looks of it, I didn't mind at all!

A ___________ B ___________ C ___________

D ___________ E ___________ F ___________

G ___________ H ___________ I ___________

GROUP 2

applaud beckon clap clutch pet pinch sign slap thumb wave

1. "Not again!" he said, ___________ himself on the forehead.
2. All the animals here are very gentle, so don't be afraid to ___________ them.
3. The crowd ___________ (or ___________) wildly when the rock star came on stage.
4. Without saying a word, she bent her finger and ___________ him to come with her.
5. As the train pulled out, the couple ___________ goodbye.
6. From the way he's ___________ his nose closed, that sneaker must be really smelly!
7. You'd be ___________ your money too if you'd been listening to the news lately.
8. When his car broke down in the middle of nowhere, he was forced to ___________ a ride.
9. Their mother was deaf, so the twin brothers learned to ___________ before they could talk.

J ___________ K ___________ L ___________

M ___________ N ___________ O ___________

P ___________ Q ___________ R ___________

6 Vocabulary Consolidation

VEXING VERBS

A Common Collocations – Complete each phrase with a word from the box.

accumulate *bask* *cater* *comfort* *compile* *decipher* *scorch* *unravel*

1. ______________ a wedding
2. ______________ a code
3. ______________ a complicated mystery
4. ______________ a fortune
5. ______________ in the sun
6. ______________ articles for an anthology
7. ______________ a silk blouse
8. ______________ a grieving friend

B Fine-Tuning Your Knowledge – The numbers below refer to questions in the Vocabulary section of Practice Test 6. After reviewing the words, fill in each blank with the correct form of the appropriate verb.

111. devote immerse pursue throw	**a.** The geologist is currently ______________ her interest in giant crystal formations. She has totally ______________ herself into her work. I've never known anyone to be so ______________ in what they do. She has ______________ herself totally to her work.
118. dabble probe speculate tinker	**a.** The government has appointed a committee to ______________ into the scandal. **b.** We can ______________ about the election all we want, but it won't change the result. **c.** He's not a serious artist, but he does enjoy ______________ in watercolors. **d.** He loves to ______________ with old car engines in his spare time.
126. bear cross pick rack	**a.** ______________ in mind that he's only been here a week. He's still learning the ropes. **b.** I've been ______________ my brains all day, and I still can't remember his name. **c.** Is this a good time to ______________ your brains about buying a new laptop? **d.** It did ______________ my mind that perhaps you'd have to work late tonight.
129. billow incinerate smolder spew	**a.** ______________ used tires is not the best way to dispose of them as the process ______________ tons of contaminants into the environment every year. **b.** We watched the last log ______________ in the fireplace, then we went up to bed. **c.** It's a beautiful clear day, with just a few fluffy clouds ______________ in the distance.
137. dissolve hover plummet reflect	**a.** A mirror ______________ your image in it. **b.** When heat is applied, the salt ______________ into the liquid. **c.** Shot by the hunter's bullet, the bird seemed to ______________ in the air for a moment before ______________ to its death.
144. compel dispel expel repel	**a.** The mosquitoes at the lake will be a problem at this time of year. What should we use to ______________ them? **b.** If the student's disruptive behavior continues, the principal will be ______________ to ______________ him. **c.** The huge diamond engagement ring she is now wearing should ______________ any notion that people had about whether or not the couple is breaking up! **d.** Discrimination of any kind ______________ her.

NOTORIOUS NOUNS

A Amusing Associations – Find the word or phrase in the box that is suggested by each prompt.

cash transfusion *energy conservation* *lucky lacerations* *presence of mind*
proficiency deficiency *quantifiable quips* *the razor's edge* *whale's scales*

1. ______________________ – You've got this if you haven't passed the Michigan ECPE Final yet.
2. ______________________ – You'll learn a lot by reading *Moby Dick*, but don't expect to find these. They don't exist!
3. ______________________ – You'll want to achieve this when you realize you're not as young as you used to be.
4. ______________________ – If you come through an accident with minor cuts, you might refer to them as these.
5. ______________________ – You'll need this from your parents if you're away at school and overspend your budget.
6. ______________________ – You'll be interested in making these if you want to prove how funny you are.
7. ______________________ – You'll wish you exercised this if you ever lose your temper in a work situation.
8. ______________________ – Metaphorically speaking, you're living dangerously if you like to live on this.

B Fine-Tuning Your Knowledge – The numbers below refer to questions in the Vocabulary section of Practice Test 6. After reviewing the words, fill in each blank with the appropriate word.

115. **conservation** **diversity** **ecology** **pollution**	**a.** ____________ relates to the protection of the environment, while ____________ is the study of the interrelation between plants and animals in their natural habitats. **b.** The enormous ____________ of plant and animal life on the Earth is being endangered by air, water, and soil ____________ resulting from human activity.
119. **hemorrhage** **laceration** **seizure** **transfusion**	**a.** The child has epilepsy and is on medication to control ____________ s. **b.** The driver sustained cuts and a ____________ or two but otherwise he's fine. **c.** He's lost a lot of blood. After they locate the source of the ____________ , he'll need a ____________ to replenish his blood supply.
124. **avalanche** **earthquake** **hurricane** **volcano**	**a.** Late summer is ____________ season in the Caribbean. Save your cruise for spring or fall if you want to avoid these high-speed windstorms. **b.** Several ski hotels suffered snow damage in the ____________ . **c.** Smoke and ash spewed from the mouth of the erupting ____________ . **d.** A massive, underwater ____________ was what triggered the deadly tsunami.
128. **dearth** **deficiency** **deficit** **profusion**	**a.** In spring, the countryside is awash in a ____________ of wildflowers. **b.** The child is suffering from anemia caused by a ____________ of iron in her diet. **c.** Congress has proposed spending cuts to reduce the budget ____________ . **d.** Last year's terrorist attack has resulted in a ____________ of tourism this year.
136. **border** **limit** **line** **margin**	**a.** The child apologized to his teacher for having been out of ____________ . **b.** Meg is wearing a dress with a pretty flowered ____________ . **c.** The speed ____________ on the Interstate Highway is 65 miles per hour. **d.** The company plans to reduce costs in hopes of increasing its profit ____________ .

AUDACIOUS ADJECTIVES

A Common Collocations – Complete each phrase with a word from the box.

blood-curdling *compact* *murky* *plump* *scrap* *toxic* *translucent* *trim*

1. ______________ cars
2. ______________ waters
3. ______________ athletes
4. ______________ screams
5. ______________ curtains
6. ______________ cheeks
7. ______________ waste
8. ______________ metal

B Fine-Tuning Your Knowledge – The numbers below refer to questions in the Vocabulary sections of Practice Test 6. After reviewing the words, fill in each blank with the appropriate word.

113. curious distinctive pensive resourceful	**a.** The ______________ child knew exactly who to call when his grandmother fell. **b.** I'm ______________ to know what happens. Call me as soon as you know. **c.** The ______________ young man was deep in thought, as usual. **d.** It's hard to describe him. There's absolutely nothing ______________ about him.
116. back-breaking blood-curdling eye-catching heartwarming	**a.** The film began with a ______________ scream that set my hair on end. **b.** He dreaded the ______________ task of moving the piano to their new home. **c.** Seeing Anna with her newborn child was a ______________ sight. **d.** I'm not sure I like the painting, but its bright colors certainly make it ______________ .
121. gangly plump slender stout	**a.** The wrestler had a ______________ , solid build, but he was by no means fat. **b.** He was a short, slim child, but now he's a ______________ teenager, all arms and legs. In contrast, his sister is ______________ , graceful, and all in all much better proportioned. **c.** I wouldn't call her fat; pleasantly ______________ is a nicer way to put it.
132. mundane murky translucent unruffled	**a.** We expected more from the film, but unfortunately it was rather ______________ . **b.** We decided not to go swimming in the ______________ lake. The muddy water was not at all appealing. **c.** The windows are frosted, making them ______________ rather than transparent. In other words, light can pass through them, but you can't see out. **d.** I expected the boss to lose his temper, but to his credit he remained ______________ .
135. conscious efficient lucid risky	**a.** Surgery is always ______________ with elderly patients. Grandma hadn't been ______________ when they brought her back to her room, but within the hour she was fully awake, completely ______________ , and complimenting the nurses on how ______________ they were.
138. average characteristic compact mediocre	**a.** Sparseness of vegetation and low rainfall are ______________ of desert habitats. **b.** ______________ cars are much more fuel-efficient than larger, gas-guzzling SUVs. **c.** The young novelist was understandably upset when the critic described his first two books as below-______________ , ______________ efforts. **d.** Murphy is of ______________ height and build. When he was younger, he had the ______________ coloring of a typical Irishman: pale skin and bright, carrot-red hair.

PRICKLY PREPOSITIONS AND PARTICLES

The following extracts are taken from passages that you have encountered in Practice Test 6. Read each one quickly, and then fill in the blanks with an appropriate preposition or particle.

1. Many tall office buildings leave their lights on ________ night – a wasteful practice that has lethal consequences ________ migrating birds. Confused ________ the lit windows, millions ________ birds slam ________ tall buildings and die every year. ... The deaths place an additional strain ________ declining species such ________ wood thrushes.

2. ________ historical drawings ________ the Hope's ancestors – the Tavernier and the French Blue – computer models were created ________ each stone. These were then used to carve facsimiles ________ the historic jewels ________ ________ cubic zirconia, which ________ turn were used to create plastic molds ________ each stone. Placing the reproduction French Blue ___________ the mold ________ the Tavernier, Post then proceeded to fill ________ the leftover spaces ________ hot, liquid wax. When dry, the wax represented the material that had to have been cut ________ to make the French Blue. He then repeated the process ________ the facsimile ________ the Hope, placing it ___________ a mold ________ the French Blue. What he found was that there wasn't enough material left ________ either case to make diamonds more than a carat or two; and even that wouldn't have been possible because the crude cutting ________ use ________ the 20th century would have reduced the excess material ________ dust.

3. Moyamoya is a rare disease that creates blockages ________ arteries deep ___________ the skull, cutting ________ blood circulation ________ parts ________ the brain. The name is Japanese ________ "puff ________ smoke," which is what the disorder looks ________ ________ X-rays: a wispy cloud ________ fragile blood vessels that develop ________ the brain where normal vessels are blocked. ... ________ moyamoya, the inner surface ________ the arteries and the muscle ________ the artery walls grow thicker until the vessels actually close ________ . The shutdowns occur ________ a limited but vital area near the base ________ the brain, a loop ________ vessels ________ the size ________ a coin 2.5 cm ______ diameter, called the Circle ________ Willis. It looks a bit ________ a traffic circle – ________ branches that provide nearly all ________ the brain's circulation.

4. FDR was loved because, though patrician ________ birth, upbringing, and style, he believed ________ and fought ________ plain people ... . He was loved because he radiated personal charm, joy ________ his work, optimism ________ the future. Even Charles de Gaulle, who well knew Roosevelt's disdain ________ him, succumbed ________ the "glittering personality." ... An optimist who fought his own brave way back ________ polio, he brought confidence and hope ________ a scared and stricken nation.

5. The destruction was especially visible ________ Latin America, where great masses ________ susceptible individuals were congregated ________ cities such as Tenochtitlān and Cuzco, not to mention the innumerable towns and villages of the countryside. As the indigenous population in the Caribbean plummeted, Spaniards resorted ________ slave raids ________ the mainland ________ what is now Florida to bolster the work force. When the time came that this, too, proved insufficient, they took ________ importing West Africans to work the cane fields and silver mines. ... Those Native Americans who did survive were often assigned, ________ an entire village or community, ________ a planter or mine operator ________ whom they would owe all their services. The *encomienda* system, as it came to be known, amounted ________ virtual slavery. This too, broke the spirit and health ________ the indigenous peoples, making them all the more vulnerable ________ the diseases brought ________ the Europeans.

Practice Test 7

Writing 30 minutes

- You may write in pen or pencil.
- You will have 30 minutes to write on one of the two topics. If you do not write on one of these topics, your paper will not be scored. If you do not understand the topics, ask the examiner to explain them.
- You may make an outline if you wish, but your outline will not count toward your score.
- Write about one-and-a-half to two pages. Your essay will be marked down if it is extremely short.
- You will not be graded on the appearance of your paper, but your handwriting must be readable. You may change or correct your writing, but you should not recopy the whole essay.
- Your essay will be judged on clarity and overall effectiveness, as well as on topic development, organization, and the range, accuracy, and appropriateness of your grammar and vocabulary. Your essay will be graded at the University of Michigan.

TOPICS For help in writing these compositions, see *Writing Tutorial*, pages 213-214.

1. Some people live nearly all their lives in the same place. Others may make one or more major moves, whether it's in search of better opportunity or simply "change." What are some of the advantages and disadvantages of each lifestyle? Assuming you had a choice, which would you prefer? Support your ideas with reasons and examples.

2. Some people are good at multitasking. They often do more than one thing at the same time, whether it's listening to music and doing homework or working on two or more tasks simultaneously at the office. Others prefer to focus on just one thing at a time, without distractions. Consider one of the two styles, and discuss why that style works or doesn't work for you. Support your ideas with reasons and examples.

CRITERIA REVIEW - Grammar and Vocabulary

GRAMMAR

✓ good variety/control of simple and more complex structures

✓ correct use of verbs (tense, voice, agreement with subject)

✓ adequate control of word forms

VOCABULARY

✓ wide range of basic and advanced lexis, including phrasal verbs and idiomatic language where appropriate

✓ word choice generally appropriate and suitable to topic

✓ message communicated richly and clearly

Listening approx. 35-40 minutes

This section of the examination tests your understanding of spoken English. The listening section has three parts. There are 50 questions. Mark all your answers on the separate answer sheet. Do not make any stray marks on the answer sheet. If you change your mind about an answer, erase your first answer completely.

Part I

In this part, you will hear short conversations. From the three answer choices given, choose the answer which means about the same thing as what you hear, or that is true based upon what you hear.

For problems 1 through 17, mark your answers on the separate answer sheet. No problems can be repeated.

Please listen carefully. Do you have any questions?

When in doubt, use process of elimination to rule out the most obviously wrong choice, and then guess if you have to. Remember that you're not penalized for wrong answers on this or any other part of the exam.

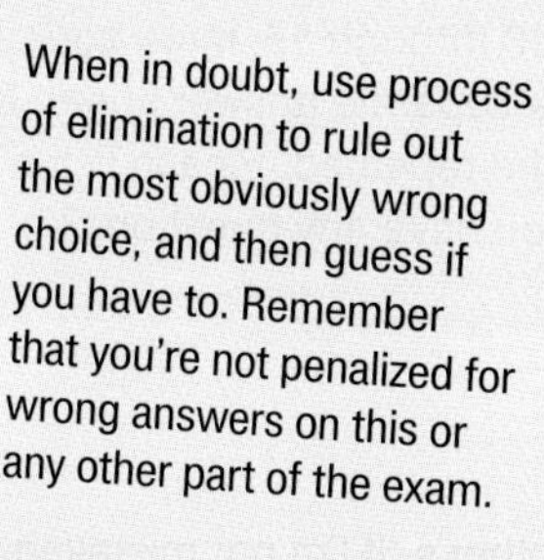

1. **a.** She's going to remind Tom.
b. He thinks it's not a good idea.
c. Tom doesn't like taking chances.

2. **a.** She's about to go on a trip.
b. She can't afford a computer.
c. She needs a new computer.

3. **a.** They paid a lot for the concert.
b. The performers were aging rock stars.
c. They'd never been to a rock concert before.

4. **a.** They're at a library.
b. His house isn't well heated.
c. She thinks he should see a doctor.

5. **a.** She was at a printer's.
b. She was working overtime.
c. She was out shopping.

6. **a.** He's not as good a student as she is.
b. She's got good reason to be worried.
c. She thinks he's better prepared than she is.

7. **a.** She thinks her current instructor is great.
b. She won't register with the same instructor.
c. She has doubts about the new instructor.

8. **a.** She's intending to take a walk in the park.
b. He thinks she could be more careful at times.
c. He'd like to get to know her better.

9. **a.** He's dressed too casually.
b. She thinks he'll never change.
c. They've been invited to a barbecue.

10. **a.** The delivery men came too early.
b. The delay is acceptable to her.
c. She's ready to cancel the order.

11. **a.** She no longer buys things at craft fairs.
b. Her kids went to her first craft fair.
c. She gave up sculpting to raise a family.

12. **a.** The ad was as good as they hoped.
b. She should have followed her instincts.
c. She was certain the ad would be a hit.

13. **a.** They're about to do a lot of shopping.
b. They'll take the train into town.
c. They shouldn't have trouble parking.

14. **a.** He hates helping her in the kitchen.
b. They recently bought a dishwasher.
c. They now have a housekeeper.

15. **a.** Their son is a college art student.
b. Their son is artistically inclined.
c. Their son's grades have improved recently.

16. **a.** The team has been on a winning streak.
b. The team is sure to win its next game.
c. The team is starting to get discouraged.

17. **a.** She hopes the professor will reconsider.
b. She thinks the professor was being unfair.
c. The student is just making excuses.

Part II

In this part, you will hear a question. From the three answer choices given, choose the one which best answers the question.

For problems 18 through 35, mark your answers on the separate answer sheet. No problems can be repeated. Please listen carefully. Do you have any questions?

Who's (Who is)* vs. *Who's (Who has)* vs. *Whose

Expect one or more items to test your ability to discriminate the meaning of these items in conversation.

They all sound alike when spoken, but if you can't tell one from the other, you're bound to fall into the test-makers' trap!

How to cope? Before choosing your answer, try to figure out which of the three is being used ... and then answer accordingly.

18. **a.** His mother's, if I'm not mistaken.
b. Sorry, I can't hear what they're saying.
c. His cousin Arlene, I think.

19. **a.** You know you can.
b. At last count there were five of us.
c. I know, but I just wasn't able to.

20. **a.** I know. I grew up in Chicago.
b. More than I ever imagined.
c. Not really. I like being single.

21. **a.** It was called off.
b. Yes, but I told them.
c. Something came up.

22. **a.** It's a cactus, so don't water it a lot.
b. In the garden.
c. At the florist's around the corner.

23. **a.** Really? He usually comes by bus.
b. Haven't you heard? He won the lottery.
c. No, but I'll ask him if you like.

24. **a.** Yes, there are several in the area.
b. There's one on the next corner.
c. Yes, it's within walking distance.

25. **a.** None, whatsoever. We'd better ask.
b. He'll let us know when we finish
c. Yes, but he didn't say.

26. **a.** That's my husband. Haven't you met?
b. No, I've never driven one.
c. The boss's, I believe. He just got it.

27. **a.** Mr. Jones from the Tax Office.
b. Can you connect me with Mr. Jones?
c. I'm calling to inquire about the ad.

28. **a.** I had dreams of becoming a doctor.
b. Funny how things work out, isn't it?
c. I always wanted a talking doll.

29. **a.** No, have you seen them?
b. They're Tom's, I believe.
c. Yes, they are. Thanks.

30. **a.** I wish they hadn't.
b. I hope so for your sake.
c. Not really. I have no regrets.

31. **a.** As soon as the game is over.
b. Until about 5, I think.
c. It's too late, I know.

32. **a.** The kids have. I'll make some more.
b. They're for Tommy. He just loves them.
c. They're mine. Do you like them?

33. **a.** You have my word. I won't tell a soul.
b. Not at all. I think you're right to be strict.
c. I promise. Nothing will come between us.

34. **a.** I think you're doing fine.
b. If you ask me, she's amazing.
c. At times I don't think I can.

35. **a.** What did you have in mind?
b. Great, I'll bring over some of my DVDs.
c. Good idea. I'm free Wednesday night.

Part III

In this part, you will hear three short segments from a radio program. The program is called "Learning from the Experts." You will hear what three different radio guests have to say about three different topics.

Each talk lasts about two minutes. As you listen, you may want to take some notes to help you remember information given in the talk. Write your notes in the test booklet.

After each talk, you will be asked some questions about what was said. From the three answer choices given, you should choose the one that best answers the question according to the information you heard.

Remember, no problems can be repeated. For problems 36 through 50, mark all your answers on the separate answer sheet. Do you have any questions?

SEGMENT 1

36. What problem related to bottled water does Jeremy Turnbull say he would rather NOT focus on in today's broadcast?
- **a.** the growth potential of the industry
- **b.** the industry's negative environmental impact
- **c.** the industry's misleading advertising practices

37. Worldwide, on average, how many tons of plastic go into the making of plastic water bottles each year?
- **a.** 155 billion
- **b.** 2.7 million
- **c.** 1.5 million

38. What is the main point that Jeremy Turhbull makes about the overall process of producing and transporting bottled water?
- **a.** The process is not at all friendly to the environment.
- **b.** The process is overly dependent on crude oil.
- **c.** Something should be done to make the process less polluting.

39. Why does Jeremy mention the BIOTA company?
- **a.** They have launched a unique recycling scheme.
- **b.** Their bottles take longer than most to degrade.
- **c.** They are trying to improve the situation.

40. According to Jeremy, what is it that most people don't realize about bottles made from recycled plastic?
- **a.** So few of these bottles are actually recycled.
- **b.** There is much more new plastic in them than recycled plastic.
- **c.** Huge amounts of energy are used to ship them back from China.

SEGMENT 2

41. According to Ann Struthers, what piece of conventional wisdom has recently been verified by scientific evidence?
- **a.** The word *satiety* means the feeling of being full.
- **b.** Fullness is a feeling that comes from the the stomach.
- **c.** Slow eaters need less food to feel full than fast eaters do.

42. At which meal during the 2004 study did subjects eat the most?
- **a.** the meal where they ate at their normal pace
- **b.** the meal that was partially controlled by beeps
- **c.** the meal that was totally controlled by beeps

43. In the 2006 study, what happened when the subjects slowed down their eating rate by chewing each mouthful 20 times?
- **a.** Their feeling of fullness was short-lived.
- **b.** They ate more food in less time.
- **c.** They ate less, and felt full for a longer time.

(Segment 2 continues at top of next page)

44. Approximately how long does it take the body to signal the brain that it has had enough food?
    a. an average of 29 minutes
    b. up to 20 minutes
    c. about 60 minutes

45. According to the scientific explanation, what must happen before the body alerts the brain that it is full?
    a. The eater must stop taking bites.
    b. The stomach must be empty of food.
    c. Food must reach the intestines.

SEGMENT 3

46. What is the medical name for the crusty material that forms inside the walls of the arteries as a result of atherosclerosis?
    a. pasty sludge
    b. cholesterol
    c. plaque

47. What may result if some of this crusty material breaks away from the walls of the artery?
    a. atherosclerosis
    b. blood clots
    c. diabetes

48. Which of the following is something that is not yet completely understood by the medical community?
    a. why diabetes impairs the body's ability to combat plaque-forming substances
    b. the strong link between diabetes, cardiovascular disease, and death
    c. the reason people with heart disease often develop type 2 diabetes

49. Why did researchers decide to focus on calcium build-up in the arteries of their diabetic subjects?
    a. It is a better indicator of diabetes than a patient's glucose level.
    b. It is rarely present in the arteries of people with type 2 diabetes
    c. It's a main ingredient of plaque and is easily seen on CAT scans.

50. From what the results of the study showed, which group would be least likely to benefit from a program of intensive glucose control?
    a. diabetics with low levels of plaque in their arteries
    b. diabetics with high levels of plaque in their arteries
    c. diabetics who are diagnosed at a young age

Grammar – Cloze – Vocabulary – Reading 75 minutes

This section of the examination contains 120 problems, numbered 51 through 170. There are 40 grammar, 20 cloze, 40 vocabulary, and 20 reading comprehension problems. If you do not understand how to do the problems, raise your hand, and a proctor will explain the examples to you. None of the actual test problems can be explained.

Each problem has only one correct answer. Do not spend too much time on any one problem. If you do not know the answer to a problem, you may guess. Work quickly but carefully. You have one hour and 15 minutes (75 minutes) to answer all 120 problems. If you finish before the time is over, you may check your answers within the GCVR section only. Do not go back to the Listening section of the exam.

GRAMMAR

51. The sound of the power lawn mower prevented _____ any work done today.
- **a.** me to get
- **b.** me from getting
- **c.** getting me
- **d.** that I get

52. The article they're going to publish _____ a Pulitzer-Prize-winning journalist.
- **a.** has written
- **b.** which wrote
- **c.** what was written by
- **d.** is being written by

53. He had to admit that _____ about the woman he was planning to marry.
- **a.** it was little known
- **b.** he knew little
- **c.** the little he knew
- **d.** little he knew

54. His visit to Colorado last year was his first; in fact, _____ anywhere in the state before.
- **a.** never would he have been
- **b.** he wouldn't have been
- **c.** he'd never been
- **d.** never has he been

55. Smoking is not _____ anywhere on the hospital premises.
- **a.** permitting
- **b.** permission
- **c.** permissible
- **d.** permissive

56. We advise you to hire the first interviewee. Everyone believes _____ the best candidate.
- **a.** her to be
- **b.** she be
- **c.** her being
- **d.** who is

57. How do you expect me to serve the ice cream when it's still _____ ?
- **a.** hard freezing
- **b.** hardly frozen
- **c.** frozen hard
- **d.** freezing hard

58. From _____ , he hasn't made any changes to the report. The old errors are still there.
- **a.** what I can see
- **b.** I can see
- **c.** that I can see
- **d.** which I can see

59. She may not be able to go. Her father is being difficult _____ giving her permission.
- **a.** by
- **b.** in
- **c.** to
- **d.** about

60. He read somewhere that cancer occurs in smokers more than twice _____ nonsmokers.
- **a.** as much for
- **b.** as often as in
- **c.** than that of
- **d.** than it does in

61. Do you have any idea _____ to renew a driver's license?
- **a.** that it takes long
- **b.** does it take long
- **c.** how long it takes
- **d.** it takes how long

62. I'm starting to worry about them; they _____ here over an hour ago.
- **a.** ought to be
- **b.** must have been
- **c.** were to have been
- **d.** supposed to have been

63. The older children get, _____ they become.
   a. the more mature
   b. the greater maturity
   c. more matured
   d. maturing

64. Going to college is a great opportunity, so I'm determined to _____ .
   a. making it the most
   b. making more of it
   c. make the most of it
   d. make more of it

65. With only a few days at our disposal, our trip to Toronto _____ hardly saw anything.
   a. was too short to
   b. was short so
   c. wasn't long enough to
   d. was so short that we

66. Mr. Adams suggests that he _____ Richard that he's out of a job.
   a. is someone who'll tell
   b. be the one to tell
   c. was one telling
   d. is the one telling

67. _____ the decision would have a major impact on his political career.
   a. Did he realize little
   b. A little he realized
   c. Little did he realize
   d. Realizing little

68. I hear the Smiths are having _____ a new home that they can afford.
   a. difficulty finding
   b. it difficult to find
   c. difficulty to find
   d. it difficult finding

69. My friend _____ at Harvard Law School is now working for a famous judge.
   a. studied law
   b. studying law
   c. that studied law
   d. who she studied law

70. I'd be happy to suggest a consultant, but _____ is going to be very expensive.
   a. whoever I recommend
   b. if I recommend someone
   c. however recommended, it
   d. he who recommended

Get into the habit of taking a few extra seconds to read each question stem four times, trying a different choice in the blank each time. This ensures that you avoid making careless mistakes on item types that you've seen over and over again.

71. Put forth in 1921, the physicist's theory has _____ to be proven wrong.
   a. since
   b. yet
   c. ever
   d. soon

72. Despite _____ two jobs, he still finds it difficult to make ends meet.
   a. he has
   b. that he has
   c. having
   d. of his having

73. Thankfully, the child was OK, having suffered _____ a few scratches.
   a. little more than
   b. little or nothing
   c. little by little
   d. for a little

74. He'd be an excellent candidate for promotion _____ his hot temper.
   a. if not
   b. if it wasn't
   c. if only
   d. if it weren't for

75. I thought the play was good, but for every person who liked it, _____ didn't.
   a. someone else
   b. another one who
   c. one another
   d. anyone else

76. I need to tell you something. Please don't make this difficult _____ me.
   a. to
   b. at
   c. by
   d. for

77. I know it's hard, but I wish _____ kinder to him.

a. you're being
b. you'd be
c. you'd been
d. you should have been

78. Michelangelo _____ his frescoes on the ceiling of the Sistine Chapel.

a. had better remember about
b. well remembered
c. better remembers
d. is best remembered for

79. Not only is he capable, but he'll also get the job done _____ than we can.

a. fast and more accurate
b. the faster, the more accurately
c. fast and more accurate
d. faster and more accurately

80. I never had any friends in the building _____ Meg moved in last year.

a. by the time
b. unless
c. until
d. since

81. It's clear that global warming _____ urgent problem.

a. becomes increasingly an
b. is becoming an increasingly
c. has been increasing an
d. is increasingly being an

82. The restaurant has excellent food, so it's no wonder _____ so crowded.

a. why is it always
b. is it always
c. whether it's
d. it's always

83. I'm surprised to see Ted here. _____ to the meeting in Boston?

a. Shouldn't he have gone
b. Had he not gone
c. Must he not go
d. Couldn't he have gone

84. It's warm enough to swim in this area _____ year round.

a. every
b. all
c. whole
d. each

85. Sadly, there are many more poor people in the world _____ rich people.

a. than there are
b. more than
c. of which few are
d. than they are

86. He hasn't contacted me yet, but _____ , you'll be the first one I tell.

a. having done so
b. should he do so
c. the sooner he does so
d. after doing so

87. The family is great in a crisis. When her mother was ill, _____ helped out.

a. all them
b. they all
c. them all
d. all they

88. Whenever my car is being repaired, _____ me use hers.

a. she would let
b. so she let
c. she lets
d. she's letting

89. If I were you, I'd encourage _____ a doctor as soon as possible.

a. that he see
b. he's being seen by
c. him seeing
d. him to see

90. I try to have fun on the weekends, so _____ time I get together with my friends.

a. most
b. the most
c. the most of the time
d. most of the

When you come across a sentence with 2–3 blanks, it's helpful to analyze the structure. Ask yourself questions like:

- How many clauses does the sentence have?
- What is the subject and verb of each clause?
- What element is missing in each blank?

As you fill in the blanks, make sure your choices suit the grammar and meaning of the sentence and the surrounding text.

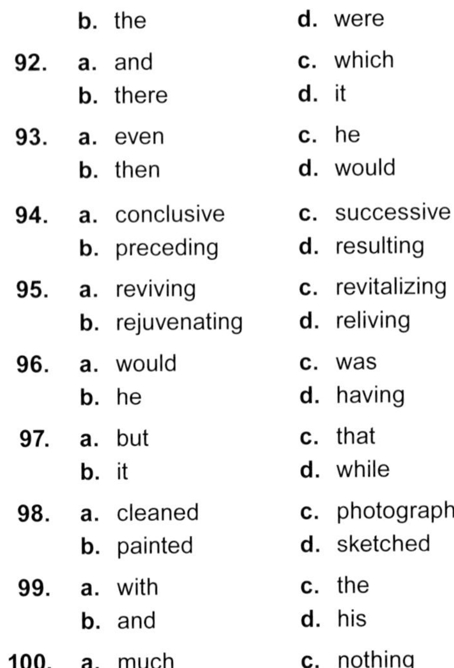

CLOZE

Passage 1 is about John James Audubon.

For over half a century, John James Audubon (1785–1851) was America's foremost wildlife artist. Today his name remains synonymous with birds and bird conservation the world over.

Not many of the birds Audubon drew stood still for him, nor ___(91)___ cameras or binoculars yet been invented. To study and draw birds, ___(92)___ was necessary to shoot them. Audubon's predecessors typically skinned their specimens, preserved the skins with arsenic, stuffed them with frayed rope, and ___(93)___ set them up on branches in order to draw them. But the ___(94)___ drawings looked as stiff and as dead as their subjects. Audubon dreamed of ___(95)___ his subjects, and while still a young man, ___(96)___ found a way to mount freshly killed specimens on sharpened wires set into a gridded board ___(97)___ allowed him to place them in lifelike positions. He ___(98)___ them first, and then filled in his drawings ___(99)___ watercolor that he rubbed with a cork to imitate the metallic cast of their feathers. The results were ___(100)___ less than magnificent.

91.	**a.** had **b.** the	**c.** when **d.** were
92.	**a.** and **b.** there	**c.** which **d.** it
93.	**a.** even **b.** then	**c.** he **d.** would
94.	**a.** conclusive **b.** preceding	**c.** successive **d.** resulting
95.	**a.** reviving **b.** rejuvenating	**c.** revitalizing **d.** reliving
96.	**a.** would **b.** he	**c.** was **d.** having
97.	**a.** but **b.** it	**c.** that **d.** while
98.	**a.** cleaned **b.** painted	**c.** photographed **d.** sketched
99.	**a.** with **b.** and	**c.** the **d.** his
100.	**a.** much **b.** even	**c.** nothing **d.** not

Passage 2 is about wolverines.

The wolverine is the largest North American member of the weasel (or Mustelidae) family. Although big males rarely ___(101)___ 40 pounds, the animals are ___(102)___ with vocal cords like those of a grizzly bear, providing them with a handy defensive mechanism that ___(103)___ off larger predators. Wolverines are primarily opportunistic scavengers, particularly during the colder months ___(104)___ they ___(105)___ on mostly winter-killed carrion. In ___(106)___ to wolves and other pack animals, ___(107)___ follow big-game herds to winter ranges for a dependable food supply, wolverines are more solitary creatures that can travel dozens of miles in a matter of days, up and over peaks and ridge tops in ___(108)___ of food. The physical makeup of wolverines – particularly their strong jaws and large incisor teeth – enhance their ___(109)___ to chew on bones. In fact, their viselike* jaw muscles sometimes ___(110)___ them to chew their way through traps or cages.

* **viselike:** like a vise (a metal tool with two jaw-like pieces that are designed to hold an object firmly in place while work is being done on it). **Note:** In British English, the tool is called a vice.

101.	**a.** weighing **b.** exceed	**c.** gain **d.** over
102.	**a.** constructed **b.** possessed	**c.** adorned **d.** equipped
103.	**a.** carries **b.** takes	**c.** scares **d.** calls
104.	**a.** unless **b.** when	**c.** until **d.** although
105.	**a.** hunt **b.** look	**c.** feed **d.** hunger
106.	**a.** relation **b.** regard	**c.** contrast **d.** order
107.	**a.** which **b.** that	**c.** they **d.** and
108.	**a.** view **b.** order	**c.** search **d.** case
109.	**a.** ability **b.** need	**c.** instinct **d.** desire
110.	**a.** prevent **b.** strengthen	**c.** enable **d.** cause

VOCABULARY

111. Everyone turned to admire the confident young man as he _____ down the street.
- **a.** strove
- **b.** staggered
- **c.** strode
- **d.** struck

112. Had the judge not been so _____ , the teenager would be serving a prison sentence now.
- **a.** lenient
- **b.** sober
- **c.** merciless
- **d.** austere

113. The doctor said that it was all right for him to drink red wine in _____ .
- **a.** mediocrity
- **b.** modesty
- **c.** mediation
- **d.** moderation

114. The car skidded on a patch of ice, spun out of control, and _____ rest on the edge of a cliff.
- **a.** put to
- **b.** stopped to
- **c.** was laid to
- **d.** came to

115. Einstein was a great physicist and one of the truly outstanding _____ of the 20th century.
- **a.** intellectuals
- **b.** attributes
- **c.** temperaments
- **d.** mentalities

116. Realizing her small son was no longer at her side, the young mother became _____ with fear.
- **a.** frantic
- **b.** erratic
- **c.** hectic
- **d.** chaotic

117. Please don't think I was _____ , but I couldn't help overhearing what you said.
- **a.** gossiping
- **b.** eavesdropping
- **c.** monitoring
- **d.** speculating

118. John is a(n) _____ worker who never leaves the office until his work is done.
- **a.** malicious
- **b.** conscientious
- **c.** indolent
- **d.** ambitious

Remember: If you do moderately well on the other sections of the GCVR, then you'll have plenty of room for error on the Vocabulary section.

See page 13 (top) for an explanation of how the math is on your side!

119. The investigation proved that the accident had resulted from the employer's _____ .
- **a.** aloofness
- **b.** negligence
- **c.** prudence
- **d.** intolerance

120. Her well-developed _____ instinct told her that the child was not quite telling the truth.
- **a.** matriarchal
- **b.** material
- **c.** maternal
- **d.** materialistic

121. The wounded soldier was awarded a medal for _____ in battle.
- **a.** virtue
- **b.** conduct
- **c.** valor
- **d.** ardor

122. Competition in today's job market is extremely _____ .
- **a.** fierce
- **b.** vindictive
- **c.** innovative
- **d.** inhibited

123. One can't help but feel _____ for the people who lost their homes in the earthquake.
- **a.** leniency
- **b.** compassion
- **c.** mercy
- **d.** heart

124. The guard managed to _____ the bank robber by knocking him unconscious.
- **a.** wrestle
- **b.** compose
- **c.** smash
- **d.** subdue

125. The new teacher has had her share of difficulties with the _____ young students.
- a. literate
- b. boisterous
- c. diligent
- d. obedient

126. He has too _____ to go up to a woman at a party and ask her to dance.
- a. much arrogance
- b. many inhibitions
- c. many vices
- d. much intelligence

127. He asked the dentist to give him a local anesthetic because he has a low _____ of pain.
- a. tolerance
- b. endurance
- c. level
- d. capacity

128. She was a capable yet _____ woman who was not fond of talking about her feelings.
- a. abashed
- b. intimidating
- c. reticent
- d. fragile

129. Imagine the politician's _____ when the scandal was exposed in the press.
- a. integrity
- b. humiliation
- c. humility
- d. impertinence

130. His parents were _____ with pride as he walked across the stage to accept the award.
- a. exploding
- b. gasping
- c. shivering
- d. bursting

131. If you don't water those plants soon, they're going to _____ .
- a. shrink
- b. shrivel
- c. wrinkle
- d. wilt

132. The old house was infested with rats and virtually _____ .
- a. uninhibited
- b. unpalatable
- c. uninhabitable
- d. unimpressive

133. We're planning on doing lots of hiking, so make sure you bring _____ shoes.
- a. sentimental
- b. sensible
- c. sensational
- d. sensitive

134. The doctor advised the elderly couple to move to a warmer environment with less _____ .
- a. humidity
- b. moisture
- c. climate
- d. atmosphere

135. His sense of humor has never been one of his most attractive _____ .
- a. characters
- b. traits
- c. properties
- d. tendencies

136. After hours of debate, there was still no _____ among the committee members.
- a. contention
- b. convention
- c. conviction
- d. consensus

137. The agile mouse _____ away before the cat could catch it.
- a. scampered
- b. lumbered
- c. lurched
- d. stumbled

138. Her parents objected, but nothing would _____ her from marrying him.
- a. defer
- b. deter
- c. deprive
- d. divert

139. The foreigners were amazed at the _____ variety of goods in the huge department store.
- a. complex
- b. confused
- c. beleaguered
- d. bewildering

140. He's thinking of taking on a second job to _____ his income.
- a. accumulate
- b. cultivate
- c. supplement
- d. implement

141. The museum owns an impressive _____ of Neolithic tools and eating utensils.
   a. demonstration
   b. array
   c. variation
   d. manifestation

142. She swore she would never again baby-sit for the ill-behaved, _____ children.
   a. noxious
   b. toxic
   c. obnoxious
   d. exhaustive

143. He's incapable of making a firm decision. I've never met a more _____ person.
   a. diverse
   b. vacillating
   c. various
   d. adaptable

144. The old woman _____ her wrinkled reflection in the mirror.
   a. contemplated
   b. preened
   c. squinted
   d. distorted

145. The scrawny young boy had _____ into a tall, muscular young man.
   a. evolved
   b. progressed
   c. modified
   d. developed

146. The vicious watchdog growled and _____ its teeth when the stranger approached.
   a. barked
   b. bared
   c. picked
   d. moistened

147. Be careful! The stem of that flower is covered with _____ .
   a. petals
   b. splinters
   c. thorns
   d. points

148. The cat _____ contentedly as the girl held it in her lap and gently stroked it.
   a. shrieked
   b. roared
   c. purred
   d. hissed

149. He drove through a puddle and accidentally _____ a woman with mud.
   a. sprinkled
   b. spattered
   c. dispersed
   d. scattered

150. The family spent the afternoon hiking in the nature _____ .
   a. preservation
   b. reserve
   c. conservation
   d. shelter

READING

After you skim for gist, it's also useful to take a few seconds to survey the first and last sentences of each paragraph so you know generally what each paragraph is about. This will help you narrow your search to a particular paragraph when you begin to answer the questions.

Passage 1 is about nicotine.

The old belief that tobacco soothes the throat, cures colds, and quenches thirst has long been replaced with evidence that cigarettes can instead cause lung cancer, heart disease, and early death. But one claimed benefit of tobacco still stands: that tobacco – or more precisely, nicotine – improves memory. Nicotine, at the levels in a smoker's bloodstream after only one cigarette, has long been known to increase recall in simple psychology tests. But no one knew exactly what nicotine did in the brain. Now researchers claim to have solved the mystery. Nicotine, they have found, strengthens communication between neurons in the hippocampus, a structure in the brain involved in learning and memory.

Nicotine seems to work by increasing the strength of messages zipping around the brain. These messages take the form of electrical impulses. As an impulse travels along a neuron, it eventually reaches the end. The next neuron lies across a gap called a synapse. In order for the message to leap the synapse, molecules known as neurotransmitters must be released into the gap. If enough of these molecules reach the neuron on the other side, they spark an electrical impulse in it and the message continues on through the brain circuit. What researchers have found is that nicotine increases the amount of neurotransmitters that are released. That greatly increases the odds that the message will reach the neuron on the other side. The more messages that get through, the more the neurons in a circuit change, becoming the physical embodiment of a memory. In fact, a 1991 study found that the risk of Alzheimer's disease is lower in smokers. Another recent study found that nicotine seems to inhibit formation, at least in the test tube, of the plaques that gum up the brains of Alzheimer patients.

The problem with using nicotine as a memory aid, of course, is that the delivery system contains 400 known carcinogens. But people at risk for Alzheimer's, or just plain forgetfulness, may not have to choose between cancer and senility. In 1995, a study found that nicotine delivered by a transdermal patch improves the performance of Alzheimer patients on learning tests.

151. What is the main idea of the passage?
- **a.** Tobacco is not as harmful as people once believed.
- **b.** Nicotine damages the electrical circuitry of the brain.
- **c.** Nicotine may aid in improving memory and learning.
- **d.** Memories can only be formed in the presence of nicotine.

152. What function do neurotransmitters perform?
- **a.** They directly increase memory and learning.
- **b.** They are able to leap across the gap between neurons.
- **c.** They release specialized molecules into nerve synapses.
- **d.** They enable messages to pass from one neuron to another.

153. What has research demonstrated about nicotine?
- **a.** It helps neurons to transfer electrical impulses more efficiently.
- **b.** It does not deserve the negative image that people have of it.
- **c.** It is able to send strong electrical impulses throughout the body.
- **d.** It can improve the strength and efficiency of neuron tissue.

154. The writer suggests that memories are created when ...
- **a.** nicotine increases the release of neurotransmitters.
- **b.** certain changes occur in the neurons of a brain circuit.
- **c.** a single message successfully reaches the hippocampus.
- **d.** a synapse fills with an adequate number of neurotransmitters.

155. What basic fact is implied in the passage?
- **a.** The majority of people who smoke are immune to Alzheimer's disease.
- **b.** Alzheimer patients who smoke do not form plaque in their brains.
- **c.** Alzheimer's disease affects a person's ability to learn and remember.
- **d.** Alzheimer patients are at greater risk from cancer than other people.

Passage 2 is about archaeology and modern technology.

Here is a tale of ancient texts and modern technology. In 1899, spurred by the discovery of the first papyrus manuscripts in Egypt, archaeologists from Oxford and the University of California at Berkeley were eager to scour the desert for more. After months of searching, the team seemed to strike pay dirt at the ancient settlement of Tebtunis, west of the Nile. Workers had uncovered some mummified crocodiles. Knowing that the reptiles were held sacred to the crocodile god Sobek, the archaeologists surmised that it wouldn't be long before they found human mummies and perhaps papyri too. But after several weeks the team realized it had stumbled upon a crocodile cemetery filled with thousands of mummified crocs but hardly any human mummies. And, so it seemed, hardly any papyri.

Then one day a workman who had exhumed yet another crocodile tossed it aside. The mummy's wrappings broke open, revealing that the reptile inside was covered with papyri – apparently to preserve its shape. Among the manuscripts, some dating from the third century B.C., were works by Homer, Virgil, and Euripides, and a fragment of a lost play by Sophocles. The surprised archaeologists saved the papyri and dumped the crocodiles, except for a few that remain today at Berkeley.

Sixty years ago, conservators mounted the papyri between flexible transparent sheets of vinyl. It seemed like a good strategy at the time, but over the decades the vinyl cracked. Even worse, it attracted static electricity, causing the fragile papyri to stick to it. This made it nearly impossible to separate the papyri from the vinyl without tearing them. The curator of Berkeley's rare manuscript collection turned to the university's engineering school to help solve the problem. The engineers knew of a machine that might prove helpful. The machine consisted of a modest six-inch fan that blows ionized air and is normally used to control static during the manufacture of silicon chips. The machine indeed worked extremely well on the papyri, making it possible to safely remove them from their aging vinyl covers. About 200 of the ancient documents are now securely mounted in glass, and the collection has thousands more, which may include lost works of ancient literature.

156. After the first mummified crocodiles were found at Tebtunis, what did archaeologists believe?

- **a.** They were close to uncovering the ancient temple of Sobek.
- **b.** They were about to uncover a rare crocodile cemetery.
- **c.** Their expedition had been a total waste of time and money.
- **d.** They would soon unearth papyri as well as human mummies.

157. Why were the archaeologists so eager to find papyrus manuscripts?

- **a.** They wanted to outdo their colleagues from a rival university.
- **b.** They knew they would probably receive extra payment if they did.
- **c.** They were motivated by a recent discovery by other Egyptologists.
- **d.** They wanted to prove how well their advanced technology worked.

158. The papyri were finally discovered ...

- **a.** right where they predicted.
- **b.** entirely by accident.
- **c.** after years of digging.
- **d.** by a conscientious workman.

159. How does modern technology come into the story?

- **a.** It was used to preserve the rare manuscripts when they first arrived at Berkeley.
- **b.** It was used in the second attempt to preserve the papyri after the first failed.
- **c.** It was used to undo problems created by early attempts to preserve the papyri.
- **d.** The Berkeley curator got the idea to use it while visiting a silicon chip factory.

160. What did the machine accomplish?

- **a.** It protected the papyri by permanently sealing them between silicon chips.
- **b.** It got rid of static electricity, allowing the safe separation of papyri and vinyl.
- **c.** It created a strong current of air that blew the cracked vinyl right off the papyri.
- **d.** It blew ionized air over the papyri, insuring their preservation for years to come.

Passage 3 is about the research of a skunk expert.

Ask Travis Quirk and he'll tell you that not everything is black and white when it comes to skunks. One example: You have to work hard to get a skunk to cut loose with its pungent spray. Quirk should know. A rare bird among mammalogists, he's studied the familiar striped skunk over the past four years near Manitoba's Delta Marsh. And while he's handled hundreds of wild and captive skunks, he's been doused only a few times.

Quirk's 30-square-mile study site lies in an area that once was among the most productive duck-breeding regions in Manitoba. But in recent decades nest success has fallen well below the level needed to maintain the duck population, and research shows that the main culprits are the growing numbers of nest-raiding skunks, raccoons, foxes and mink. Waterfowl managers estimate that predators typically destroy around 90 percent of upland duck nests across the northern prairie breeding grounds, along with countless songbird nests. When predator numbers climb, nest success declines in lockstep. Tellingly, on a smaller research plot within Quirk's area, only 1 percent of the nests of mallard ducks produced ducklings when the skunk population doubled from two to four skunks per square mile.

Quirk's study, in particular, is shedding light on how food abundance and diet affect skunk populations. "The size and fat condition of females in the fall goes a long way towards determining their reproductive success," he explains. "Bigger, well-conditioned females have a better chance of having an early litter with larger offspring and higher survival rates." To facilitate data collection, it's important that Quirk knows exactly where the skunks live. To this end, he temporarily immobilizes his subjects, and then weighs and measures them, fits them with ear tags and radio collars, and implants microchips. Once radio signals reveal a nesting site, he places a sensor at the site's entrance to monitor the comings and goings of the mother and her young. He also collects blood, hair, and droppings from around the site, which provide important clues to the animals' diet.

Although Quirk's study focuses only indirectly on the interrelationship between skunks and ducks, the conservation organization that sponsors it hopes that research by Quirk and others will lead to practical ways to offset the impact of nest-raiding skunks on duck populations other than by trapping or more lethal means.

161. According to the writer, what is the main focus of Quirk's research?
- **a.** the effect of nest-raiding skunks on local duck populations
- **b.** how skunk populations vary with food availability and a skunk's diet
- **c.** finding ways to achieve a balance between duck and skunk populations
- **d.** the role that food and diet play in successful duck breeding

162. What commonly held misconception is dispelled in paragraph 1?
- **a.** that most skunks are black and white
- **b.** that a skunk's spray rightly deserves its bad reputation
- **c.** that skunks are quick to release their foul-smelling spray
- **d.** that few scientists study skunks because of their smell

163. What happened when the skunk population in one area went from two to four skunks per square mile?
- **a.** There was no appreciable effect on the new duckling population.
- **b.** It had a disastrous effect on all but a few duck nests in the area.
- **c.** Quirk was called in to find out what had caused the increase.
- **d.** The duck population increased right along with it.

164. According to the writer, what are Quirk's sponsors hoping to do?
- **a.** protect the duck population in Delta Marsh at all costs
- **b.** increase the duck population by trapping and killing off skunks
- **c.** avoid having to intervene to save the ducks from nest-raiding skunks
- **d.** find ways to protect duck nests without reducing the skunk population

165. What is true of the way Quirk collects his data?
- **a.** He relies exclusively on remote monitoring.
- **b.** He uses both remote and hands-on techniques.
- **c.** He avoids nesting sites once sensors are in place.
- **d.** He only monitors the animals in the fall.

Passage 4 is about educating medical students.

For all of modern medicine's arsenal of sophisticated diagnostic machinery, there is one invaluable tool that is often overlooked and just as frequently underappreciated. That tool is the human eye.

To address this, Jefferson Medical College and the Pennsylvania Academy of the Fine Arts have begun collaborating to teach aspiring doctors to closely observe, describe, and interpret the subtlest details with the eye of an artist. The institutions recently launched their first two-hour "Visual Perception" workshop with a group of 18 white-coated medical students visiting the academy's museum to study a dynamic representation of their profession: Thomas Eakins' masterpiece "The Gross Clinic" (1875), which depicts an operation in progress. The students heard how to take a "visual inventory" by paying attention to overall elements of the painting, such as texture and brightness, and specifics, such as body language and facial expressions. The idea is for students to learn to fine-tune their attention to detail. Other workshops in the offing are "Accuracy and Perception," "Hand-Eye Coordination," and "Sculpture and Surgery."

Apparently, this attempt to wed medicine and visual art is not the first. An article published in the *Journal of the American Medical Association* in 2001 reported that medical students in a similar program at Yale acquired more astute observational skills than their colleagues who didn't take the courses. Besides enabling doctors to better assess their patients' well-being during office visits and make better diagnoses, finely honed visual abilities can also allow practitioners to spot subtle changes in X-rays over time, for example. Interestingly, the trend seems to be spreading to other areas of the humanities as well. The Association of American Medical Colleges reported recently that an increasing number of medical schools nationwide are requiring students to study literature, music, and the performing arts.

While fine art may be unexplored territory for some Jefferson medical students, their artistic counterparts at the fine arts academy are no strangers to the world of science. "Our upper-level students have been attending anatomy labs at Jefferson for years," said the head of the academy's painting department, "but this is the first time we've hosted the medical students. It's been long overdue."

166. What is true of the program described in the second paragraph?

- **a.** It is the first of its kind in the USA.
- **b.** It is typical of a growing trend among American med schools.
- **c.** It is designed to instill a love of art in medical students.
- **d.** It was not as successful as the college had hoped.

167. Which statement best describes the writer's main idea?

- **a.** Artists and doctors have more in common than was once believed.
- **b.** A well-trained eye is the best diagnostic tool that medical science has to offer.
- **c.** Patients will benefit if doctors are trained to be more attuned to fine detail.
- **d.** Medical colleges that do not offer art courses are doing their students a disservice.

168. What is the purpose of having students of Jefferson Medical College attend the two-hour workshop?

- **a.** to improve their knowledge of anatomy
- **b.** to teach them how to read X-rays better
- **c.** to refine their powers of observation
- **d.** to show them how to enjoy a painting's fine detail

169. What do the findings of an article published in 2001 suggest?

- **a.** Yale medical students benefited more than their Jefferson counterparts.
- **b.** Medical students who take such courses could benefit greatly from them.
- **c.** The impact of such programs on medical students is difficult to assess.
- **d.** Medical students should take courses in all areas of the humanities.

170. Which of the following best sums up the point of the last paragraph?

- **a.** Both art and medical students can benefit by selectively studying each other's field of study.
- **b.** Students of fine art understand anatomy better than their medical student counterparts.
- **c.** It's a shame that art students are only now beginning to socialize more with medical students.
- **d.** Art students are much better observers than most medical students.

7 Vocabulary Enhancement

Searching and Throwing

Who would have thought there were so many ways to search for and throw things in English? For example, *Reading Passage 2 talks about archaeologists who* ***scour*** *the desert for papyrus manuscripts and a workman who* ***tosses aside*** *yet another uninteresting crocodile mummy. Here's a closer look.*

A **Ways of Searching** – Study the explanations, and then underline the correct choices in the sentences that follow.

If we **seek** something (e.g., a job, advice, happiness), we **search for** it and try to obtain it. If we **scour** or **comb** a place, we search it thoroughly, looking for something. (Note that **scour** can also mean "clean the surface of something by rubbing hard" – e.g., **scour** the floor or a dirty pot.) If we **scan** something, we pass our eyes over it thoroughly, looking for something specific (e.g., we can **scan the horizon** looking for land or we can **scan a crowded room** looking for someone we know). We can also **scan** something written, which means "read quickly, looking for specific information." **Scan** can also mean "pass a beam of light over or through something with a scanner or scanning device" (e.g., a product's bar code in a supermarket). If we **probe** something, we examine or explore a place that is difficult to reach (e.g., a doctor **probes** a wound, rockets **probe** outer space). We can also **probe** a person by asking questions intended to reveal information. If we **delve into** a subject or a mystery, we search deep within it to discover new information. We can also **delve into** things that have depth, trying to find something (e.g., a purse or a closet). If we **ransack** something, we look through it, desperately trying to find something and often damaging or messing things up in the process (e.g., burglars may **ransack** a house looking for money). Less desperate is to **rummage**, which means "search by moving things around in a careless, hurried way" (e.g., **rummage** through the attic, looking for an old book.). The word **forage** is used to mean "search for food or supplies" and is often used for animals or soldiers.

1. I can't think of anything worse than having to **scan / rummage / delve** around in a garbage dumpster looking for something that you shouldn't have thrown away!
2. In his spare time, he likes to **probe / comb / ransack** the beach looking for coins with his metal detector.
3. I hate it when the dentist asks me a question as soon as he begins to **probe / scan / seek** around in my mouth.
4. What's the name of that hi-tech machine that allows doctors to **scour / seek / scan** your body?
5. If we **search / probe / ransack** through these personnel files, I'm sure we'll find all the information we need.
6. The burglar **delved / probed / rummaged** through the upstairs of the house. Finding nothing of value, he intensified his efforts and **scanned / ransacked / sought** the living room downstairs. What a mess!
7. Everyone was relieved when the **seek / search / comb** and rescue operation ended successfully.
8. "**Combing / Foraging / Delving** is always such a chore," thought the young squirrel. "But Mother was right. **'Seek / Rummage / Scan** and ye shall find!'"

Now match the base form of the target word(s) in sentences 1-8 with the photos that illustrate them.

1 ____________

2 ____________

3 ____________

4 ____________

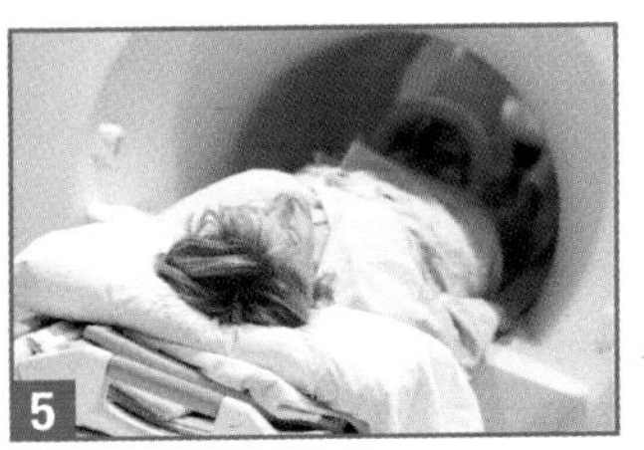
5 ____________

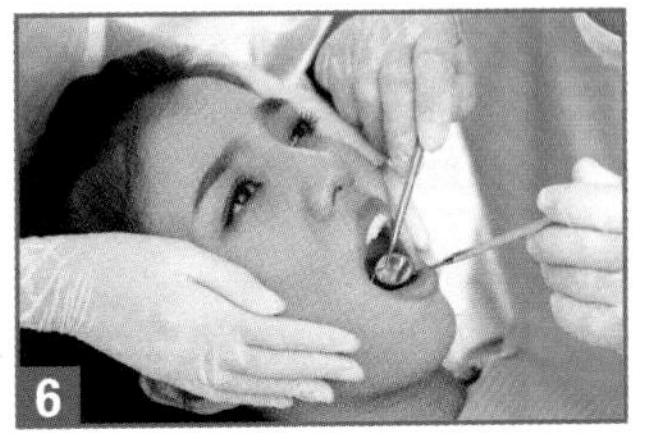
6 ____________

7 ____________

8 ____________

B Ways of Throwing – Study the explanations, and then underline the correct choices in the sentences that follow.

If we **toss** something, we throw it lightly (e.g., we can **toss** bread to the ducks or **toss** a coin to see who goes first). **Toss** can also mean "throw / move from side to side or up and down" (e.g., we **toss** in our sleep, the wind or waves **toss** an object from side to side, and a horse can **toss** its rider to the ground). Going to the other extreme, we can **hurl** something, which means "throw violently" (e.g., rioters **hurl** stones at the police). If we **heave** something, we throw something heavy with great effort (e.g., a murderer **heaves** a body into a river). If we **fling** something (irregular: *fling - flung - flung*), we throw it with force (usually with a sideways movement of the arm) because the object is light enough to do so (e.g., **fling** a cup across the room). It can also mean "throw or move all or part of the body" (e.g., **fling** our arms around somebody we love or **fling** your hair back to get it out of your eyes). Don't confuse this with **sling** (irregular: *sling - slung - slung*), which means to "throw or hang carelessly or loosely" (e.g., **sling** a purse over your shoulder or your coat on a chair). If we **dump** something, we throw it down carelessly, heavily, or in a mass (e.g., **dump** the garbage into the bin). **Cast** (irregular: *cast - cast - cast*) is a formal word with many uses, most of which relate to "throwing": e.g., a fisherman **casts** his line into the water; we **cast** a look at someone; objects **cast** shadows; we **cast** doubt on something. And for those who know something about baseball, you'll know that **pitch** means "throw the ball to the batter," but it also means, simply, "throw" (e.g., **pitch** a horseshoe).

1. The soldiers marched through the forest with their rifles **pitched / hurled / slung** over their shoulders.
2. I'm tired of you **heaving / casting / dumping** your clothes all over the floor. Get this place cleaned up!
3. The furious teacher was tempted to **hurl / cast / toss** a book at the insolent student.
4. The sea grew rough, **slinging / tossing / dumping** the small boat up and down like a cork.
5. He always **flings / tosses / casts** himself into a new project with great enthusiasm.
6. Anxious about the exam, she spent a sleepless night **tossing / casting / pitching** and turning.
7. He **tossed / cast / heaved** an angry glance at me and **dumped / cast / heaved** the papers in the trash.
8. He walked in the door and, without saying a word, **flung / tossed / pitched** himself on the couch.

Now look at the photos and choose the word that best suits each one.

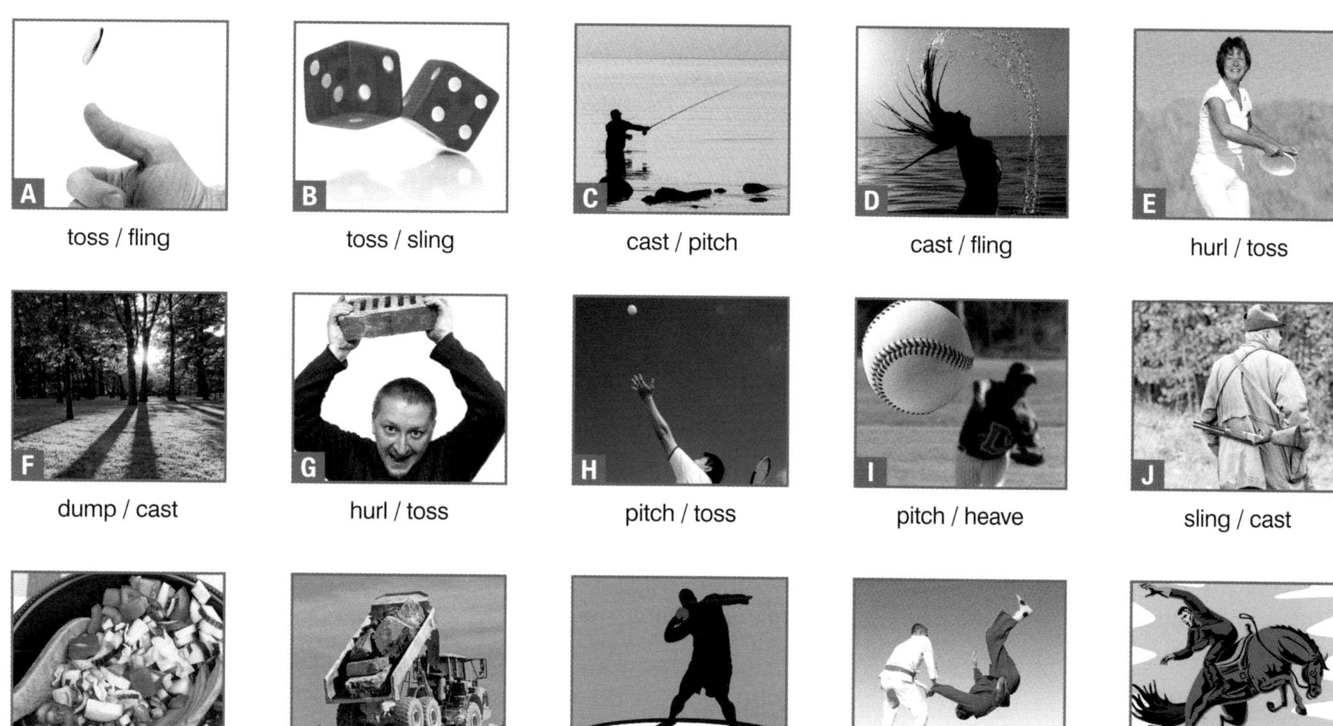

A toss / fling

B toss / sling

C cast / pitch

D cast / fling

E hurl / toss

F dump / cast

G hurl / toss

H pitch / toss

I pitch / heave

J sling / cast

K fling / toss

L dump / heave

M toss / heave

N throw / sling

O toss / pitch

7 Vocabulary Consolidation

VEXING VERBS

A Common Collocations – Complete each phrase with a word from the box.

bare	bark	compose	eavesdrop	moisten	monitor	smash	wrestle

1. ______________ the front end of your car
2. ______________ with your conscience
3. ______________ a command at someone
4. ______________ yourself before an interview
5. ______________ on a conversation
6. ______________ a student's progress
7. ______________ your lips
8. ______________ your teeth in anger

B Fine-Tuning Your Knowledge – The numbers below refer to Vocabulary items in Practice Test 7. After reviewing the words, fill in each blank with the correct form of the appropriate verb.

111. stagger stride strike strive	**a.** The manager's plan ______________ them as an excellent idea. **b.** The injured athlete ______________ off the field and slumped to the ground. **c.** The young applicant ______________ into the room with confidence. **d.** People with ambition ______________ to succeed.
130. burst explode gasp shiver	**a.** The audience ______________ into laughter when the clowns entered the ring. **b.** When we found the lost child, he was crying and ______________ with fear. **c.** We usually say that balloons ______________ , but dynamite ______________ . **d.** She ______________ with astonishment when she heard the terrible news.
138. defer deprive deter divert	**a.** It is a violation of the Geneva Convention to ______________ prisoners of war of food. **b.** If he loses his job, they'll have to ______________ their decision to buy a new car. **c.** Nothing would ______________ her from going to college. **d.** One shoplifter ______________ the jeweler while the other made off with the ring.
140. accumulate cultivate implement supplement	**a.** The bank will be ______________ its new interest rates on January 1st. **b.** It's amazing how quickly dust ______________ if you don't clean your house regularly. **c.** You may get fewer colds if you ______________ your diet with vitamin C. **d.** It takes time and effort to ______________ new relationships.
145. develop evolve modify progress	**a.** He'll sign the contract, but only if we ______________ the final due date. **b.** The idea that humans ______________ from apes is still controversial in some quarters. **c.** The company has ______________ several new products in the past year. **d.** If the disease ______________ , the surgeon will have to operate.
149. disperse scatter spatter sprinkle	**a.** Did you cook pasta again? The stove top is ______________ with tomato sauce. **b.** It didn't take long for the child to ______________ his toys all over the floor. **c.** She ______________ the top of the cake with powdered sugar and cinnamon. **d.** Nowadays, information is ______________ instantaneously by satellites and other forms of telecommunication.

NOTORIOUS NOUNS

A **Amusing Associations** – Find the word in the box that is suggested by each prompt.

ardor *compassion* *endurance* *intelligence* *moderation* *modesty* *tolerance* *valor*

1. ______________ – If you display this, you've probably got good grades and do well in school.
2. ______________ – If you lack this, you've probably got an inflated ego and/or a swelled head.
3. ______________ – If you usually display this, people describe you as passionate and enthusiastic.
4. ______________ – If you lack this, no one will ever mistake you for being open-minded or unbiased.
5. ______________ – If you always eat with this, you'll never have to worry about weight control.
6. ______________ – If you don't have this, forget about ever being able to complete a marathon.
7. ______________ – If you have this, you would probably make a good nurse or social worker.
8. ______________ – If you lack this, don't ever expect to win any medals for bravery in battle.

B **Fine-Tuning Your Knowledge** – The numbers below refer to Vocabulary items in Practice Test 7. After reviewing the words, fill in each blank with the appropriate word.

113. mediation **mediocrity** **moderation** **modesty**	**a.** ______________ is not Ed's strong suit. He's one of the most arrogant people I know. **b.** If labor and management cannot agree, the dispute will have to be solved by ______________ . **c.** I was disappointed by the ______________ of the famous actor's performance. I expected much more of him. **d.** She's just bouncing back from a back injury, which is why the doctor cautioned her to exercise in ______________ .
119. aloofness **intolerance** **negligence** **prudence**	**a.** ______________ was not the cause of the fire; the home's wiring was in perfect condition. **b.** Racism is one of the worst forms of ______________ . **c.** He's extremely shy, so don't be offended by his ______________ . **d.** New investors should approach the stock market with ______________ .
129. humiliation **humility** **impertinence** **integrity**	**a.** His ______________ is refreshing; it's rare for a successful person to be so modest. **b.** The team's 10-0 loss was only a temporary ______________ ; they bounced back to win the next ten games and the league championship. **c.** The student's ______________ earned him frequent trips to the principal's office. **d.** The judge prides herself on her ______________ ; she would never accept a bribe.
135. character **property** **tendency** **trait**	**a.** He has a ______________ not to respect other people's personal ______________ . **b.** One ______________ of water is that it boils at 212° F. **c.** Honesty and integrity have never been among the criminal's strongest ______________ s. **d.** Her true ______________ always shines through in a crisis.
136. consensus **contention** **convention** **conviction**	**a.** The doctor will be attending a medical ______________ next week. **b.** The politician is a Democrat with very strong ______________ s. **c.** Inheritances are a matter of ______________ in many families. **d.** It's the mayor's ______________ that the City Council will not be able to reach a ______________ of opinion on this issue. Let's see if he's correct.
147. petal **point** **splinter** **thorn**	**a.** She hates getting ______________ s, so she never walks barefoot on wooden floors. **b.** Be careful! Those roses have ______________ s. **c.** The child drew a star with five ______________ s. **d.** She pulled the flower apart ______________ by ______________ , chanting "He loves me, he loves me not."

AUDACIOUS ADJECTIVES

A Common Collocations – Complete each phrase with a word from the box.

fragile *noxious* *obnoxious* *reticent* *sensible* *sensitive* *unpalatable* *wilted*

1. feel sick after inhaling ________________ fumes
2. refuse to babysit a(n) ________________ child
3. be ________________ to discuss a private matter
4. water a ________________ plant (and hope it revives!)
5. cover up if you have ________________ skin
6. shatter a(n) ________________ vase
7. refuse to eat a(n) ________________ meal
8. wear ________________ shoes on a long hike

B Fine-Tuning Your Knowledge – The numbers below refer to Vocabulary items in Paractice Test 7. After reviewing the words, fill in each blank with the appropriate word.

116. chaotic erratic frantic hectic	**a.** You'd be ______________ too if you saw the value of your retirement account drop by 25% in just a few weeks! **b.** The patient has an ______________ heartbeat, so his doctor says he may need a pacemaker to make it more regular. **c.** She's a competent businesswoman whose life is very ______________ . Luckily, she's well organized, which prevents things from getting out of control and ______________ .
118. ambitious conscientious indolent malicious	**a.** He's the most hard-working person I know; he has no idea what it means to be ______________ . **b.** That was a(n) ______________ , spiteful thing to say! Apologize at once! **c.** She's too ______________ if you ask me; she'd do anything to succeed. **d.** He's loyal and ______________ , and doesn't mind staying late to get the job done.
120. material materialistic maternal matriarchal	**a.** It's often been said that we live in a ______________ society which places too much emphasis on the acquisition of ______________ goods. **b.** The archaeologist is a leading expert on ______________ societies. **c.** The ______________ instinct is so powerful that most women would do anything to protect their children.
122. fierce inhibited innovative vindictive	**a.** Nowadays cell phone companies are in ______________ competition with each other. **b.** He used to be shy and ______________, but now he never stops talking! **c.** She's usually very forgiving; it's not like her to be so ______________ . **d.** The company has come up with a(n) ______________ sales campaign. Let's hope it works; it's a totally unique idea.
132. unimpressive uninhabitable uninhibited unpalatable	**a.** The steak I ordered was so ______________ that I couldn't eat it. **b.** The house is in such a state of disrepair that it's virtually ______________ . **c.** Don't bother with his first novel; it's boring and ______________ compared to his later work. **d.** I wish you weren't so ______________ ; it's going to get you in trouble some day.
143. adaptable diverse vacillating various	**a.** Ann is very ______________ , so she shouldn't have a problem adjusting to her new school. **b.** His ______________ nature makes it very difficult for him to make a decision and stick to it. **c.** The school has a(n) ______________ population, with students from more than 50 nations. **d.** ______________ people in his class have expressed a desire to study Chinese.

PRICKLY PREPOSITIONS AND PARTICLES

The following extracts are taken from passages that you have encountered in Practice Test 7. Read each one quickly, and then fill in the blanks with an appropriate preposition or particle.

1. As an impulse travels _________ a neuron, it eventually reaches the end. The next neuron lies _________ a gap called a synapse. _________ order _________ the message to leap the synapse, molecules known _________ neurotransmitters must be released _________ the gap. If enough _________ these molecules reach the neuron _________ the other side, they spark an electrical impulse _________ it and the message continues on ____________ the brain circuit. What researchers have found is that nicotine increases the amount _________ neurotransmitters that are released. That greatly increases the odds that the message will reach the neuron _________ the other side. The more messages that get _________, the more the neurons _________ a circuit change, becoming the physical embodiment _________ a memory. _________ fact, a 1991 study found that the risk _________ Alzheimer's disease is lower _________ smokers. Another recent study found that nicotine seems to inhibit formation, _________ least _________ the test tube, _________ the plaques that gum _________ the brains _________ Alzheimer patients.

   The problem _________ using nicotine _________ a memory aid, _________ course, is that the delivery system contains 400 known carcinogens. But people _________ risk for Alzheimer's, or just forgetfulness, may not have to choose _________ cancer and senility. _________ 1995, a study found that nicotine delivered _________ a transdermal patch improves the performance _________ Alzheimer patients _________ learning tests.

2. Then one day a workman who had exhumed yet another crocodile tossed it aside. The mummy's wrappings broke _________, revealing that the reptile inside was covered _________ papyri – apparently to preserve its shape. _________ the manuscripts, some dating _________ the third century B.C., were works _________ Homer, Virgil, and Euripides, and a fragment _________ a lost play _________ Sophocles. The surprised archaeologists saved the papyri and dumped the crocodiles, except _________ a few that remain today _________ Berkeley.

   Sixty years ago, conservators mounted the papyri _________ flexible transparent sheets _________ vinyl. It seemed like a good strategy _________ the time, but _________ the decades the vinyl cracked. Even worse, it attracted static electricity, causing the fragile papyri to stick _________ it. This made it nearly impossible to separate the papyri _________ the vinyl _________ tearing them.

3. Quirk's study, _________ particular, is shedding light _________ how food abundance and diet affect skunk populations. ... To facilitate data collection, it's important that Quirk knows exactly where the skunks live. _________ this end, he temporarily immobilizes his subjects, and then weighs and measures them, fits them _________ ear tags and radio collars, and implants microchips. ... He also collects blood, hair, and droppings _________ around the site, which provide important clues _________ the animals' diet. ... Although Quirk's study focuses only indirectly _________ the interrelationship _________ skunks and ducks, the conservation organization that sponsors it hopes that research _________ Quirk and others will lead to practical ways to offset the impact _________ nest-raiding skunks _________ duck populations other than _________ trapping or more lethal means.

4. The institutions recently launched their first two-hour "Visual Perception" workshop _________ a group _________ 18 white-coated medical students visiting the academy's museum to study a dynamic representation _________ their chosen profession: Thomas Eakins' masterpiece "The Gross Clinic" (1875), which depicts an operation _________ progress. The first- and second-year med students heard how to take a "visual inventory" _________ paying attention _________ overall elements _________ the painting, such _________ texture and brightness, and specifics, such _________ body language and facial expressions. The idea is _________ med students to learn _________ the masters _________ order to fine-tune their attention _________ detail. Other workshops _________ the offing are "Accuracy and Perception," "Hand-Eye Coordination," and "Sculpture and Surgery." The courses are a mix _________ demonstrations, lectures, and hands-______ art lessons.

8 Practice Test 8

Writing 30 minutes

- You may write in pen or pencil.
- You will have 30 minutes to write on one of the two topics. If you do not write on one of these topics, your paper will not be scored. If you do not understand the topics, ask the examiner to explain them.
- You may make an outline if you wish, but your outline will not count toward your score.
- Write about one-and-a-half to two pages. Your essay will be marked down if it is extremely short.
- You will not be graded on the appearance of your paper, but your handwriting must be readable. You may change or correct your writing, but you should not recopy the whole essay.
- Your essay will be judged on clarity and overall effectiveness, as well as on topic development, organization, and the range, accuracy, and appropriateness of your grammar and vocabulary. Your essay will be graded at the University of Michigan.

TOPICS For help in writing these compositions, see *Writing Tutorial*, pages 215-216.

1. Deciding what career to pursue is one of the most important and difficult choices a young person has to make. The options may seem endless, and it's sometimes difficult to know where to start. Imagine you are a high school career counselor. What strategies would you recommend to help your students begin to narrow down their options? Support your ideas with reasons and examples.

2. Thomas Edison suggested that he would devote his energies to perfecting an invention only if he could see that invention "in terms of the service that it might give others." Choose one of the following and discuss how you think it achieved Edison's requirement. Support your ideas with reasons and examples.

airplane television telephone computer communications satellites

CRITERIA REVIEW - Mechanics

✓ accurate spelling, especially of easily confused words like *its–it's, there–their–they're, be–been–being,* and *to–two–too*

✓ sentences starting with a capital and ending with proper end punctuation (. ? !)

✓ proper use of commas: e.g., in lists, after introductory subordinate clauses and adverbials, before/after nonrestrictive relative clauses

✓ proper use of apostrophes in possessive nouns (*Mary's, the children's, the boys'*) and in contractions (*don't, they're, aren't*)

FINAL PROOFREAD (2-3 minutes)

✓ spelling and punctuation

✓ subject-verb agreement

✓ verb tense usage

✓ vocabulary upgrade, if possible

Listening approx. 35-40 minutes

This section of the examination tests your understanding of spoken English. The listening section has three parts. There are 50 questions. Mark all your answers on the separate answer sheet. Do not make any stray marks on the answer sheet. If you change your mind about an answer, erase your first answer completely.

Part I

In this part, you will hear short conversations. From the three answer choices given, choose the answer which means about the same thing as what you hear, or that is true based upon what you hear.

For problems 1 through 17, mark your answers on the separate answer sheet. No problems can be repeated.

Please listen carefully. Do you have any questions?

SUMMARY: Part I - Main Question Types

- ✓ recognize gist/summary
- ✓ identify context from speakers' word choice
- ✓ interpret tone of voice/feelings
- ✓ paraphrase idioms/phrasal verbs
- ✓ interpret grammatical clues

1. **a.** He's panicking about a deadline.
b. She thinks he shouldn't work so hard.
c. He doubts she'll be able to help.

2. **a.** They're stuck in traffic near the mall.
b. They're about to pull off the highway.
c. They're trying to find a parking spot.

3. **a.** He's afraid she may let him down.
b. He's relieved that she can help him.
c. He's sorry he disappointed his wife.

4. **a.** His plans were completely ruined.
b. He'll go away next weekend instead.
c. His flight was the only one canceled.

5. **a.** The party was a big hit.
b. The party hasn't happened yet.
c. The party wasn't a surprise.

6. **a.** His team lost the game.
b. The other team won in overtime.
c. The game ended in a tie.

7. **a.** She thinks he doesn't believe her.
b. She needs to take computer lessons.
c. She realizes she made a big mistake.

8. **a.** She wants Bernie to repair something.
b. She's hoping to make the repair herself.
c. She'd rather pay someone to do the repair.

9. **a.** Both kids are busy on Saturday morning.
b. Both kids will stay home on Sunday.
c. The soccer tournament is next weekend.

10. **a.** Tommy's been delayed at the dentist.
b. Tommy promised to clean his room today.
c. She doubts he'll be home in time to help.

11. **a.** She didn't hear what he said.
b. She thinks he's being sarcastic.
c. She agrees with him wholeheartedly.

12. **a.** He offers to drive her to the airport.
b. He offers to pick her up.
c. He suggests she take a cab.

13. **a.** She'd rather cook dinner herself.
b. He's going to prepare the meal.
c. He'll arrange for dinner to be delivered.

14. **a.** She likes the sound of the car.
b. She's going to make an offer on the car.
c. She'll get her mechanic to inspect the car.

15. **a.** She's moving to a new house.
b. He's already found someone to help her.
c. He's sorry he'll miss seeing her parents.

16. **a.** She wants to break up with him.
b. He's angry with her.
c. Her phone isn't working properly.

17. **a.** He doesn't like fruits and vegetables.
b. They only buy organic produce.
c. They object to paying extra for organic produce.

Part II

In this part, you will hear a question. From the three answer choices given, choose the one which best answers the question.

For problems 18 through 35, mark your answers on the separate answer sheet. No problems can be repeated. Please listen carefully. Do you have any questions?

SUMMARY: Part II - Things to Listen for

- ✓ function
- ✓ structure: *wh-* word or helping-verb
- ✓ speaker's tone of voice
- ✓ time frame
- ✓ potentially confusing grammar (e.g., hypothetical language, conditionals)
- ✓ target idioms and/or phrasal verbs

18. **a.** You're right. I'll see to it next week.
b. I shouldn't have, but I did.
c. No, I've got plenty of gas.

19. **a.** You're right. I need to be there.
b. I can't let myself think about it.
c. The plane took off without me.

20. **a.** Soon, I hope.
b. As long as everyone helps out.
c. We've made good progress so far.

21. **a.** No thanks. I just ate.
b. That would be nice. Thanks.
c. Order me a large, please.

22. **a.** Yes. Shall I stop at the bank?
b. No, I haven't cashed my paycheck yet.
c. No, I bought some yesterday.

23. **a.** You're right. My eyes do need a rest.
b. Sorry, I didn't mean to be rude.
c. Soon. My vacation's next month.

24. **a.** Would you like it?
b. It's beautiful. Thank you so much!
c. No, but I haven't worn it for a while.

25. **a.** He's getting married in the spring.
b. He's the one in the blue jacket.
c. Thanks. I'll send him your regards.

26. **a.** Yes, tomorrow, I suppose.
b. Please don't forget. It's urgent.
c. Yes, but he called to reschedule.

27. **a.** I suppose there will be.
b. I drove.
c. I haven't figured it out yet.

28. **a.** No, mine's working fine.
b. Is it plugged in?
c. Sorry, it wasn't my idea.

29. **a.** Actually, I took the bus.
b. It'll be five years next month.
c. It won't be long now.

30. **a.** Sarah's, I believe.
b. On Lake Street.
c. Be there at 8:00 sharp!

31. **a.** They may decide to fire him.
b. He hasn't been very happy here.
c. He had to pick up his son at school.

32. **a.** Somebody let the cat out of the bag.
b. I thought you told her.
c. Don't worry. I won't tell them.

33. **a.** I hope so.
b. It would've been nice.
c. I'd like that.

34. **a.** It must be our new neighbor.
b. It kept me awake all night.
c. They had a great time at the party

35. **a.** He must be having a rough day.
b. You shouldn't have bothered.
c. Not that I know of.

Part III

In this part, you will hear three short segments from a radio program. The program is called "Learning from the Experts." You will hear what three different radio guests have to say about three different topics.

Each talk lasts about two minutes. As you listen, you may want to take some notes to help you remember information given in the talk. Write your notes in the test booklet.

After each talk, you will be asked some questions about what was said. From the three answer choices given, you should choose the one that best answers the question according to the information you heard.

Remember, no problems can be repeated. For problems 36 through 50, mark all your answers on the separate answer sheet. Do you have any questions?

SUMMARY - Part III

Before you listen

✓ Skim the questions and choices for gist.

During the program phase

✓ Use the choices to organize your listening.

✓ Focus on the broad details, and don't panic if you hear unknown words.

During the question phase

✓ Watch out for distractors that are true but do not answer the question.

✓ Use process of elimination, and guess if you must.

SEGMENT 1

36. What is true regarding the sinking of the *Explorer* off the coast of Antarctica?
- **a.** It took the Antarctic Treaty countries by surprise.
- **b.** Observers had predicted the likelihood of such an event.
- **c.** The incident was a disaster of tragic proportions.

37. What point does Ronald Dolan make about the growth of ship tourism to Antarctica?
- **a.** It is roughly four times greater than in the early 1990s.
- **b.** It has decreased since the sinking of the *Explorer*.
- **c.** It has leveled off at about 28,000 visitors a year.

38. According to Ronald Dolan, what impact has the sinking of the *Explorer* had on Antarctica's fragile ecosystem?
- **a.** It was responsible for the loss of hundreds of lives.
- **b.** It resulted in an oil spill of over 48,000 gallons.
- **c.** It has had no impact as yet, but dangers exist.

39. What makes it particularly difficult to control tourism in Antarctica or make plans for rescue operations or environmental clean-ups, should they become necessary?
- **a.** There has not been a government in Antarctica since 1959.
- **b.** Resolutions of the Antarctic Treaty nations are not legally binding.
- **c.** Bad feelings exist between the Antarctic Treaty nations.

40. In the opinion of the observers that Ronald Dolan interviewed, which of the following could make the most impact in terms of establishing strict guidelines for tourism in the area?
- **a.** the Antarctic Treaty nations
- **b.** the International Association of Antarctica Tour Operators
- **c.** the governments of countries who send tourists to the region

SEGMENT 2

41. According to the often-quoted medical saying mentioned at the beginning of the program, what is the best way to reduce the length of a common cold?
- **a.** Symptoms should be treated aggressively.
- **b.** Symptoms should be ignored completely.
- **c.** Neither method is effective; the cold must simply run its course. *(Segment 2 continues at top of next page)*

42. What did the two studies demonstrate about nasal sprays containing alpha-inteferon?
   - a. Cold sufferers should always use them at the first sign of a cold.
   - b. Families who use them suffer 40% fewer colds than those who don't.
   - c. They are an extremely effective way of minimizing cold symptoms.

43. According to Dana Hodgkins, what is the major drawback of the treatment?
   - a. its affordability
   - b. its side effects
   - c. the time it will take to get approved

44. Which group is least likely to experience the benefits of alpha-interferon in the near future?
   - a. school children
   - b. asthma sufferers
   - c. cancer patients with low resistance

45. Which of the following best summarizes the main idea discussed in the last part of the program?
   - a. Colds are caused by a potentially dangerous form of bacteria.
   - b. Antibiotics should not be taken to combat the common cold.
   - c. More and more bacteria are becoming resistant to antibiotics.

SEGMENT 3

46. What technical-sounding name do experts give to the vast expanse of rubbish floating around in the Pacific Ocean?
   - a. the Great Pacific Garbage Patch
   - b. the trash vortex
   - c. plastic soup

47. What is one of the points that Tom Fields makes about the plastic in the vast expanse of garbage?
   - a. It never gets close enough to land to come on shore.
   - b. The swirling currents pull it to the bottom of the ocean floor.
   - c. The great majority of it comes from land-based activities.

48. According to oceanographer Charles Moore, what must happen to prevent the Great Pacific Garbage Patch from doubling in size over the next decade?
   - a. People need to reduce their use of disposable plastic.
   - b. Boats should be banned from entering the Garbage Patch.
   - c. A massive clean-up effort needs to be organized.

49. What are nurdles?
   - a. a biodegradable form of plastic
   - b. tiny bits of fragmented plastic
   - c. plastic found in the stomachs of sea animals

50. Which of the following best summarizes the main idea discussed in the last part of the program?
   - a. Nurdles have pushed marine animals to the edge of extinction.
   - b. Nurdles may contain deadly amounts of DDT and other toxins.
   - c. Nurdles are a threat to the entire food chain, including humans.

Grammar – Cloze – Vocabulary – Reading 75 minutes

This section of the examination contains 120 problems, numbered 51 through 170. There are 40 grammar, 20 cloze, 40 vocabulary, and 20 reading comprehension problems. If you do not understand how to do the problems, raise your hand, and a proctor will explain the examples to you. None of the actual test problems can be explained.

Each problem has only one correct answer. Do not spend too much time on any one problem. If you do not know the answer to a problem, you may guess. Work quickly but carefully. You have one hour and 15 minutes (75 minutes) to answer all 120 problems. If you finish before the time is over, you may check your answers within the GCVR section only. Do not go back to the Listening section of the exam.

GRAMMAR

51. I ran to answer the phone, but _____ , it had stopped ringing.
- **a.** no sooner I got to it
- **b.** while I was doing so
- **c.** before I could get to it
- **d.** until I'd got to it

52. The spaghetti needs to cook a bit more; it's not _____ soft enough.
- **a.** still
- **b.** very
- **c.** quite
- **d.** fairly

53. I'm ashamed to say that his remarks were so rude that they are not _____ .
- **a.** repetitious
- **b.** repeatable
- **c.** repetitive
- **d.** repeated

54. _____ a student has found it difficult to write research papers.
- **a.** Too much
- **b.** Hardly
- **c.** A lot
- **d.** Many

55. _____ here before, they shouldn't have any trouble finding the house.
- **a.** Have they been
- **b.** Having been
- **c.** To have been
- **d.** They've been

56. The food at the new restaurant is delicious, _____ beautifully presented.
- **a.** not to mention
- **b.** but also
- **c.** as well
- **d.** moreover

57. The company's new policy affects each and _____ of you.
- **a.** everybody
- **b.** every one
- **c.** every single
- **d.** every last

58. I'm disappointed in you. There was no reason _____ in that manner.
- **a.** as to your behaving
- **b.** of your behaving
- **c.** that you behaved
- **d.** for you to behave

59. Please believe me when I say that _____ offending you.
- **a.** I did not intend to
- **b.** I had no intention of
- **c.** it was not my intention of
- **d.** it was not my intent on

60. He's such an excellent tennis player _____ anyone beat him.
- **a.** whom I haven't ever seen
- **b.** that I've yet to see
- **c.** that never I have seen
- **d.** to whom I still haven't seen

61. The president's advisors admit to _____ about the economy.
- **a.** having concerns
- **b.** having concerned
- **c.** be concerned
- **d.** concerning

62. Everyone I know finds that new comedian _____ entertainer.
- **a.** a most amusing
- **b.** a highly amused
- **c.** the most amused
- **d.** so amusing an

63. I doubt he'll call, but _____ , please remind him about the party.
   a. should he do
   b. when he does
   c. if he did
   d. in case he does

64. I called the twins yesterday, but _____ of them was at home.
   a. none
   b. nobody
   c. neither
   d. both

65. Would you happen to know where _____ after the professor has graded our exams?
   a. would post the results
   b. the results will be posted
   c. the results are posting
   d. would be posted the results

66. If you're looking for an exotic vacation spot, Bali is the place _____ .
   a. to go
   b. you went
   c. for going
   d. you should go there

67. _____ if you checked with Ann to find out when the meeting starts.
   a. It would be better
   b. You'd better
   c. You'd have been better
   d. It was better

68. _____ to move to California was something that surprised all of us.
   a. After her decision
   b. Having decided
   c. Her deciding
   d. She decided

69. In the old days, people _____ use a hand crank to start their cars.
   a. were used to
   b. used to
   c. would have been used to
   d. got used to

70. _____ her, I can't possibly tell you what I think of the new assistant.
   a. Not having met
   b. Because of not meeting
   c. To have not met
   d. So as not to meet

REMEMBER:

The answer you choose must fit into the question stem both grammatically and logically. If you've chosen "b" for item 63, you'd better think again!

71. For some people, traveling is all about _____ new places and cultures.
   a. to discover
   b. the discovering
   c. discovered
   d. discovering

72. The boss is really angry. _____ he ask her to correct the mistake, but twice!
   a. Not only did
   b. Not once did
   c. Not only once
   d. Once didn't

73. Her students' unexpected birthday gift made the teacher feel _____ .
   a. appreciable
   b. appreciating
   c. appreciatively
   d. appreciated

74. Of the ten used cars we've seen, _____ is worth the asking price.
   a. and none of them
   b. not one of them
   c. none of which
   d. which none of them

75. He couldn't help but notice how kind _____ in the days following his wife's death.
   a. had everyone been
   b. of everyone to be
   c. everyone had been
   d. that was everyone

76. To trace the package, you need to know the exact address of the person _____ .
   a. that sent
   b. to whom you sent
   c. it was sent to
   d. you sent to

77. Did you hear about that up-and-coming actor? _____ on Broadway next month.
  a. He appears as if he's
  b. He's appearing
  c. He appears that he's
  d. It appears to be

78. We'll be able to get back to work _____ the power goes on.
  a. once
  b. since
  c. unless
  d. by the time

79. I'd like the next laptop I buy _____ super thin and light as a feather.
  a. to be one that is
  b. which is one that will be
  c. will be one that is
  d. it will be

80. The roof of a skyscraper is a great vantage point _____ view the entire city.
  a. that you can
  b. from which one can
  c. so as to
  d. where you are to

81. His rude behavior is a perfect example of _____ a new employer.
  a. not impressing
  b. not to impress
  c. what not to impress
  d. how not to impress

82. I hear Jonathan is trying to buy the house _____ grew up.
  a. that he
  b. from which
  c. in which he
  d. where

83. She's hoping to study abroad, but her parents aren't _____ agreement.
  a. of
  b. in
  c. with
  d. on

84. _____ he's just lost his job, they will probably not be going on vacation next month.
  a. Provided
  b. Given that
  c. On condition that
  d. As a result of

85. When she promised to pay you back next week, did you actually believe _____ ?
  a. her doing it
  b. that she did it
  c. she would
  d. her to do it

86. The company's objective _____ its sales over the next two years.
  a. is to double
  b. will be doubling
  c. will have doubled
  d. has doubled

87. I enjoyed the writer's new thriller, but it wasn't _____ story as his last one was.
  a. a more exciting
  b. so exciting a
  c. as exciting a
  d. such an exciting

88. He _____ to leave his bike unlocked in such a tough neighborhood.
  a. had known better
  b. had better know
  c. would have been better if he were
  d. should have known better than

89. Mary's been abroad for two months, but she'll be home _____ the next few days.
  a. between
  b. among
  c. within
  d. by

90. _____ about the danger, we might never have taken the risk.
  a. Had we stopped to think
  b. Having stopped thinking
  c. Could we have stopped thinking
  d. Stopping to think

"Clozing" remarks

Don't spend too much time on any one question. If you're not sure of an answer, guess and move on. Plan to spend about 10 minutes total on the two passages. Any more, and you're using up time that could be put to better use on the four Reading passages.

CLOZE

Passage 1 is about the Bibliotheca Alexandrina.

After two decades of planning and construction, the Bibliotheca Alexandrina now stands on Alexandria's waterfront, just 130 feet from the sea. Opened to the __(91)__ on April 23rd, 2002, the library was designed as a tilting disk __(92)__ from the ground. __(93)__ seven levels above ground and four below, the scale of the building is thus minimized at close quarters, __(94)__ it does not overwhelm the visitor. __(95)__ to be an architectural signature like Australia's Sydney Opera House and Spain's Guggenheim Museum in Bilbao, the library is __(96)__ worldwide attention, not only for its bold architecture __(97)__ for its __(98)__ to the site of the most famous library of the ancient world.

But can Egypt, a poor country by any standard, __(99)__ a library __(100)__ of the one that housed the wisdom of Ancient Greece? "Creativity and culture are sound bases for development," responded the library's former project manager. "We make our buildings," he said, quoting Churchill, "and after, our buildings make us."

91. **a.** public **b.** society **c.** audience **d.** population

92. **a.** reaching **b.** rising **c.** leaping **d.** increasing

93. **a.** Elevated **b.** Its **c.** All **d.** With

94. **a.** so **b.** because **c.** when **d.** unless

95. **a.** Seeming **b.** Intended **c.** Designing **d.** Going

96. **a.** become **b.** having **c.** attracted **d.** drawing

97. **a.** but **b.** even **c.** just **d.** and

98. **a.** association **b.** location **c.** proximity **d.** similarity

99. **a.** build **b.** attend **c.** achieve **d.** maintain

100. **a.** proud **b.** capable **c.** worthy **d.** aware

Passage 2 is about mosquitoes and malaria.

In the United States, an encounter with summer's most annoying pest – the mosquito – is trouble enough, but in many parts of the world, it can be deadly. Malaria __(101)__ 300 to 500 million people every year and kills nearly 3 million, __(102)__ 1 million children. A single mosquito bite can __(103)__ the disease, which causes fever, chills, nausea and, in some __(104)__, death. This disease, which was eradicated in the United States during the 1950s, is one of the world's biggest __(105)__ of children.

The greatest problem impeding the struggle against malaria is the rise of resistance to the drugs that treat the disease. In many parts of the world, the drugs __(106)__ commonly used to treat malaria no __(107)__ work, and doctors are __(108)__ to more expensive alternatives – and in some countries __(109)__ these are failing to work. As a result, countries that had previously seen a __(110)__ in malaria cases are now seeing a resurgence.

101. **a.** contacts **b.** injures **c.** infects **d.** influences

102. **a.** particularly **b.** including **c.** about **d.** even

103. **a.** spread **b.** emit **c.** give **d.** catch

104. **a.** times **b.** occasions **c.** instants **d.** cases

105. **a.** threats **b.** killers **c.** victims **d.** fears

106. **a.** were **b.** which **c.** most **d.** it

107. **a.** longer **b.** sooner **c.** more **d.** further

108. **a.** using **b.** turning **c.** experimenting **d.** going

109. **a.** which **b.** where **c.** only **d.** even

110. **a.** rise **b.** decline **c.** tendency **d.** cure

VOCABULARY [**Note:** This vocabulary section is a review of words introduced in Practice Tests 5-7.]

111. He's usually very serious, but this time we could see _____ of amusement in his eyes.
- **a.** an omen
- **b.** a hint
- **c.** a hunch
- **d.** a fantasy

112. You'd better put the potato chips away or else they'll get _____ .
- **a.** frothy
- **b.** crunchy
- **c.** chewy
- **d.** soggy

113. He hadn't planned to steal the CD; he just did it on _____ .
- **a.** collision
- **b.** impulse
- **c.** impact
- **d.** contact

114. John's report was thorough and insightful. He deserves a real _____ .
- **a.** slap on the wrist
- **b.** pat on the back
- **c.** peck on the cheek
- **d.** pain in the neck

115. It's hard to tell what he's feeling as he rarely _____ any emotion.
- **a.** signals
- **b.** points
- **c.** waves
- **d.** displays

116. It's natural for students to worry about whether they will _____ or not at a new school.
- **a.** measure up
- **b.** sprout up
- **c.** show up
- **d.** stand up

117. Your theory is just that – a theory unsupported by facts. It just doesn't _____ .
- **a.** make waves
- **b.** hold water
- **c.** keep pace
- **d.** stay afloat

118. As the youngest of five children, she's used to wearing clothes that have been _____ to her.
- **a.** handed down
- **b.** handed in
- **c.** handed out
- **d.** handed over

Look before you leap!

Always work carefully and take nothing for granted! In item 112, for example, if you just zoom in on "potato chips" and ignore the rest of the stem, you might be tempted to choose "crunchy" as the answer. If you read the stem carefully, you'll see that the context requires a word that means just the opposite!

119. It would be nice if we could _____ , but he has a bad habit of stretching the truth.
- **a.** take him down a peg or two
- **b.** take him up on it
- **c.** take him at his word
- **d.** take him for granted

120. I'm so sorry. I didn't mean to leave your name off this list. It was done _____ .
- **a.** aggressively
- **b.** vehemently
- **c.** inadvertently
- **d.** graciously

121. As more and more clues came to light, the mystery began to _____ .
- **a.** surmise
- **b.** accumulate
- **c.** persevere
- **d.** unravel

122. The _____ of the city surprises her. She's met people from all walks of life.
- **a.** diversity
- **b.** exuberance
- **c.** abundance
- **d.** quantity

123. My friend Michael eats so much that you'd think he was a _____ pit!
- **a.** buoyant
- **b.** overflowing
- **c.** bottomless
- **d.** irrepressible

124. I heard on the news this morning that the dictator was _____ by a military coup.
- **a.** receded
- **b.** toppled
- **c.** inundated
- **d.** scorched

125. The _____ teenager looked a bit like a scarecrow: all arms and legs!

a. gangly
b. stout
c. flabby
d. plump

126. The new president vows to cut spending to make up for the _____ in the budget.

a. deficit
b. dearth
c. profusion
d. deficiency

127. The flags outside the stadium were _____ in the breeze.

a. smoldering
b. spewing
c. billowing
d. incinerating

128. The military base is restricted and strictly _____ to unauthorized civilians.

a. within limits
b. out of line
c. on edge
d. off limits

129. No one could explain why her blood pressure _____ to such a dangerously low level.

a. dissolved
b. reflected
c. hovered
d. plummeted

130. The Rosetta Stone enabled experts to _____ many elements of hieroglyphic writing.

a. conjecture
b. decipher
c. deduce
d. compile

131. The widower named his only son as the _____ of his life insurance policy.

a. beneficiary
b. descendant
c. benefactor
d. consequence

132. The bad odor coming from the sewer _____ everyone who walked by it.

a. dispelled
b. expelled
c. repelled
d. compelled

133. After working out at the gym, she always takes a hot shower to _____ her aching muscles.

a. alleviate
b. comfort
c. console
d. relieve

134. Her friends cautioned her that starting a new job would be _____ with difficulties.

a. fraught
b. confronted
c. endowed
d. afflicted

135. On Saturday morning the busy open-air market is always _____ with activity.

a. crowded
b. clogged
c. swarming
d. congested

136. Alternative energy must be exploited to compensate for the world's _____ coal and oil reserves.

a. deceased
b. dwindling
c. perishable
d. vulnerable

137. After working on his car engine all morning, his hands were covered in _____ .

a. soot
b. fumes
c. smog
d. grease

138. The fire was so intense that it literally _____ the building and everything in it.

a. incinerated
b. generated
c. kindled
d. induced

139. The children shrunk in fear as the _____ police officer approached them.

a. fragile
b. abashed
c. intimidating
d. reticent

140. The survivors of the crash took _____ in the fact that they had come out alive.

a. pains
b. aim
c. heart
d. pity

141. An actor with an artistic _____ is said to be difficult to deal with.
- **a.** temperament
- **b.** conduct
- **c.** mentality
- **d.** integrity

142. The rumor going around is nothing but _____ gossip. Don't believe a word of it!
- **a.** conscientious
- **b.** buoyant
- **c.** distinguished
- **d.** malicious

143. Please don't drive home from the party unless you are 100% _____ .
- **a.** lenient
- **b.** austere
- **c.** sober
- **d.** frantic

144. The dispute is currently in _____ . A settlement is expected in the next few days.
- **a.** moderation
- **b.** mediation
- **c.** consensus
- **d.** jeopardy

145. The nervous job candidate took a deep breath and tried to _____ herself.
- **a.** subdue
- **b.** compose
- **c.** wrestle
- **d.** strike

146. If you want to look good after a long flight, wear clothing that doesn't _____ .
- **a.** wilt
- **b.** shrivel
- **c.** wrinkle
- **d.** shrink

147. The driver braked hard, and the car _____ to a halt just in time to avoid an accident.
- **a.** lurched
- **b.** lumbered
- **c.** scampered
- **d.** stumbled

148. The children _____ with laughter when the clowns rushed onto the stage.
- **a.** barked
- **b.** purred
- **c.** shrieked
- **d.** hissed

149. She's a vain woman who can't help _____ herself whenever she passes a mirror.
- **a.** preening
- **b.** immersing
- **c.** cultivating
- **d.** modifying

150. The children looked forward to their upcoming vacation with great _____ .
- **a.** valor
- **b.** conduct
- **c.** virtue
- **d.** ardor

READING

Never turn in your answer sheet with unanswered questions. If you're running out of time, fill in an answer for any item you haven't done. You have a 25% chance of guessing correctly, and you won't be penalized for mistakes. (Experts recommend using the same choice for all your guesses - e.g., all b's or all c's.)

Passage 1 is about college career centers.

College career centers are a student's best link to local employers and alumni networks. Many centers have job search websites that allow employers to peruse student résumés and post job openings aimed specifically at the college population. They are also a central resource for helping students complete work-study requirements and find part-time jobs and internships that could easily give them the edge in landing a competitive position while they are still in school.

Jason, a senior at a Texas university, wishes he had turned to his school's career center sooner than he did. Jason had been working his way through school, but until his third year, he rarely made more than $7 an hour. And the work – waiting tables and doing grunt work for professors – was hardly on a professional track. Fed up, he posted his résumé on the campus career center's website. Within a week, he had landed a summer internship with the strategic planning department of the international division of a large American telecommunications firm. Not only did he earn $15 an hour, but he also learned about the company and got to travel to Puerto Rico for work. "I was making a few thousand a month last summer, which will now cover rent, gas, and my cell phone bills this year," he says.

Indeed, it is the career centers' connection to internships that makes them an essential stop for the ambitious student. The centers post internship opportunities, help with applications, and arrange for students to receive course credit for their work. "Doing an internship pays off not only with salary and class credit, but it pays big advantages when students enter the job market," says the director of the internship office at a university in Utah. Employers rated internships as one of the most effective ways to attract and hire college graduates, according to a recent study by the National Association of Colleges and Employers. The study also found that employers extended full-time offers to 58 percent of their interns and offered higher starting salaries to graduates with internship experience.

151. What is true of college career centers?

- **a.** They advise employers on which students would make good employees.
- **b.** They guarantee that every student will find a full-time job after graduation.
- **c.** They make it possible for students and employers to find each other.
- **d.** They help students find full-time employment while they are still in school.

152. Why had Jason become discouraged?

- **a.** It had taken a long time for anyone to notice his résumé on the website.
- **b.** He hadn't realized that the career center could find him an internship.
- **c.** He was convinced that his professors were taking advantage of him
- **d.** The jobs he had done were low-paying and unrelated to his career plans.

153. What does Jason regret?

- **a.** having had to spend the summer working
- **b.** having had to work his way though school
- **c.** not having utilized the career center earlier
- **d.** having to work the summer to earn extra money

154. According to the study, what is true of students who do internships?

- **a.** More than half are offered positions with the same company.
- **b.** They are inclined to be more ambitious than their classmates.
- **c.** They are usually more highly paid than regular employees.
- **d.** They are not paid until after they graduate from college.

155. How can students find out about internship possibilities?

- **a.** by posting their résumé with their college's career center
- **b.** by calling the National Association of Colleges and Employers
- **c.** by searching listings on the website of a school's career center
- **d.** by first having completed their work-study requirements

Passage 2 is about ecotourism.

Since the early 1980s, more and more people are embracing ecotourism, leading many travel observers to regard it as wildly successful. But recent studies show a more complicated picture.

Take the case of the ecotourism industry that's grown up around the endangered rock iguana on Allen Cay in the Bahamas. When researchers arrived in the mid-1970s, male iguanas outnumbered females two to one, an imbalance they attributed to poaching by local fishermen. Historically, fishermen captured iguanas to sell or eat, and females were easier to trap because they would guard their nests rather than flee intruders. Enter ecotourism. As protection of the island's main attraction increased, poaching declined and the gender imbalance quickly righted itself. But then it tipped the other way: as ecotourism increased, male iguana numbers declined. To quantify this, in the year 2000 researchers tagged the largest male iguanas in two ecotourism areas. By 2005, the number of tagged iguanas at one site had fallen from 30 to 9. Using death rates calculated from the previous 20 years, the researchers had predicted that 16 would survive. At the other site, researchers found none of the 17 tagged iguanas, though they had expected 9 animals to remain. Since males tend to be aggressive and interact more with human visitors than females do, researchers surmised that the missing males had fallen prey to visitors who had left behind hazardous and potentially lethal material such as spoiled food or Styrofoam. But when some of the males were spotted on nearby islets that they couldn't possibly have reached themselves, it became clear that other forces were also at work. Further investigation bore out that well-meaning ecotour guides had removed many of the large, aggressive males from the most popular sites – an action that might bode ill for another endangered species. To wit, some of the tagged reptiles were found on islets that are home to an endangered species of seabirds called Audubon's shearwaters. Because the iguanas and the birds require similar nesting territories, researchers now fear the iguanas might crowd out the seabirds.

In other words, ecotourism sometimes rescues one species at the expense of others. But this is just the tip of the iceberg. Over-visitation can lead not only to declining animal populations, but also to environment-threatening waste-disposal problems, not to mention the displacement of local populations and other woes. It's not always a win-win situation.

156. What surprised the researchers when they first counted the tagged iguanas in 2005?

- **a.** that there were even fewer tagged males than they had predicted.
- **b.** that so many had been killed by the actions of thoughtless ecotourists.
- **c.** that many of the tagged males had swum to nearby islets.
- **d.** that fishermen were now starting to poach males more than females.

157. What is true of the rock iguana population on Allen Cay in the mid-1970s?

- **a.** Males were more highly prized by poachers because they were harder to catch.
- **b.** There were an equal number of male and female iguanas.
- **c.** The female iguana population was half that of the male population.
- **d.** They were the main attraction of the local ecotourism industry.

158. Which phrase best sums up the main idea of the passage?

- **a.** There is now ample proof that ecotourism is a huge success.
- **b.** Ecotourism on Allen Cays has saved the rock iguana from extinction.
- **c.** Ecotourists need to be better educated and strictly monitored.
- **d.** Ecotourism often brings with it a host of unforeseen local problems.

159. What does the writer imply about the ecotour guides in paragraph 2?

- **a.** They knowingly tried to sabotage the researcher's efforts.
- **b.** They did not like that fact that the iguanas had been tagged.
- **c.** They should not have moved the male iguanas off the main island.
- **d.** They were afraid that the male iguanas would harm the tourists.

160. What do researchers believe?

- **a.** The iguanas have already taken over the nests of the Audubon's shearwaters.
- **b.** It is unlikely that Audubon's shearwaters will thrive in the presence of iguanas.
- **c.** Audubon's shearwaters are a serious threat to male iguanas.
- **d.** The shearwaters will quickly adapt to the presence of the iguanas.

Passage 3 is about Rosalind Franklin.

By 1952, much was known about DNA. What was not yet known was what the elusive molecule looked like or how it performed its amazing hereditary function. This would change in the course of a single year. The now familiar double helical structure of DNA and the base-pairing crucial to its hereditary function were deciphered in 1953. The individuals most commonly associated with this remarkable feat are James Watson and Francis Crick. Maurice Wilkins also played a crucial role in the discovery, for which he would later share the 1962 Nobel Prize for Physiology and Medicine with Watson and Crick. But another important figure remains, without whom the discovery might not have been possible: the brilliant but short-lived Rosalind Franklin.

Born in July of 1920, Franklin went to work as a research associate for John Randall at King's College in 1951. A well-respected chemist, she had already made vital contributions to the understanding of the structure of graphite and other carbon compounds. In *The Double Helix*, James Watson's account of the discovery of DNA's structure, Franklin is depicted as an underling of Maurice Wilkins, but in fact the two scientists were peers in Randall's lab. And it was to Franklin that Randall had given the task of elucidating DNA's structure. The technique with which she set out to do this is called x-ray crystallography. In the early 1950s, scientists were just learning how to apply the technique to map biological molecules. After complicated analysis, she discovered (and was the first to state) that the sugar-phosphate backbone of DNA lies on the outside of the molecule. She also elucidated the basic helical structure of the molecule.

Randall presented Franklin's data and conclusions at a routine seminar and – without his knowledge – her work was passed on to Watson and Crick, her competitors at Cambridge University. The scientists used her data and that of others to build their ultimately correct and detailed description of DNA's structure in 1953. Franklin was not bitter but pleased, and quickly published an article corroborating the Watson-Crick model. Many have concurred that it is a shame she never received due credit for her essential role in determining DNA's structure, either during her lifetime or after her untimely death at age 37 due to cancer.

161. Why is the year 1952 so notable in the history of DNA research?
- **a.** Researchers discovered the existence of DNA.
- **b.** Scientists began to explore DNA's role in heredity.
- **c.** Rosalind Franklin discovered the structure of DNA.
- **d.** Major progress was made in understanding DNA's structure.

162. According to the writer, why did Randall task Franklin with determining the structure of DNA?
- **a.** He wanted to show she was just as capable as the men in his lab.
- **b.** He was angry at Watson for portraying her unfairly in his book.
- **c.** She had done work on the structure of other carbon compounds.
- **d.** She was the only scientist who had ever used x-ray crystallography.

163. How did Franklin react when she learned of Watson and Crick's discovery?
- **a.** She wrote an article in support of their historic findings.
- **b.** She was angry, but did not do anything to discredit them.
- **c.** She did everything she could to disprove their theories.
- **d.** She criticized them for having used her data unethically.

164. What does the passage imply about Watson and Crick?
- **a.** They should not have been awarded the Nobel Prize in 1962.
- **b.** They were justified in not having shared the credit with Franklin.
- **c.** Their attitude was partly responsible for Franklin's untimely death.
- **d.** Their access to the data of Franklin and others aided their efforts.

165. What point does the writer make about Rosalind Franklin's role in DNA history?
- **a.** Her work, though outstanding, was ignored because she was a woman.
- **b.** Her research was promising but not as significant as Watson and Crick's.
- **c.** She ought to have been given more credit for her role in the discovery.
- **d.** It's a shame that ill health prevented her from making the discovery.

Passage 4 is about methane.

There are two key things to know about methane and its relationship to global warming. It is about 20 times more potent as a greenhouse gas than carbon dioxide, and there are massive stores of it locked away under the permafrost of the northern hemisphere. Methane is produced naturally by the decay of water-logged vegetation. Over thousands of years, it has accumulated underground at northern latitudes and has effectively been taken out of circulation by the permafrost acting as an impermeable lid. Now there are signs that this lid is leaking.

Like carbon dioxide, methane concentrations in the atmosphere have risen significantly since the Industrial Revolution, increasing from about 700 parts per billion in 1800 to about 1,790 parts per billion today. Much of the increase is attributed to human activities, notably oil and gas exploration and agriculture. At the start of the 21st century, average global methane concentrations seemed to level out, probably due to advances in Russian gas exploration. However, in 2007, for the first time in more than a decade, scientists recorded a spike in global levels, putting everyone on their toes. A year later, scientists on a research ship that sailed the length of Russia's northern coast reported extreme concentrations of methane – sometimes 100 times more than normal – over several areas covering thousands of square miles of the Siberian continental shelf. In some places, they observed areas of sea foaming with gas bubbling up through "methane chimneys" rising from the sea floor - a sign that the sub-sea layer of permafrost has melted, allowing methane to rise from underground deposits formed before the last ice age.

What makes methane so potentially dangerous is that its release from under the permafrost could accelerate global warming. This in turn would speed the thawing of the permafrost, releasing even more methane. Scientists believe this has happened in the geological past with devastating consequences for the global climate and life.

The good news is that methane degrades quickly in the environment, with an average lifetime of about 12 years compared to the 100 years of carbon dioxide. The bad news is that we do not understand how the methane stores in the north will behave as the region experiences more extensive thaws. The fear is that the amounts released will make global warming far worse than expected.

166. According to information in the text, what is true about methane?
- **a.** It degrades at the same rate as carbon dioxide.
- **b.** It is not a significant by-product of human activity.
- **c.** It has the potential to speed global warming.
- **d.** It was not present in the atmosphere prior to 1800.

167. What has given scientists new cause for concern?
- **a.** evidence that methane has begun to seep through the once-solid permafrost
- **b.** the discovery of previously unknown deposits of methane under the sea
- **c.** recent developments in Russia's gas exploration efforts
- **d.** signs that methane levels are continuing to level off

168. What fact does geological evidence seem to point to?
- **a.** The melting of the permafrost is not unprecedented.
- **b.** The problem is not quite as serious as it sounds.
- **c.** Carbon dioxide is a greater threat than methane.
- **d.** If the earth warms, it will not cool off again.

169. What happened in 2007?
- **a.** Scientists were eye-witnesses to the melting of the permafrost.
- **b.** There was an unexpected, dramatic increase in global methane levels.
- **c.** Global methane levels dropped unexpectedly in a number of areas.
- **d.** Scientists realized that the northern coast of Russia needed to be studied carefully.

170. Which phrase best describes the tone of the article?
- **a.** cautiously optimistic
- **b.** openly critical
- **c.** factual and objective
- **d.** subjective and alarmist

Vocabulary Enhancement

Edges, Limits, and Other Fine Lines

*In Reading Passage 1, the phrase "internships could easily **give students the edge**" (i.e., give them a distinct advantage) brings to mind a number of other expressions with the words **edge, limit**, and **line**. The words, of course, are close in meaning, but let's see if we can give you a good feel for the distinct ways in which each is used.*

A **Basic Distinctions** – Fill in each blank with one of the words in the box. One of the words is used less frequently than the other two.

edge *limit* *line*

1. ______________ In geometry, it's a thing that connects two points.
2. ______________ On a knife, ax, or sword, it's the sharp cutting part of the blade.
3. ______________ On a contract, it's what you sign your name on at the end (e.g., *a dotted or solid ~*).
4. ______________ On a cliff, table, or chair, it's the outer boundary. Don't go beyond, or you'll fall off.
5. ______________ At the bank or the bus stop, it's a row of people; in a poem or book, it's a row of words.
6. ______________ People who shave know that this is what a razor blade has, which is either sharp or dull.
7. ______________ At home, it's what you hang your laundry out to dry on if you don't use a clothes drier.
8. ______________ On the road, it's the greatest amount of speed that's allowed by law; it's also a point or series of points beyond which sth does not extend (e.g., *the city ~, the ~ of sb's patience*).

B **Power of Suggestion** – Combine each word in the box with *edge, limit,* or *line* to form the compound noun or phrases suggested by each photo.

bottom *check-out* *credit* *clothes* *competitive* *cutting* *dotted* *life* *product* *production* *serrated* *sky* *speed* *time* *water's*

A ______________

B ______________

C ______________

D ______________

E ______________

F ______________

G ______________

H ______________

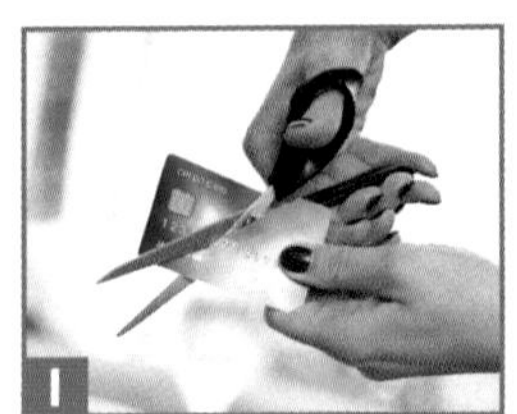
I ______________

J ______________

K ______________

L ______________

M ______________

N ______________

O ______________

C **Expressions with *Edge*** – For each group, fill in each blank with one of the expressions.

on edge | *on the edge of* | *on/at the cutting edge of* | *over the edge*

1. Understandably, the latest terrorist attacks have everyone ______________________ (i.e., worried, anxious).
2. If he doesn't find a job soon, it will push him right ______________________ (i.e., past his breaking point).
3. The firm prides itself on being innovative; it's been ______________________ . (i.e., at the forefront, in a leading position) of cancer research for decades. Apparently, they're ______________________ (i.e., just about to experience, on the verge of) a big breakthrough.

be edged out | *be edged with* | *have an edge* | *take the edge off*

1. You can tell she's still upset. Her voice ______________________ (i.e., is tinged or colored with) anger.
2. Have an apple. It will ______________________ (i.e., reduce, lessen) your appetite.
3. You've been here the longest so you ______________________ (i.e., have an advantage) over us. But it looks like Ed wants your job. Be careful or you'll ______________________ (i.e., be pushed out little by little).

D **Expressions with *Line* and *Limit*** – Fill in each blank with the correct form of one of the expressions.

be out of line | *be on the line* | *draw the line* | *lay it on the line* | *toe the line*

1. You ______________________ (i.e., acted inappropriately) at today's meeting. The bosses are friendly types, but they ______________________ at (i.e., refuse to tolerate) being openly criticized.
2. Let me just ______________________ (i.e., talk frankly and openly). If you want to keep your job, you'll have to ______________________ (i.e., obey orders, do what's expected of you). If you don't, your job ______________________ (i.e., is at risk).

off limits | *The sky's the limit!* | *to the limit* | *within limits*

1. She's trying to lose weight, so most high-calorie foods are strictly ______________________ (i.e., not allowed). Other than that, she can eat pretty much anything – ______________________ (i.e., in moderation), of course.
2. The factory has a lot of orders at the moment, so everyone is working ______________________ (i.e., to the maximum degree possible).
3. The boss wants to go all out on the fall ad campaign. He told me himself: "I don't want you to spare any expense this time. ______________________ !" (i.e., There is no limit!)

E **Free Association** – In your notebooks, write 2-3 sentences to describe each photo. Use words and expressions that you've met in tasks A-D. Get creative. The possibilities are limitless!

A

B

C

D

Vocabulary Consolidation

PASSAGES IN REVIEW

This section reviews a sampling of words you have met in the Cloze and Reading passages in Practice Tests 5-8. For each group, fill in the blanks with the appropriate words. For verbs, remember to use the correct form.

A Notorious Nouns

causes *champion* *collapse* *concentrations* *culprit* *dynamics* *odds* *reaches* *swing*

1. The end of 2008 saw experts scrambling to avoid the ______________ of the global economy. To many, it seemed like drastic actions were being taken before the ______________ of the crisis were fully understood.
2. The Hubble Space Telescope has captured images of the far ______________ of the universe.
3. The young senator is widely recognized as a ______________ of civil rights and other humanitarian ______________. He is exciting voters young and old. Observers say that the ______________ are good that his candidacy will create a ______________ of support away from the president's party.
4. Scientists are concerned about rising ______________ of methane in the atmosphere. They believe that the gas is a worse ______________ than carbon dioxide when it comes to global warming.

B Vexing Verbs

absorb *bolster* *evaporate* *oversee* *quench* *radiate* *soothe* *trigger* *undergo*

1. The job of a plant's roots is to ______________ water from the soil.
2. She served them a nice tall glass of iced tea to ______________ their thirst.
3. Her son was fascinated to learn that the sun ______________ heat, which in turn warms the earth and can even cause puddles to ______________ back into the air.
4. He'll have to ______________ tests so his doctors can determine exactly what ______________ the heart attack. Meanwhile, he's taking medication to ______________ his chest pains.
5. John has been asked to ______________ a multi-million-dollar government project. The hope is that thousands of jobs will be created, which will help ______________ the local economy.

C Addling Adjectives

declining *devastating* *dormant* *evasive* *idle*
indigenous *migratory* *prone* *sufficient* *vulnerable*

1. Ed's parents were understandably upset by his ______________ answers. They've decided to ground him until he comes up with a more ______________ explanation as to why he had stayed out so late.
2. Our guide told us that the birds we had been observing were ______________ birds that were just passing through on their way south. They are not ______________ to this area.
3. The volcano, ______________ for over 100 years, has recently begun to show signs of activity beneath the surface. An eruption would have ______________ consequences on the area.
4. I'd take what she says with a grain of salt. She's ______________ to exaggeration and you, my friend, are obviously ______________ to her considerable charm!
5. In response to ______________ orders, the company has shut down several of its factories. The high-tech machinery is just sitting there, lying ______________ and gathering dust.

COMIC RELIEF

This section reviews words you have met in Vocabulary Enhancements 5-8.

A Amusing Associations – For each group, find the word or phrase in the box that is suggested by each prompt.

a fog *a marathon* *hail* *honey* *steam* *time*

1. ______________ – You'll have this coming out of your ears if a friend breaks your favorite CD.
2. ______________ – It's what retired people hope to have on their hands (but usually don't).
3. ______________ – It's something people like to drizzle on toasted bread, over yogurt, or in tea.
4. ______________ – Prepare to feel like someone is hurling pebbles at you if you get caught in a storm of this.
5. ______________ – You might feel like you're in one of these if you're coming down with a head cold.
6. ______________ – You're probably feeling dehydrated if you've just run one of these.

hand over fist *like the back of your hand* *on edge* *on the line* *over the edge* *to the limit*

1. ______________ – It's where your job will be if you don't finish that report on time!
2. ______________ – It's where you'll be pushed if your teacher tells you to learn 500 new words a day!
3. ______________ – It's how every business person hopes to make money.
4. ______________ – It's how you'll probably feel on the morning you take the ECPE.
5. ______________ – It's how people work when they really want to achieve something.
6. ______________ – It's how you should know someone before you agree to marry them!

B A Dozen Daffy Definitions – Match the sentence endings (a-l) to the sentence beginnings (1-12) to form logical (if sometimes unusual) statements. Be ready to explain your answers.

1. ______ A strict disciplinarian
2. ______ An obedient office worker
3. ______ An impertinent child
4. ______ A nosy detective
5. ______ A job-hungry college graduate
6. ______ A well-fed squirrel
7. ______ An ill-prepared job candidate
8. ______ A conscientious accountant
9. ______ An energetic housewife
10. ______ A wilted houseplant
11. ______ A parched landscape
12. ______ A concerned cosmetician

a. has finely-tuned foraging skills.
b. is concerned about a company's bottom line.
c. lacks a distinct competitive edge.
d. is usually dying to be watered.
e. offers hydrating remedies for wrinkled skin.
f. scours pots and pans till they shine.
g. is frequently out of line.
h. almost always toes the line.
i. frequently lays it on the line.
j. probes into people's pasts.
k. seeks employment wherever it might arise.
l. is often the result of a prolonged drought.

PRICKLY PREPOSITIONS AND PARTICLES

The following extracts are taken from passages that you have encountered in Practice Test 8. Read each one quickly, and then fill in each blank with an appropriate preposition or particle

1. Opened _________ the public _________ April 23rd, 2002, the library was designed _________ a tilting disk rising _________ the ground. _________ seven levels _________ ground and four _________ , the scale _________ the building is thus minimized _________ close quarters, so it does not overwhelm the visitor. Intended to be an architectural signature _________ Australia's Sydney Opera House and Spain's Guggenheim Museum _________ Bilbao, the library is drawing worldwide attention, not only _________ its bold architecture but _________ its proximity _________ the site _________ the most famous library _________ the ancient world.

2. College career centers are a student's best link _________ local employers and alumni networks. … Jason, a senior _________ a Texas university, wishes he had turned _________ his school's career center sooner than he did. Jason had been working his way _________ school, but until his third year, he rarely made more than $7 an hour. And the work – waiting tables and doing grunt work _________ professors – was hardly _________ a professional track. Fed _________ , he posted his résumé _________ the campus career center's website. _________ a week, he had landed a summer internship _________ the strategic planning department _________ the international division _________ a large American telecommunications firm.

3. Since males tend to be aggressive and interact more _________ human visitors than females do, researchers surmised that the missing males had fallen prey _________ visitors who had left behind hazardous and potentially lethal material. … But when some _________ the males were spotted _________ nearby islets that they couldn't possibly have reached themselves, it became clear that other forces were also _________ work. Researchers suspected that well-meaning ecotour guides had removed many _________ the large, aggressive males _________ the most popular sites – an action that might bode ill _________ another endangered species. To wit, some _________ the tagged reptiles were found _________ islets that are home _________ an endangered species of seabirds called Audubon's shearwaters. Because the iguanas and the birds require similar nesting territories, researchers now fear the iguanas might crowd _________ the seabirds. … _____ other words, ecotourism sometimes rescues one species _________ the expense _________ others. But this is just the tip _____ the iceberg. Over-visitation can lead not only _________ declining animal populations, but also _________ environment-threatening waste-disposal problems, not to mention the displacement _________ local populations and other woes.

4. By 1952, much was known _________ DNA. What was not yet known was what the elusive molecule looked _________ or how it performed its amazing hereditary function. This would change _________ the course _________ a single year. The now familiar double helical structure of DNA and the base-pairing crucial _______ its hereditary function were deciphered _______ 1953. The individuals most commonly associated _________ this remarkable feat are James Watson and Francis Crick. Maurice Wilkins also played a crucial role _________ the discovery, _________ which he would later share the 1962 Nobel Prize _________ Physiology and Medicine _________ Watson and Crick. But another important figure remains, _________ whom the discovery might not have been possible.

5. _________ thousands _________ years methane has accumulated underground _________ northern latitudes and has effectively been taken _________ _________ circulation _________ the permafrost acting _________ an impermeable lid. Now there are signs that this lid is leaking. … _________ the start _________ the 21st century, average global methane concentrations seemed to level _________ , probably due _________ advances _________ Russian gas exploration. However, _________ 2007, _________ the first time _________ more than a decade, scientists recorded a spike _________ global levels, putting everyone _________ their toes.

PUZZLE TIME

The crossword is based on words you encountered in the Cloze and Reading passages of Tests 5-8. Use the words in the box and the Across and Down clues to help you solve the puzzle. The photos on the right should help you form a mental image of some of the answers. Write the words under the pictures to help you remember them for future use.

beckon career cast clarity clench concept core cork disdain entrepreneur frayed glittering gravity impact lethal palm pat pay dirt ransack scan scour sleet steam thaw transient vulnerable wave wilt

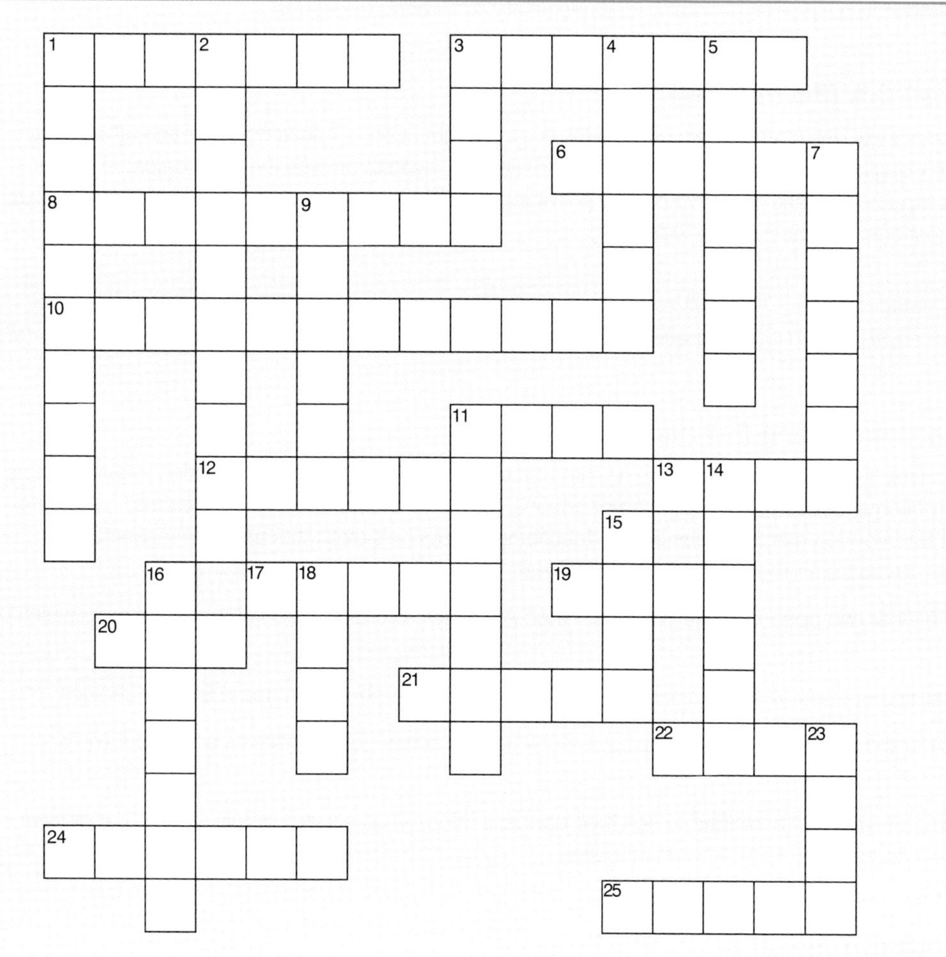

A ____________

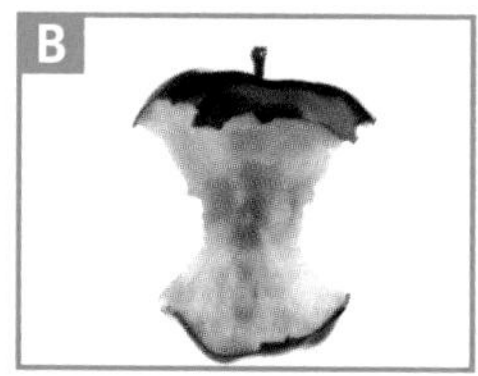

B ____________

C ____________

D ____________

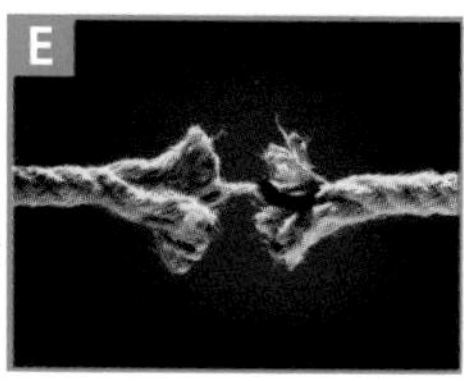

E ____________

F ____________

ACROSS

1. Without this, we'd float away.
3. general idea or principle
6. like an old rope or worn-out jeans
8. like a wandering beggar
10. ambitious business person
11. the bit at the center
12. potentially deadly, like poison
13. supermarket check-out activity
17. search carefully
19. hello or goodbye hand signal
20. a _____ on the back
21. tea kettle by-product
22. post-winter melt-down
24. signal someone to come near
25. frozen rain

DOWN

1. bright, shining
2. liable to be hurt or damaged
3. Sunbeams do this to shadows.
4. e.g., teacher, doctor, lawyer
5. It's your lucky day; you've struck this.
7. Arrogant people display lots of this.
9. what grenades do: explode on _____
11. the state of being clear
14. Do this to your hand to make a fist.
15. hand part
16. search desperately
18. Pop this to get to the champagne.
23. droop, like a thirsty plant

NOTE: Highlighted numbers denote clues with related picture clues.

Speaking Tests

WHAT TO EXPECT

The ECPE Speaking Test is designed to allow candidates to demonstrate their speaking ability by taking part in a five-stage task between two or three candidates and two examiners. (The three-candidate format is used only if there is an uneven number of candidates present at the testing center on the day of the test.)

The test consists of an introductory phase followed by a four-phase decision-making task. The stages are designed so that the candidates have a chance to speak individually as well as to engage in discussion. During Stages 1 and 5, one of the examiners will participate in the discussion. During Stages 2, 3, and 4, however, the candidates will do all of the talking related to the task. Examiner involvement in Stages 2, 3, and 4 is limited to giving instructions and, if necessary, answering questions.

Stage 1: Introduction and Small Talk (3-5 minutes)

This stage of the test is an ice-breaker activity designed to help candidates relax and get used to speaking with each other. When candidates enter the room, Examiner 1 begins with introductions and then initiates a conversation with the candidates on one or more general topics. Candidates are expected to take an active part by providing detailed responses and, if the opportunity arises, to ask each other and Examiner 1 questions. Topics might include:

school	family	hobbies	interest	vacation plans
work	friends	hometown	ambitions	travel

Stage 2: Summarizing and Recommending (5-7 minutes)

After briefly introducing the task, Examiner 1 hands each candidate an information sheet. Candidate A's information sheet contains two options; and Candidate B's information sheet contains two different options, for a total of four options. (In the three-candidate format, there is a total of six options.) Each option has 5-7 bullet points describing the option's strengths and weaknesses. Candidates are then given 2-3 minutes to read over their own information sheet.

Candidate A begins by summarizing his/her two options, while B listens. When A finishes, B offers a recommendation as to which of the two options is better.

Next, Candidate B summarizes his/her two options, while A listens and then makes a recommendation about B's two choices.

Finally, both candidates silently consider the recommendation they have received and decide for themselves which of their two options they prefer and why.

NOTE: During Stages 2 and 3, candidates are NOT permitted to see their partner's information sheet. For this reason, candidates are permitted to take notes, if they wish, to help them remember key points.

Stage 3: Reaching a Consensus (5-7 minutes)

Candidates A and B take turns reporting to each other which of their own two options they think is best. Then, together, they compare and contrast the options they have chosen until they come to an agreement on one single option.

Stage 4: Presenting and Convincing (5-7 minutes)

The goal of Stage 4 is for the candidates to present and justify their choice to Examiner 2, who takes on the role of a person of relatively high status: e.g., a school principal or company director.

First, the candidates are given 2-3 minutes to work together and plan a short presentation justifying the option they decided on. Each candidate should present two different reasons in support of their choice. At this point, candidates may look at each other's information sheets if they wish.

Then the candidates present the option and their reasons to Examiner 2.

Stage 5: Justifying and Defending (5-7 minutes)

In this stage, Examiner 2 questions the candidates about the decisions they have made. Together, the candidates justify and defend their decision.

HELPFUL HINTS

General

- The examiners are rating you on your ability to take part in an extended conversation. This means that, where possible, you should support your ideas with reasons and not just answer with a word or two. Throughout the task you should try to be as expansive as possible.
- Candidates are expected to contribute equally to the speaking activity, so try not to be either too dominant or too passive. If you sense your partner is hesitant to speak, be sensitive to this and ask his/her opinion after you finish speaking to help the conversation move forward.
- Remember to make eye contact with your partner and the examiners when they are involved in the task. It helps if you don't stare constantly at your information sheet and you keep your hair out of your eyes.
- Don't panic if you make an occasional mistake. Remember that fluency and your ability to make yourself understood are more important than 100% accuracy.

Stage 2

- As you begin the task, remember that there is no set answer; all four options are possible. In the end, the examiners are more concerned about the appropriateness and quality of the language you produce as you and your partner go through the process of narrowing down the choices and justifying your choice to the examiner.
- When you describe the options to your partner, try to summarize the list of features in your own words instead of just reading what is on the information sheet.
- You will not be allowed to look at your partner's information sheet during Stages 2 and 3, so when it's your turn to listen, you may want to take notes to help you recall what was said.

Stages 3-5

- Try to use a variety of strategies when you compare and contrast the options. For example, you could present the strengths of one of the options while focusing on the weaknesses of the other. Or you could begin by pointing out the advantages of both, and then examining the disadvantages. Doing this will allow you to use a wider range of functional language for speech events: e.g., considering both sides of an argument, stating opinions and preferences, making generalizations, expressing doubt and certainty, and so on. (For a list of common expressions, see "Fluency Builders" on page 194.)
- After presenting your opinion, it's always a good idea to invite your partner to comment on your ideas with phrases like "What do you think?" or "Do you agree?" This shows that you are making a conscious effort to include your partner and that you are taking an active role in developing the conversation.
- When building on what your partner or Examiner 2 has said, it's also a good idea to begin by acknowledging what was just said with polite phrases of agreement or disagreement. For example, "I totally agree because …" or "That's a good point, but I think we should also consider …" .

PAGE GUIDE TO SPEAKING TESTS

	Candidate A	Candidate B
Speaking Test 1	p. 195	p. 196
Speaking Test 2	p. 195	p. 196
Speaking Test 3	p. 195	p. 196
Speaking Test 4	p. 197	p. 198
Speaking Test 5	p. 197	p. 198
Speaking Test 6	p. 197	p. 198
Speaking Test 7	p. 199	p. 200
Speaking Test 8	p. 199	p. 200

Fluency Builders – Common Linking Expressions to Use When Speaking

Expressing an Opinion
To my mind, ...
As I see it, ...
It seems to me that ...
Personally speaking, ...
In my opinion, ...
If it were up to me, I'd say that ...
I feel strongly that ...

Recommending
I recommend choosing X instead of Y because ...
I'd suggest that you choose X over Y since ....
Perhaps you should/ought to consider ...
I'd advise you to choose X because ...

Stating Preferences
I think X is much better qualified than Y.
I prefer ...-ing to ... -ing
There's no comparison. I'd much rather ...
To be honest, I'd prefer to see ...

Giving Reasons/Justifying
I say this because ...
The main reason for my saying this is that ...
One of the reasons I decided on X is that ...

Sequencing Your Ideas
Well, for one thing ...
Another thing is that ...
I also believe that ...
What's more, ...
Finally, ... / Last but not least, ...

Considering Both Sides
On the one hand, ... On the other hand, ...
Some people might say that ..., but others say ....
Although it's true that ..., it could also be argued that ...
One way to look at the situation is to ... But you might also say that ...
It's true that ..., but there's also a downside/a major disadvantage to ...

Making Generalizations/Conclusions
All in all, ...
On the whole, ...
Finally, ...
To sum up, ...
When all is said and done, we think that ...

Expressing Certainty
Without a doubt, I'd say that ...
I'm certain/positive that ...
There's no doubt in my mind that ...

Expressing Uncertainty
It's a bit hard to say, but ...
I suppose that ...
My guess is that ...
It's possible that ..., but ...
I'm not sure, but if I had to say one way or the other ...

Asking for Clarification
Would you mind repeating that, please?
I'm sorry. What do you mean by ... ?
I'm sorry, I didn't quite catch/get that.
Sorry, I'm not sure I understood. Do you mean ...?

Adding Clarification
What I mean is, ...
What I'm trying to say is that ...
In other words, ...

Agreeing with Partner/Examiner
I totally agree. To my mind, ...
I'd have to go along with you there because ...
I'm strongly in favor of that as well because ...
You're quite right. That's exactly how I feel.

Politely Disagreeing with Partner/Examiner
I'm not so sure about that because ...
I'm afraid I don't totally agree. I say this because ...
Perhaps there's another way to see it. In my opinion ...
I see it a bit differently. You see, ...

Acknowledging Partner's/Examiner's Input
That's an interesting point. What I think is that ...
Well, it's a bit difficult to say but ...
I've always thought that myself.
Do you really think so? What about ...
Well, I suppose you've got a point, but ...
That's very interesting, but in my opinion ...

Fillers to Avoid Long Awkward Gaps
Just a second ... / Hold on a sec ...
Hmm, it's on the tip of my tongue ...
Umm - as I was saying ...
What's the word I wanted ... - oh, yes ...
You know, uh ... ,

SPEAKING TEST 1 Candidate A

Deciding on the Best Tourism Project for a Developing Country

Bella Beach Hotel

This is a list of points about the Bella Beach Hotel.

- 600 rooms; medium-priced
- Initial investment: $10 million
- 800-900 employees, 80% from local community
- Two towers, 20 floors each
- Golf course, casino, swimming pools, fine dining
- Environmental impact: high water usage and sewage issues

Tom's Rainforest Lodge

This is a list of points about Tom's Rainforest Lodge.

- 25 luxury bungalows; expensive
- Initial investment: $3 million
- 50-75 employees, 90% from local community
- Rafting, kayaking, treetop tours via elevated walkways
- Eco-friendly building; no living trees cut down
- Accessible only by air, private landing field

SPEAKING TEST 2 Candidate A

Choosing a Home for a Family with an 8-Year-Old Girl and 14-Year-Old Boy

Home 1

This is a list of points about Home 1.

- 2-bedroom apartment: $400,000
- In good location near city center
- Within walking distance of parents' jobs
- Good schools nearby
- Close to cultural attractions (museums, theaters, etc.)
- Busy neighborhood, sometimes noisy

Home 2

This is a list of points about Home 2.

- 3-bedroom home with yard: $250,000.
- In pleasant suburban area on outskirts of city
- 45-minute commute to work by public transportation ($12 a day)
- Good schools in the community
- Many parks and recreational areas nearby
- Large multiplex movie theater a mile away

SPEAKING TEST 3 Candidate A

Choosing a High School Student to Receive a $20,000 Science Scholarship

Student A

This is a list of points about Student A.

- Has a 3.9 grade point average (out of 4.0)
- Aptitude test scores (out of 800): 700 (math), 675 (reading)
- President of the school science club
- Won first prize at the senior science fair
- Tutors disadvantaged students twice a week
- 3 years ago, suspended for a week for smoking in school

Student B

This is a list of points about Student B.

- Has a 3.4 grade point average (out of 4.0)
- Aptitude test scores (out of 800): 760 (math), 740 (reading)
- Plays on high school soccer team
- Works weekends at local science research lab
- Has spent last 3 summers at a marine biology summer camp
- Acts bored and sometimes disrupts class

SPEAKING TEST 1 Candidate B

Deciding on the Best Tourism Project for a Developing Country

Hotel Belle Vue

This is a list of points about Hotel Belle Vue.

- 100 luxury rooms; very expensive
- Initial investment: $8 million
- About 250 employees, 75% from abroad
- Spa, fine dining, swimming pools, deep sea fishing
- Committed to protecting local nature reserve
- Beach only for hotel guests; not open to locals

Cloud Forest Cabins

This is a list of points about Cloud Forest Cabins.

- 30 cabins; priced for budget traveler
- Initial investment: $500,000
- About 50 employees, all local
- Showers and toilets in separate building
- Opportunities for guests to participate in environmental studies
- Accessible only by boat along jungle river

SPEAKING TEST 2 Candidate B

Choosing a Home for a Family with an 8-Year-Old Girl and 14-Year-Old Boy

Home 3

This is a list of points about Home 3.

- Large 3-bedroom apartment: $300,000
- Located in slightly run-down area of city
- 30-minute commute to work by public transportation ($5 a day)
- Schools OK, but not the best
- A lot of young families moving into neighborhood
- Not many recreational facilities for children

Home 4

This is a list of points about Home 4.

- 4-bedroom home with big garden: $225,000
- Located in beautiful rural area outside city
- 1-hour commute into city by car
- Schools small but good
- Many outdoor activities for whole family (fishing, hiking, etc.)
- Children far away from old friends

SPEAKING TEST 3 Candidate B

Choosing a High School Student to Receive a $20,000 Science Scholarship

Student C

This is a list of points about Student C.

- Has a 4.0 grade point average (out of 4.0)
- Aptitude test scores (out of 800): 760 (math), 725 (reading)
- Contributes occasionally to school newspaper
- Was semifinalist in national science fair last year
- Enjoys hiking and camping
- Does not actively participate in after-school clubs or activities

Student D

This is a list of points about Student D.

- Has a 3.6 grade point average (out of 4.0)
- Aptitude test scores (out of 800): 760 (math), 725 (reading)
- Plays cello in the school orchestra
- Created/marketed successful computer game
- Weekend volunteer at ecological research center
- Has had several unexcused absences from school this year

SPEAKING TEST 4 Candidate A

Deciding on a Chain Store to Open in a Small City of 50,000 People

Bargain Blast

This is a list of points about Bargain Blast.

- Large discount store (clothing, home decor, etc.)
- Would employ 500-600 people
- Low prices, good for consumers
- Would generate significant tax revenue for city
- Pay and benefits for employees are low
- Will force some local stores out of business

Fab Furniture

This is a list of points about Fab Furniture.

- Huge seller of inexpensive furniture of all kinds
- Would employ about 300 people
- Has a profit-sharing plan for employees
- Supports community recycling programs
- Known for poor quality of some products
- Will create traffic and congestion problems

SPEAKING TEST 5 Candidate A

Choosing the Best $15,000 Used Vehicle for a Family of Five

Hybrid Car

This is a list of points about the standard-size hybrid car.

- Seats 6
- 3 years old
- 35,000 miles on the speedometer
- Gas mileage: 42 miles per gallon
- Excellent sound system
- Car was repaired after a minor accident

Compact Economy Car

This is a list of points about the compact economy car.

- Seats 5
- New
- Gas mileage: 28 miles per gallon
- Basic model with few extras
- Good security system
- Engine not very powerful

SPEAKING TEST 6 Candidate A

Deciding on a Math Tutor or Tutoring Program for 12-Year-Old Marissa

Amanda

This is a list of points about Amanda.

- 18 years old, senior in high school
- Charges $25 an hour
- Honor roll student
- Wants to major in math in college
- Lives next door to family
- Busy with after-school activities so would need to keep lesson times flexible

Mildred Robinson

This is a list of points about Mildred Robinson.

- Recently retired high-school math teacher
- Charges $40 an hour
- Will come to the home
- Reputation: dedicated, hard-working
- Works to supplement retirement income
- Old-fashioned and boring, according to Marissa's best friend

SPEAKING TEST 4 Candidate B

Deciding on a Chain Store to Open in a Small City of 50,000 People

Champion Sporting Goods

This is a list of points about Good Sports.

- Sells sports equipment and sports clothing
- Would employ about 150 people
- No other sporting goods store in community
- Sponsors a number of free sports programs for local schools
- Quiet, non-polluting business
- Has recently had economic problems

Good Foods

This is a list of points about Good Foods.

- Large supermarket specializing in fresh produce and organic foods
- Would employ about 200 people
- Pay and benefits for employees above average
- No other store like this in the community
- Prices higher than at other supermarkets
- Doesn't buy from local farmers

SPEAKING TEST 5 Candidate B

Choosing the Best $15,000 Used Vehicle for a Family of Five

Sport Utility Vehicle (SUV)

This is a list of points about the SUV.

- Seats 9
- 4 years old
- 60,000 miles on the speedometer
- Gas mileage: 17 miles per gallon
- Very large trunk
- Known problems with SUVs

European Luxury Car

This is a list of points about the European luxury car.

- Seats 6
- 7 years old
- 100,000 miles on the speedometer
- Gas mileage: 22 miles per gallon
- Excellent safety rating
- Leather seats showing signs of wear

SPEAKING TEST 6 Candidate B

Deciding on a Math Tutor or Tutoring Program for 12-Year-Old Marissa

Study, Study

This is a list of points about Study, Study.

- Commercial, for-profit tutoring program
- Cost: $50 an hour plus materials and fees
- Uses standardized tests to measure progress
- All classes on company site
- Tutors trained by company
- Parents report being pressured to accept expensive "extras"

Tutoring.com

This is a list of points about tutoring.com.

- Online tutoring available, 7 a.m.–11 p.m., 7 days a week
- Cost: $230 for 500 minutes
- Contact with students via Instant Messaging
- No need to schedule in advance
- Sessions as long or as short as needed
- Different tutor for each session

SPEAKING TEST 7 Candidate A

Choosing a Diet Program for a 40-Year-Old Adult Who Wants to Lose 25 Pounds

Diet 1

This is a list of points about Diet 1.

- Based on eating meals supplied by the company
- Cost of food + service = $400 a month
- Fruits, vegetables, and dairy products must be purchased by customer
- Eating out while on diet not recommended
- Weekly private counseling part of program
- Encourages exercise as part of program

Diet 2

This is a list of points about Diet 2.

- Based on food group guidelines and easy point system
- $40-$50 monthly for meeting fees and materials
- Lots of recipes for all eating styles/tastes
- Point system makes it easy to eat out and stay on diet
- Weekly meetings with public weigh-ins/discussion
- Workout/exercise ideas online

SPEAKING TEST 8 Candidate A

Giving Job Advice to a Computer Software Engineer with Two Teenage Children

Job 1

This is a list of points about Job 1.

- Software developer for multinational telecommunications company
- Starting salary: $150,000
- Excellent health plan and retirement benefits
- 15 vacation days, 5 sick/personal days a year
- Requires move to city over 1,000 miles away
- Children unhappy about relocating

Job 2

This is a list of points about Job 2.

- Manager of IT* department of a large financial company
- Starting salary: $120,000
- Good health plan and retirement benefits
- 20 vacation days, 7 sick/personal days a year
- Requires frequent business travel
- No move required

* IT - Information Technology

SPEAKING TEST 7 Candidate B

Choosing a Diet Program for a 40-Year Old Adult Who Wants to Lose 25 Pounds

Diet 3

This is a list of points about Diet 3.

- High-protein (meat, fish, dairy), low-carb plan
- One-time fee: $50 (online recipes, weight-tracker)
- No pre-packaged meals, but meat and fresh fish diet expensive to keep up
- Easy to eat out and stay on diet
- No individual counseling or support groups
- Diet plan only; no advice about exercise

Diet 4

This is a list of points about Diet 4.

- Based on a wide selection of "light," inexpensive foods; no pre-packaged meals
- One-time fee: $75
- Excellent web site: menu planner, recipes, etc.
- OK to eat out, if careful about menu choices
- Optional support group with trained counselor
- 3-stage exercise program essential part of plan

SPEAKING TEST 8 Candidate B

Giving Job Advice to a Computer Software Engineer with Two Teenage Children

Job 3

This is a list of points about Job 3.

- Executive vice president, small start-up software company
- Starting salary: $200,000
- Health plan, but no retirement benefits
- 10 vacation days, 5 sick/personal days a year
- Company owned by good friend
- No move required

Job 4

This is a list of points about Job 4.

- Senior software developer for a small start-up Internet company
- Starting salary: $100,000
- Health plan and retirement benefits
- 20 days a year for vacation/sick leave
- Can work from home 3 days a week
- In city about 50 miles from current home

Practice Test 1

TOPIC 1 – Local Solutions with Global Applications

Problem/Solution (Type 2)

A Before You Begin

1. Either in pairs or in small groups, brainstorm **3 problems** in your area that negatively affect people's quality of life, and write them in the chart below. Then brainstorm possible **solutions** for each. Finally, think about how these local solutions might benefit communities all over the world and the world as a whole.

	1	2	3
Problem	▪ ______________	▪ ______________	▪ ______________
Solution(s)	▪ ______________ ▪ ______________	▪ ______________ ▪ ______________	▪ ______________ ▪ ______________
Global Benefit(s)	▪ ______________ ▪ ______________	▪ ______________ ▪ ______________	▪ ______________ ▪ ______________

2. Review your notes and decide which two of the three areas you feel most comfortable writing about. Questions to ask yourself: Which two can I best develop with one or two reasons and examples? Which two allow me to best show off my knowledge of vocabulary and grammar?

B Suggestions for Development

INTRODUCTION – Tell them what you're going to tell them

- Restate the topic in your own words, perhaps by starting with a comment on "global issues" and then establish the background by commenting on the "quality of life" in your own area. For example:

  We all want to do something "big" to save the Earth, but sometimes it makes good sense to start small by ... .

- Conclude by mentioning problems/solutions generally and suggesting that they have global implications.
  Recently, though, problems have arisen with ... . The solutions, however, might benefit people everywhere.

MAIN BODY (2 paragraphs) – Tell them

Devote one paragraph to each problem and its solution(s).

- Start each paragraph with a clear topic sentence that announces one of the problems. Use introductory phrases such as:
  The first problem is that …
  Perhaps the greatest problem of all is that …
  Another problem is that …
  The second area that I think we should focus on is …
- Develop the first part of each paragraph by elaborating on the problem (giving examples of it or reasons why it exists) and/or mentioning other problems that may result from it:

  In other words, …
  The city says … , but …
  This means that …
  This not only affects … , but also …
  This may lead to …
  If nothing is done, then …

- Shift to the second part of the paragraph with a clear transition statement. Then go on to offer one or more solutions, elaborating with reasons, examples, and results. Use linking phrases such as:

  There are a number of ways to overcome this. For example, …
  The effect of this would be to …
  One low-cost solution would be to …
  This would lead to …

CONCLUSION – Tell them what you told them

- Summarize, perhaps by suggesting how quality of life would improve if these problems were solved.
- End with a dramatic statement about how the world would benefit if solutions were applied globally.

Practice Test 1

TOPIC 2 – Should Music and Art Be Required Subjects?

Opinion (Type 4b)

When an essay question presents you with a statement and asks whether you agree or disagree with it, a good way to structure your response is to explore both your own point of view as well as the opposite point of view.

A Before You Begin

1. In small groups or as a class, examine the status of music and art in your school system: e.g., Are the subjects required? Are they offered as "electives" (i.e., subjects that students can choose to take or not)? Are they offered at all? What about after school activities related to these activities (e.g., school choir or orchestra, art club, etc.)? How might a young person benefit from studying these subjects?
2. Alone or in small groups, brainstorm a list of reasons/examples for each side of the argument.

Yes, music and art should be required.	No, music and art should not be required.
a) ______	a) ______
b) ______	b) ______
c) ______	c) ______
d) ______	d) ______
e) ______	e) ______

3. Review your notes, and decide which side of the issue you will support.

B Suggestions for Development

INTRODUCTION – Tell them what you're going to tell them

- Introduce the topic in your own words, perhaps mentioning status of music and art in your school system.
- Briefly acknowledge the complexity of the issue (i.e., that there are two sides, both of which have merit) and then state briefly which side you support.

MAIN BODY (2 paragraphs) – Tell them

Conventional approach: Devote a separate paragraph to each side of the argument: one for your opinion and the other for the opposing opinion (ending with reasons why you feel this opinion is flawed).

- Start each paragraph with a clear topic sentence introducing each point of view. For example:

  Para. 2: *I feel strongly that secondary students should not be required to study music and art. …*

  Para. 3: *Of course, some people would argue that … .*

- Develop each side with a series of reasons, elaborations, and/or examples, using links such as:
  To begin with … , / In other words … , / In addition, … / Take, for example, …
  While these are all valid points, I feel strongly that …

Alternative approach: Explore the opposing side first … and then introduce your own argument by suggesting why the opposing side is flawed.

  Para. 2: *The main argument against requiring music and art is that these subjects are not …*

  Para. 3: *In my opinion, this view fails to take into account how valuable these subjects can be …*

CONCLUSION – Tell them what you told them

- Conclude by quickly acknowledging the opposing view again, and restating your opinion in a dramatic or thought-provoking way.

Practice Test 2

TOPIC 1 – Part-Time Jobs for Teenagers? Opinion (Type 4b)

Essay questions that ask you whether you think something is a good idea are similar to topics that ask you whether you agree/disagree with something (see page 202). As with "agree/disagree" topics, your essay will be more convincing if you explore both sides of the issue. In fact, both of these are similar to "For and Against" (Type 3) essays. Look at the "Summary of Main Composition Types" on page 9, and answer these questions.

a) How are Type 3 and Type 4b essays similar? – ____________________

b) What's the key difference? – ____________________

A Before You Begin

1. Ask classmates who have worked to share their experiences. Then discuss: If you were offered a job after school or on weekends, would you take it? Would your parents let you work? What problems might you have? What benefits would you gain?
2. Alone or in small groups, brainstorm a list of reasons/examples for each side of the issue.

It is a good idea for teenagers to work part-time.	It is NOT a good idea for teenagers to work part-time.
a) __________	a) __________
b) __________	b) __________
c) __________	c) __________
d) __________	d) __________
e) __________	e) __________

3. Review the chart, and decide which side you will support. Check (✓) the ideas you think you can use for each side.

B Suggestions for Development

INTRODUCTION – Tell them what you're going to tell them

- Restate the topic in your own words OR invite readers to visualize an unusual scene to capture their interest (e.g., a teen slaving over a bubbling deep-fat frier). Consider opening with one of the following:

  Have you considered what it would be like to … ?　　*Imagine how free you'd feel if …*

- Briefly acknowledge the complexity of the issue (i.e., that there are two sides, both of which have merit) and then state briefly which side you support. For example:

  There's no easy answer, but in my opinion working part-time …

MAIN BODY (2 paragraphs) – Tell them

Devote a separate paragraph to each side of the argument: one for your opinion and the other for the opposing opinion (ending with reasons why you feel this opinion is flawed).

- Start each paragraph with a clear topic sentence introducing each point of view. For example:

  Para. 2: *If teens can keep up with school, …* OR *I have several main objections to teens working.*

  Para. 3: *Of course, some people object to … .* OR *Those in favor of teens working argue that … .*

- Develop each side with a series of reasons, elaborations, and/or examples, using links such as:
  For one thing, … / For another … , / … also … / Finally, …
  Despite these objections/benefits, I feel strongly that …

CONCLUSION – Tell them what you told them

- Finish by referring to both sides again.
- Restate your opinion leaving readers, if possible with a dramatic or thought-provoking image or idea.

Practice Test 2

TOPIC 2 – Foreign-Language Teaching

Opinion (Type 4a or 4b)

A Before you Begin

1. **Discuss:** Do you think teachers spend too much time correcting errors? Do you feel you can express yourself freely in the languages you've studied? Which is more important: fluency or accuracy? What do you think the goal of language teaching/ learning should be?
2. **Exchange stories:** Talk about your successes and/or frustrations as language learners outside the classroom. How have your experiences in the classroom helped you succeed or made you stumble in real-life situations?
3. **Brainstorm:** On a separate piece of paper, alone or with your classmates, jot down a quick list of good and bad aspects of the two goals in the question. If you have a different goal in mind, add notes on that as well:

   Speaking and writing correctly *Expressing ideas fluently* *Other?*

   Also include brief notes about any details you might include about your own language-learning experience.
4. Read the question and your notes again. Check (✓) the points you think you should include, and then decide which "opinion strategy" you will use for the Main Body:
   - **4a:** Examine two aspects of what *you* think the main goal of language learning should be. OR
   - **4b:** Examine your view in one paragraph and the opposing view (including flaws) in another. (Paragraphs can be in either order.)

B Suggestions for Development

INTRODUCTION – Tell them what you're going to tell them

- Restate the topic in your own words, perhaps by rephrasing it as a rhetorical question or inviting readers to visualize a telling moment in your language-learning experience. For example:

  Which is more important in learning a foreign language: speaking and writing it correctly or expressing yourself fluently though perhaps inaccurately?

  Imagine being locked in a hotel room in a foreign country. You know how to say "Help!", but words fail you when you try to communicate to your rescuers that the doorknob has fallen off in your hand!
- Briefly acknowledge the complexity of the issue (i.e., that both are important) and then state briefly which side you support. For example:

  Although accuracy and fluency are admirable long-term goals, I'd say fluency is a higher priority.

MAIN BODY (2 paragraphs) – Tell them

- **If you choose Type 4a:** Devote one paragraph to each aspect of your argument. Start each with a clear topic sentence, supported by narrative detail and/or reasons and examples. For example:

  Para. 2: *My first encounter with American tourists taught me that grammar knowledge alone did not make me a competent English speaker. After five years of … , the problem was that … .*

  Para 3: *This experience made me rethink my ideas. I realized, for example, …*
- **If you choose Type 4b:** Devote one paragraph to your opinion and the other to the opposing view. Start with a clear topic sentence, supported by reasons, examples and, where appropriate, narrative examples.

  Para. 2: *Experience has shown me that being able to communicate is more valuable than accuracy.*

  Para. 3: *There are those, of course, who would argue that accuracy is most important. …*

CONCLUSION – Tell them what you told them

- Finish by referring to both sides again.
- Restate your opinion, leaving readers, if possible with a dramatic, amusing, or thought-provoking idea.

Practice Test 3

TOPIC 1 – Innovators: Giving More People Access

Problem/Solution (Type 2) OR
"Tell Them Prototype" (see Tip, p 82)

A Before You Begin

1. Jot down ideas for each category. Compare notes with your classmates, and add any ideas you like to your notes.

   Health and medicine: ______________________

   Alternate … energy: ______________________

   Computer technology: ______________________

   Agriculture: ______________________

2. Look at your notes and decide which area or specific breakthrough you could develop most effectively.
3. Reread the question, review your notes, and decide which strategy/structure you will use for Main Body:
   - **Type 2:** Examine (a) the overall PROBLEM(S) that innovators have met (or will meet) in giving more people access to your breakthrough area and (b) SOLUTIONS (i.e., ways that these problems can be overcome).
   - **"Tell Them" Prototype:** After establishing background in Introduction, examine two or more ways in depth that innovators can give more people access to your breakthrough area.

B Suggestions for Development

INTRODUCTION – Tell them what you're going to tell them

- Restate topic in your own words and/or briefly introduce the general or specific "breakthrough" area you have chosen to discuss. For example:

  Most people recognize the need for … . Innovators have been working on the problem for decades and there is no shortage of good ideas. But despite their progress, … is still not widely available.

- Lead into Main Body by suggesting what you will discuss, e.g., perhaps with a question/answer, as follows:
  What role can innovators play in … ? Let's look at ... for insight. / Let's look at several ways …

MAIN BODY (2 paragraphs) – Tell them

- **If you choose Type 2:** Devote one paragraph to the general problem(s) and a second to solutions (ways their innovation can be made more accessible). Start each with a clear topic sentence, and develop each with a series of reasons, examples and/or results, using linking words to connect your ideas. For example:

  Para. 2: *The problem innovators have had with electric cars is that … . The main reason for this is that … . In addition, … . Finally, ...*

  Para. 3: *There are a number of solutions that innovators might implement … . To begin with … . Once this happened, they could then … . By doing so, they would achieve … . Finally, ...*

- **If you choose the "Tell Them" Prototype:** Devote one paragraph to each solution. Develop each with a series of reasons and/or examples, using linking words to connect your ideas. For example:

  Para. 2: *The first thing innovators might focus their attention on is … . This is vital because … . One way to do this would be to …* [specific example]. *Once they achieved this, …* [result].

  Para. 3: *A second thing they could do would be to … .*

CONCLUSION – Tell them what you told them

- Summarize main idea put forward in Introduction and Main Body.
- End with a dramatic comment about the role of innovators and/or the consequences of putting your solutions into effect.

Practice Test 3

TOPIC 2 – Museum Admission Fees

For and Against (Type 3)

A Before you Begin

1. **Discuss:** Think about the major national museums, galleries, and historical sites in your country. Do most of them charge an admission fee? If they do, do you think the charge is reasonable or do you think it is high enough that some people may not be able to afford it? If they don't, how are museums funded in your country (e.g., by the government, by private donations, by voluntary admissions fees?)
2. **Brainstorm:** Alone or with your classmates, jot down a quick list of arguments for and against establishing free admission to your country's national treasures.

Museums and other nationals treasures should establish a policy of free admission.
Arguments "for" free admission ▪ ______ ▪ ______ ▪ ______ ▪ ______
Arguments "against" free admission ▪ ______ ▪ ______ ▪ ______ ▪ ______

3. **Decide:** Read your notes and decide which policy *you* think is best: charging admission or not charging?

B Suggestions for Development

INTRODUCTION – Tell them what you're going to tell them

- Restate topic in your own words, perhaps by making a statement about the purpose of museums and other cultural institutions and then posing a question about admissions fees.
- Acknowledge the complexity of the topic (i.e., that there are arguments for and against) and state that you will examine both sides. (Hold your opinion for the end.)

MAIN BODY (2 paragraphs) – Tell them

- Start each paragraph with a clear topic sentence announcing the point of view you are going to discuss. For example:

  Para. 2: *On the one hand are those who feel that cultural institutions should be free of charge.*

  Para. 3: *On the other hand are those who argue against free admission.*
- Develop each side with 2-4 points, using linking words and elaborating with reasons and examples.

CONCLUSION – Tell them what you told them

- Assess what you've said by saying you've weighed both sides and reached a decision. For example:

  On balance, I feel that although both sides have merit, … is the better option.
- End with a dramatic or thought-provoking statement of your opinion.

Practice Test 4

TOPIC 1 – Measures Reducing Congestion and Air Pollution   "Tell Them" Prototype (see Tip, p 82)

A Before You Begin

1. **Analyze the task:** Read the topic carefully. How many questions does it pose? ______ What specific thing(s) does it ask you to discuss? ____

____

2. **Discuss:** How bad is congestion and air pollution in your country's big cities? Is the situation better or worse than it was, say, ten years ago? Why do you think this is so?
3. **Brainstorm:** On a separate piece of paper, alone or with your classmates, jot down a quick list of ideas under the following headings:

   Past/current situation   *Measures taken*   *Effectiveness of measures*   *Ideas for future measures*
4. Review your notes, and check (✓) the ideas you think you can use to develop your response.

B Suggestions for Development

INTRODUCTION – Tell them what you're going to tell them

- Introduce the topic by commenting on the past or current situation in your country regarding congestion/air pollution.
- Hint briefly at how your country tackled (or perhaps ignored) the situation and suggest that even more could be done to improve the situation.

MAIN BODY (2 paragraphs) – Tell them

- Devote a separate paragraph to each question in the essay topic. Start each with a clear topic sentence and support it with a series of examples, reasons, and/or consequences, using linking words to connect your ideas. For example:

Para. 2: *To its credit, my country's government has addressed the problem with a number of measures that have greatly reduced both congestion and air pollution. Among the more effective of these was … , which had the effect of … .*

OR

Although the government was quick to enact a number of measures to control the situation, the measures have met with limited success. A big part of the problem is that … . Another contributing factor is that ... . Finally, … .

Para. 3: *Where should we go from here? In my opinion, there are a number of options that need to be explored … To begin with, I'd recommend that … . This would have the effect of … . A second idea would be to … . This would mean that … . Last but not least, … .*

CONCLUSION – Tell them what you told them

- Summarize your ideas in the Introduction and Main Body.
- End with a dramatic or thought-provoking statement about your vision of the future.

Practice Test 4

TOPIC 2 – Is Your Country's Educational System Obsolete? "Tell Them" Prototype (see Tip, page 82)

A Before you Begin

1. **Analyze the task:** Read the topic carefully. How many questions does it pose? ______ What specific thing(s) does it ask you to discuss? ____

____

2. **Discuss:** Has your country always placed a high value on education for all or is this a relatively recent phenomenon? What improvements have been made in your country's educational system since your grandparents were of school age? What do you think is the system's greatest strength? If you could correct one weakness of your country's educational system, what would it be? Do you think the system is doing a good job in preparing students to compete in the modern world?

3. **Brainstorm:** On a separate piece of paper, alone or with your classmates, jot down a quick list of ideas under the following headings:

   Strengths *Weaknesses* *Steps for the Future*

4. **Decide:** Review your notes and decide whether you will focus on the strengths or weaknesses or both. Then check (✓) the ideas you think you can use to develop your response.

B Suggestions for Development

INTRODUCTION – Tell them what you're going to tell them

- Establish the background, perhaps by commenting on the past and/or present of education in your country OR by inviting readers to consider a striking scene or statistic (e.g., improvement in literacy rate, percentage of students who go on to college, etc.).
- Conclude with 1-2 sentences that summarize your general opinion (e.g., that the system has many strengths and/or weaknesses) and that more needs to be done to ensure that future generations are prepared to compete in the modern world.

MAIN BODY (2 paragraphs) – Tell them

- Devote a separate paragraph to each question in the topic. Start each with a clear topic sentence and support it with a series of well-linked examples, reasons, and/or consequences. For example:

  Essay focusing initially on strengths:

  Para. 2: *I'm proud to say that the educational system in my country has improved tremendously since the mid 1950s. Perhaps the most striking improvement is that … . Another area is … .*

  Para. 3: *Despite these strengths, however, there are several weak spots that need to be reinforced as we move forward. For one thing, … . For another, … . Finally, … .*

  Essay focusing initially on weaknesses:

  Para. 2: *It saddens me to say that, despite some improvement, the system continues to be deficient in several areas. Perhaps the most striking problem is … . Another area where we fail to measure up is … .*

  Para. 3: *To improve the situation for future generations, it's clear that the government needs to set firm priorities. For starters, … . Secondly, more emphasis needs to be put on … . Finally, … .*

CONCLUSION – Tell them what you told them

- Summarize the ideas you set out in the Main Body.
- End with a dramatic or thought-provoking statement about the future.

Practice Test 5

TOPIC 1 – "You" as Person of the Year

"Tell Them" Prototype (see Tip, p 82)

A Before you Begin

1. **Analyze the task:** Read the topic carefully. How many questions does it pose? ______ What specific thing(s) does it ask you to discuss? ____________________
2. **Discuss:** Take an informal poll of your classmates: How many people blog or read blogs? How many people participate in social networking sights or regularly check out video sights like YouTube? Find out what benefits they feel they get from such activities. Do they believe they are taking part in activities that are somehow changing society? If so, how? If not, why not?
3. **Brainstorm:** Alone or with your classmates, quickly jot down ideas under one or both sides of the chart:

Participation in Internet is changing society	Participation in Internet is NOT changing society
■ ____________________	■ ____________________
■ ____________________	■ ____________________
■ ____________________	■ ____________________
■ ____________________	■ ____________________
Reasons to be FOR *Time*'s choice	**Reasons to be AGAINST *Time*'s choice**
■ ____________________	■ ____________________
■ ____________________	■ ____________________

B Suggestions for Development

INTRODUCTION – Tell them what you're going to tell them

- Restate topic in your own words, by establishing the context (i.e., what *Time* did in 2006).
- Briefly comment on the choice (e.g., that it was unusual, silly, commendable) and hint at your opinion, perhaps by speculating on what you think the magazine hoped to gain by making such a choice.

MAIN BODY (2 paragraphs) – Tell them

- Devote a separate paragraph to each question in the topic. (**Note:** In this case you may want to start with the second question first as a build-up to what you think of *Time*'s choice.) Start each with a clear topic sentence and support it with a series of well-linked examples, reasons, and/or consequences. For example:

Para. 2: *The main social change that the Internet has brought about is that it … . For example, … .*

Para. 3: *Was* Time *right to recognize "Us" as Person of the Year? Some might say … . Others might argue … . But on balance, I think* Time's *choice was excellent/misguided/absurd because it … .*

CONCLUSION – Tell them what you told them

- Restate your opinion about the significance/insignificance of the Internet.
- End with a thought-provoking or dramatic idea.

Practice Test 5

TOPIC 2 – Success: What Does It Come From?

Opinion (Type 4a)

A Before You Begin

Think about it: The essay task begins with a statement about two points of view about the origin of success. Then it asks what *your* opinion is. Unlike other opinion tasks we've seen so far, the question is worded in an open-ended manner, so there is no need to choose one side or the other (unless of course you want to). You may feel that success comes from something entirely different or you may feel that success depends on a *combination* of the two factors mentioned in the task. The choice is entirely up to you. Bear in mind that if you *do* choose to explore different factors, it wouldn't hurt to make a passing reference to the two viewpoints mentioned as a way of acknowledging the complexity of the issue.

1. **First Things First:** In small groups or as a class, discuss what success is. It may be helpful to start by seeing how the word is defined in a monolingual English dictionary. Success can mean different things to different people. Starting your essay with a clear definition of what *you* mean by success will help keep you and your readers on track.
2. **Brainstorm:** On a separate piece of paper, alone or with your classmates, brainstorm a list of factors that you think a person needs to achieve success. Then next to each, brainstorm examples you might use to illustrate them.
3. **Decide:** Review your notes, and put a check (✓) next to the factor(s) you want to discuss in your essay. (Remember: You can always stick with one or both of the factors mentioned in the essay topic. Then think about how you will develop the Main Body of your essay. For example, do you want to discuss: (a) one key factor in each paragraph? (b) one key factor in para. 2 and a number of secondary factors in para. 3? (c) key factors in para. 2 and factors/viewpoints you want to dismiss in para. 3? You will also need to decide whether you want to illustrate your points by looking at one extended example (e.g., a person launching a business) or by referring to a number of different examples.

B Suggestions for Development

INTRODUCTION – Tell them what you're going to tell them

- Restate the topic in your own words, perhaps by including a definition in the first sentence, asking a rhetorical question in the second, and then mentioning how others would answer the question in the third (i.e., acknowledge the complexity of the issue by hinting that there are a range of answers). For example:

  Success can be defined as … . How can it be achieved? Some say … is the key, while others say … .

- Briefly state your own opinion and hint at how you're going to explore the issue in the rest of the essay.

  In my opinion, … . Let's look at … [different aspects or an extended example] *to see how … .*

MAIN BODY (2 paragraphs) – Tell them

- Devote one paragraph to each aspect of your argument. Start each with a clear topic sentence, supported by narrative detail and/or reasons and examples. For example:

  Para. 2: *Most people would agree that … is essential for achieving success. First, … . Then, … . Finally, … . These are just a few of the traits that … . / These are just a few examples of how … .*

  Para. 3: *But … alone isn't enough. What's also required is … . For example, … . OR Those who think that … or … is the key to success might say that … . However, … .*

CONCLUSION – Tell them what you told them

- Restate your opinion with a clear summary statement.
- End with a thought-provoking or dramatic idea.

Practice Test 6

TOPIC 1 – Is Television Living Up to Its Full Potential …?

Opinion (Type 4a)

A Before You Begin

Think about it: The task asks you: (a) whether or not you think TV is living up to its potential OR (b) if you think there are more beneficial ways that TV could be used. Given the close connection between the two, you could choose to touch on both in the Main Body: e.g., one paragraph addressing the first part and a second paragraph addressing the second part. Alternatively, you could choose to explore one of the two parts in more depth, but comment on the other part in your Introduction and/or Conclusion.

1. **Discuss:** Why are people so critical of TV? Despite this, why do you think so many people spend so much time watching TV? Do you think TV's popularity will continue into the future or do you think it will "lose ground" to Internet activities? How do you think TV programming/viewing/technology will change over the next fifty years?
2. **Brainstorm:** Work alone or in small groups. Below or on a separate piece of paper jot down a quick list of ideas under the following headings:
   - *Goals of TV/Potential?* – ____________________
     ____
   - *What's bad about TV?* – ____________________
     ____
   - *What's good about TV?* – ____________________
     ____
   - *Improvements for the future?* – ____________________
     ____
3. **Decide:** Review your notes, and put a check (✓) next to the points you feel you can use in your essay. Then decide on what you will discuss in each paragraph of the Main Body:

   Para. 2: ____________________ **Para. 3:** ____________________

B Suggestions for Development

INTRODUCTION – Tell them what you're going to tell them

- Restate topic in your own words, perhaps by quickly surveying some of the reasons that people criticize television OR by commenting on what its goals should be and suggesting that it could be meeting them better. Alternatively, invite readers to consider a striking or humorous scene OR ask a rhetorical question: e.g., Is TV living up to its full potential?
- End by hinting at the two aspects you will explore in the Main Body.

MAIN BODY (2 paragraphs) – Tell them

- Devote one paragraph to each aspect of your argument. Start each with a clear topic sentence, and then support it with a series of reasons and examples. For example:

  Para. 2: *What does TV do well/badly? For one thing … . TV also … . Finally, … .*

  Para. 3: *Taking these strengths/weaknesses into account, how can TV be improved? To my mind, the answer lies in … . / there are a number of things that can be done … . To begin with, … . A second area to exploit would be … . If this happened, viewers … . In short, the key is to … .*

CONCLUSION – Tell them what you told them

- Summarize your opinion.
- End with a thought-provoking or dramatic statement about what might lie ahead in the future.

Practice Test 6

TOPIC 2 – "You Can't Always Get What You Want"

Narrative (Type 1) OR
"Tell Them" Prototype (see Tip, page 82)

A Before You Begin

Think about it: Although most essay topics that have appeared on the ECPE in recent years have been "expository" or "argumentative," occasionally you might get a topic that asks you to explore an idea based on personal experience. For example, the topic could describe a general situation and then ask you to describe a personal experience that was similar. You might then be asked to analyze and comment on one or more aspects of the situation. How should you cope? Read the topic carefully and underline what the topic asks you to do. More often than not, the phrases you underline will suggest the structure you should use in the Main Body and/or Conclusion.

1. **Analyze the task:**

   (a) What does it ask you to describe? ______________________________

   (b) What two aspects should you explore? ______________________________

2. **Discuss:** Exchange stories with your classmates about a time when something didn't work out for you.
   - Establish the time frame and the background (e.g., the circumstances surrounding your personal defeat).
   - Narrate the events that led up to your not getting what you had hoped for.
   - Describe how you felt initially and how you eventually coped with your feelings.
   - Talk about one or more of the lessons you learned.

   As you listen, think of ways that your classmates might improve their stories: e.g., by adding more detail or explanation.

3. **Brainstorm:** Working alone, use a separate piece of paper to jot down quick notes under these headings:

   Background/Key Events *How I Coped* *Lessons Learned*

4. **Decide:** Review your notes, and put a check (✓) next to the points you feel you can use.

B Suggestions for Development

INTRODUCTION – Tell them what you're going to tell them

- Restate the topic in your own words, perhaps with a brief general anecdote about people being disappointed when things don't work out.
- End by hinting that we can usually use such defeats to our advantage or by suggesting that something similar happened to you and that you managed to learn from the situation.

MAIN BODY (2 paragraphs) – Tell them

Para. 2: Establish the background to your story and narrate what happened, up to and including the moment of your defeat, failure, or disappointment. Start with a clear opening sentence that either establishes the time frame or provides a clear thematic framework for your story. To show the passage of time, use narrative time links. If desired, use direct speech for dramatic effect to show how you felt. For example:

In my last year of high school, I was an A student hoping for a college scholarship. … When I got my report card that quarter, … . "There goes my scholarship," I thought.

Para. 3: Narrate the sequence of events that occurred in the aftermath of your defeat as you began to recover. Again, use time links and, if desired, direct speech. For example:

As soon as … , … . Shortly after, … . As she spoke, … . "I can do this!" I vowed. "I'll show her."

CONCLUSION – Analyze/Explore what you told them

- Use the Conclusion to analyze and explore the lessons you learned from the incident.
- End with a dramatic, thought-provoking idea.

Practice Test 7

TOPIC 1 – Lifestyle: Stay in One Place or Move Around?

For and Against (Type 3 modified)

A Before You Begin

1. **Analyze the task:** Typical "for and against" topics ask you to explore both sides of an issue (e.g., pros and cons). How does this topic differ? ____________________ Look at the model for Type 3 topics on page 9. What changes would you make for this topic? ____________________

____

2. **Discuss:** Poll your classmates. Find out whose family has stayed in one place and whose has moved around. What are some of the reasons that people have moved/stayed? Which lifestyle would you prefer?
3. **Brainstorm:** Alone or in small groups, jot down a quick list of arguments for each lifestyle. Then compare ideas with the class as a whole.

MOVING AWAY
Arguments "for"
▪ ____________________
▪ ____________________
Arguments "against"
▪ ____________________
▪ ____________________

STAYING IN ONE PLACE
Arguments "for"
▪ ____________________
▪ ____________________
Arguments "against"
▪ ____________________
▪ ____________________

4. **Decide:** Review your notes, and check (✔) the ideas you think you can use to develop your response.

B Suggestions for Development

INTRODUCTION – Tell them what you're going to tell them

- Establish background and restate topic in your own words, perhaps by describing both lifestyles and asking a rhetorical question (e.g., *Which way is better?*).
- If desired, hint at your preference, but acknowledge that both sides have pros/cons.

MAIN BODY (2 paragraphs) – Tell them

- Devote one paragraph to each lifestyle. Start each with a clear topic sentence, and then support it with a series of reasons and examples, covering both advantages and disadvantages. For example:

Para. 2: *As a "mover, I'm sometimes envious of the "stayers" that I know. Their main advantage is that ... .*
They also … .
On the down side, however, … . That's why ... .

Para. 3: *In contrast, "movers" enjoy a broader experience of life. For example, … . The disadvantage, of course, is that … .*
In addition, … . However, … .

CONCLUSION – Analyze what you told them

- Clearly state your preference, supporting it with one or more reasons/examples.
- End with a thought-provoking or dramatic idea.

Practice Test 7

TOPIC 2 – Work Styles: Is Multitasking for You?

"Tell Them" Prototype (see Tip, page 82)

A Before You Begin

1. **Analyze the task:**
   - Underline what the task asks you to do. How many parts does the task have? ______
   - What does that suggest about how you should structure the Main Body of the essay? ____________________

   ____

2. **Discuss:** In small groups or as a class, exchange information about multitasking. Do you do it? If so, how does it benefit you? If not, what problems does it pose for you? Do you find yourself using one working style at certain times and the other working style at others? What are the main arguments for and against multitasking? What are the main arguments for and against doing one thing at a time?

3. **Brainstorm:** On a separate piece of paper, jot down quick notes under the following headings:

   THE STYLE I PREFER
   - *Why it works for many people*
   - *Why it usually works for me*
   - (Optional) *Why it sometimes doesn't work*

   THE STYLE I DON'T PREFER
   - *Why it works for many people*
   - *Why it usually doesn't work for me*
   - (Optional) *Why it sometimes works*

4. **Decide:** Review your notes, and check (✔) the ideas you think you can use to develop your response. Then check (✔) which paragraph plan you will use for the Main Body. For example:

   (a) **Para. 2:** The style that other people like / **Para. 3:** Why it does not work for me

   (b) **Para. 2:** The style I prefer: why it works for many / **Para. 3:** Why/how it works for me specifically

   (c) **Para. 2:** The style I prefer most of the time / Para. 3: Why I sometimes switch back and forth

   (d) **Para. 2:** ______________________ / **Para. 3:** ______________________

B Suggestions for Development

INTRODUCTION – Tell them what you're going to tell them

- Establish background by briefly discussing multitasking and restating topic in your own words.
- Briefly state your opinion about the two work styles mentioned and suggest that you will now go on to explore the issues more deeply. For example:

  Personally speaking, I prefer … . This is because + [general reason]. Let's take a closer look.

MAIN BODY (2 paragraphs) – Tell them

- Follow the plan you decided on in (4). Start each paragraph with a clear topic sentence, and then support it with reasons and examples. If you choose (a), for example, your essay might look something like this:

  Para. 2: *The successful multitaskers I know claim that multitasking makes them more productive because … . For example, take the case of someone who … . This person claims … .*

  Para. 3: *For me, this way of working simply doesn't work. For one thing, … . For another, … . That's because over the years I've gotten used to … . To get the job done, I find I have to … .*

CONCLUSION – Tell them what you told them

- Sum up your personal preference.
- End with a thought-provoking or dramatic statement about one or both styles.

Practice Test 8

TOPIC 2 – Strategies for Narrowing Down Career Options

"Tell Them" Prototype (see Tip, page 82)

A Before You Begin

1. **Analyze the task:**
   - How many questions does the task include? ______
   - What are you asked to do? ______________________________
   - What does that suggest about structuring the Main Body? ______________________________
2. **Discuss:** In small groups or as a class, exchange ideas and stories about how young people begin to narrow down their career choices. Ask and answer questions like: When did you start thinking about what you wanted to be when you grew up? Did/Do you get any help or guidance from teachers or administrators at your school? What strategies did they recommend? What strategies have you yourself or others close to you found useful?
3. **Brainstorm:** Alone or in groups, make a list of all the things you can think of that young people can do to begin narrowing down their career choices. Compare notes with your classmates and add any ideas that appeal.
4. **Decide and expand your notes:** Review your notes, and check (✔) the 2-3 general strategies that you would like to focus on in your response. **Note:** Keep in mind that you might be able to group together some of the strategies you wrote down under one or more broad general strategies (e.g., DO RESEARCH: go to the library, browse Internet, talk to people who are in the job). Once you decide on your broad, general strategies, make notes on a separate piece of paper: e.g., make a column for each strategy and then add reasons, examples, and/or other elaborating details that you might use to support each strategy:

   Strategy 1 *Strategy 2* [OPTIONAL] *Strategy 3*

B Suggestions for Development

INTRODUCTION – Tell them what you're going to tell them

- Establish the background and restate the topic in your own words, perhaps by posing one or more rhetorical questions … and then stating that there are several basic strategies that readers might want to consider. For example:

  Where should you start? Try considering two basic strategies that many teens have found helpful.

MAIN BODY (2 paragraphs) – Tell them

- Devote one paragraph to each broad strategy. Start each with a clear topic sentence, and then support it with a series of reasons and examples and results. For example:

  Para. 2: *The first thing you can do is … . A good way to begin is to … . You could also try … . All of these are helpful in that they … .*

  Para. 3: *The second strategy is to … . Many teenagers find this useful because … . Closely related to this is … . For example, you might … . It's also a good idea to … .*

CONCLUSION – Tell them what you told them

- Summarize the message in your Intro and Main Body: e.g., acknowledge the complexity of the issue by hinting that choosing a career is always challenging, but it can be less so if you start with a basic plan.
- End with a thought-provoking or dramatic idea.

Practice Test 8

TOPIC 2 – Inventions and the Service They Perform

"Tell Them" Prototype (see Tip, page 82)

A Before You Begin

1. Analyze the task:

- What are you asked to do? ______________________________
- What does that suggest about how you should structure the Main Body? ______________________________

____

2. Brainstorm: In small groups or as a class, discuss each invention and jot down ideas related to the "service" each invention "gives to others." Compare notes with your classmates, and add any ideas you like to your notes.

Airplane: ______________________________

____

Television: ______________________________

____

Telephone: ______________________________

____

Computer: ______________________________

____

Com. satellites: ______________________________

____

3. Look at your notes and decide which invention you think you could develop most effectively.

B Suggestions for Development

INTRODUCTION – Tell them what you're going to tell them

- Introduce the invention, perhaps by opening with a surprising or dramatic image/idea that establishes the context. For example: speculating about what was in the inventor's mind as he/she developed the invention might be an interesting way to start. If possible, mention the Edison quote from the essay topic.
- Make a broad general statement about the "service" that your choice provides.

MAIN BODY (2 paragraphs) – Tell them

- Devote a separate paragraph to each main aspect of your argument. Start each with a clear topic sentence, and then support it with a series of reasons and examples and results. For example:

Para. 2: *First consider the …'s huge impact on people's personal lives. Before … , …. .*
Once it caught on, however, … . Today, thanks to … , we're able to … in ways that [the creators of the invention] couldn't possibly have imagined.

Para. 3: *… have also changed the way that companies and governments do business. When … came along, for example, it was no longer necessary to … . In addition, … . Last but not least, … . None of these developments would have been possible, had it not been for … .*

CONCLUSION – Tell them what you told them

- Summarize the main message of the Introduction and Main Body.
- End with a dramatic or thought-provoking statement about the present and/or future.

Practice Test 1

Passage 1 (page 28)

Before You Begin – To gain insight into what Obbink does, take an A4 piece of paper which is covered in writing on one side and rip it into at least 50 tiny pieces. Scramble the pieces on a flat surface and then, using a pair of tweezers, try piecing the page together again.

1. What is it about Professor Obbink's job that stretches the meaning of "painstaking"?
2. List three reasons why scholars had so much trouble working with the Herculaneum papyri.
3. What three breakthroughs did Obbink have while working on the Herculaneum papyri?
4. What is the underlying scholarly significance of the work that Obbink and his colleagues are engaged in?

For Further Discussion – With your classmates, brainstorm a list of jobs that require painstaking attention to detail. Would you personally want to do any of these jobs? Why or why not?

Passage 2 (page 29)

Para. 1

1. Describe the typical cacao grove of a pioneer farmer.
2. According to the text, how long is such a grove productive for?
3. What problems usually set in after that?

Paras. 2-3

4. Compare the methods and benefits described in para. 2 with those described in para. 3.

Passage 3 (page 30)

1. Why does the writer think SUV drivers will be surprised at the findings?
2. How are the Jetta, Civic, Escort, and Neon similar? How are they different?
3. What conclusion can be drawn about SUVs and fuel efficiency?
4. Before the study, why was the auto industry faulted for trying to achieve higher fuel economy? How has the study changed this perception?

For Further Discussion – Do you believe car owners in your country are becoming more concerned about the environment? Support your opinion with evidence.

Passage 4 (page 31)

1. What is the topic sentence of para. 1?
2. The writer supports the topic sentence by isolating three general areas. What are they?
3. The second paragraph is about "molting." What is this? (Read the paragraph quickly; one of the sentences gives a very precise definition.)
4. Why do you think large birds such as eagles and cranes have adapted longer molting cycles?
5. Why is it logical (from a survival point of view) that new feather growth appears before migration?
6. "Preening" is defined in the last paragraph. What is it and how does a bird benefit from doing it?

For Further Discussion – Some people say bird-watching is a fascinating hobby; others think it's excruciatingly boring! Discuss the pros and cons. Can you see yourself engaging in such a hobby?

Practice Test 2

Passage 1 (page 50)

1. To appreciate the size of the crystals, consider the following: 1 foot = approx. 0.3 meters. Now do the math: How high and how wide were the crystals in meters? Could you put your arms around them?
2. Check (✓) the picture that best resembles what the miners saw when they made their discovery.

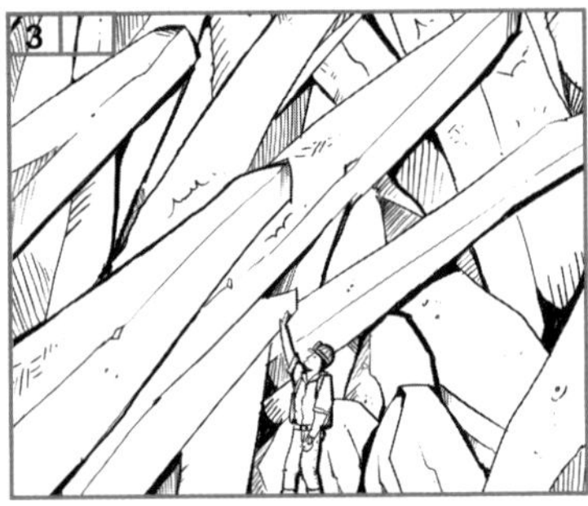

Internet Follow-up – At the time of publication, the National Geographic website had a fabulous video about the cave. Try: http://ngm.nationalgeographic.com/video/player#/?titleID=1842856752

Passage 2 (page 51)

1. What are the two ways in which species disappear?
2. How does the mass extinction of species that is currently under way differ from the other five mass extinctions that have occurred in evolutionary history?
3. In addition to hunting and "introduced predators," how else has humanity contributed to the "assault on the ecosystem"? (para. 2)
4. What role does hunting play in increasing the current "tempo of extinction" (para. 3)?
5. What specific examples of "habitat destruction" are mentioned in para. 3?

For Further Discussion – List the problems discussed in the passages. Which problems affect your country? How successful has your government been in combating these issues?

Passage 3 (page 52)

1. What is the passage about?
2. How do operations done with the cyberknife differ from conventional surgery?
3. What does the cyberknife do?
4. Explain in your own words how magnetic stereotaxis systems work.
5. What happens once the magnet reaches its destination?
6. Why does the writer mention the now primitive practice of "operating without anesthesia"?

Passage 4 (page 53)

1. Is the description in para. 1 objective and scientific or poetic and emotional? What words/phrases show this? Where does the author shift to a different tone? How does the second tone compare to the first? Do you think the shift is effective?
2. According to the text, how are auroras formed?
3. What experience did the writer share with Charles Deerh? Where was each man at the time?
4. What was unusual about the visibility of the 1989 aurora? (If possible, use a map or globe to locate an aurora's usual range of visibility, and then locate the extreme extent of the reach of the 1989 aurora).
5. List the disturbances that the aurora caused in Canada and elsewhere.

Internet Search/Further Discussion – If you've never seen an aurora borealis, do an Internet search for "aurora borealis photos."

Practice Test 3

Passage 1 (page 72)

1. What does the writer mean when she says "For anthropologists, this kind of string is a cultural marker" (lines 5-6)? What examples does she give in para. 1?
2. How do archaeologists know that string and rope were used as early as 28,000 years ago?
3. What will the "lack of string" tell future archaeologists about 21st-century Western society? What cultural markers do you think they will find in place of string?

Passage 2 (page 73)

1. Para. 1: What is the main idea in sent. 1? What example is given in sent. 2? How does the writer bring us back to the idea in sent. 3?

2. Para. 2: What kind of protozoan-like cells are discussed in the first sentence? What is the job of these cells (sents. 2-4)? What do researchers believe happens when killer cells are defective, and what has this led them to believe (sent. 5)?

3. Para. 3: What kinds of protozoan-like cells are focused on in sentence 1? How does the first type of these cells operate (sents. 2-3)? What does the second type do (sent. 4)? How do the two types work together (sents. 5-6)? What happens if they don't do a perfect job (sent. 7)?

4. Para. 4: What cells are discussed here? How do they perform their job (sent. 3)? What happens after they form a complete layer over the wounded area (sent. 4)?

For Further Discussion – The writer of the passage does an excellent job of explaining complex cell functions in everyday language. He does so by using comparison and creating a distinct, almost human personality for each cell type. What details do you find especially memorable? Which cell type is your favorite?

Passage 3 (page 74)

1. What are the three phases that characterize the "potentially absurd character of cosmic evolution"?
2. What two crises are referred to in para. 1?
3. What examples are given of man's "prodigious intellectual faculties"? (para. 2)
4. What difficult task still lies ahead?
5. What is the "awesome challenge" (end of para. 2), and what will happen if it isn't resolved?
6. What is the connection between biological evolution and "achievements of modern technology"? (para. 3)
7. Why does the writer mention "life on other planets"? (para. 4)
8. What two realities would a galactic voyage reveal?

For Further Discussion – Do you believe that mankind will destroy itself? What can governments and individuals do to try to avoid destruction?

Passage 4 (page 75)

1. What famous story is referred to in para. 1? Can you retell it in your own words?
2. What is the relationship between para. 2 and para. 1?
3. Why does the writer return to the famous story in para. 3?

For Further Discussion – Have you ever seen a "Pygmalion project" at work in real life? How does it make you feel when someone (e.g., your parents, a teacher, or a friend) tries to change you?

Practice Test 4

Passage 1 (page 94)

1. What connection does Vincent van Gogh have with the main idea of the article?
2. What is meant by the phrase "adult dabbler" (para. 1, last sent.)?
3. What is meant by the phrase "the labeling process is compromised by industry influence" (para. 2)?
4. Is the Art and Creative Materials Institute for or against exempting paints and other materials from consumer lead laws? What reasons do they give to justify their stance? Do you agree with this?
5. What health hazards do solvents pose to humans?

For Further Discussion – Does your family keep hazardous materials at home? Are their laws in your country regarding labeling and disposal of such products? What lessons can you learn from this passage?

Passage 2 (page 95)

1. Explain the phrase: "… programs are developing international talent at the expense of aspiring American athletes, not to mention America's Olympic hopes."
2. What percentage of the field do foreign athletes with scholarships currently constitute in college swimming, ice hockey, and tennis?
3. What is true of the percentage of foreigners in other sports?
4. What possible solution to the problem does the article mention? Why don't more coaches come out in favor of this?

For Further Discussion – Are there many foreigners on your national or professional teams? Are you for or against this?

Passage 3 (page 96)

1. Is *Chlamydia pneumoniae* a disease or a bacterium that causes disease?
2. How does it usually affect the body?
3. What other damage do scientists believe it causes?
4. According to the current hypothesis, how does "the bug" get into the walls of a blood vessel?
5. Describe the "vicious cycle" that may begin once the bug is in the wall of a blood vessel.
6. How are scientists using rabbits to prove their hypothesis?
7. What do scientists hope to prove about antibiotics?

For Further Discussion – The passage states that "heart attack mortality" has dropped by half since the mid-1960s, partly due to changes in lifestyle. What changes do you think these might be? What are some of the things we can do to continue improving our chances of maintaining a "healthy heart"?

Passage 4 (page 97)

Before you begin: Search the Internet for photos of and information about Mount Rushmore. Suggested search phrases: Mount Rushmore facelift, Mount Rushmore maintenance

1. Did you notice the pun (play on words) in the first paragraph? Look up the words *concrete* and *cement*, then explain why the phrase *concrete use* is so appropriate in context.
2. There's another clever pun in the last paragraph, where the writer mentions a "bacterial facial" for Mount Rushmore. Find the noun meaning of the word *facial*, read the footnote about Mount Rushmore again, then explain why the phrase would amuse a well-informed reader.

For Further Discussion – What qualities do you think are necessary for a person to be a successful researcher in microbiology or other sciences? Which do you think is a more noble profession: being a doctor or doing scientific research? If you had to pick one over the other, which would you choose?

Practice Test 5

Passage 1 (page 116)

1. What is the passage about?
2. How many main types of plants are contrasted to support the writer's main idea? How does the writer show this in the way the passage is broken into paragraphs?
3. What three basic ways does a plant have of getting rid of the heat it absorbs during the day?
4. Why do plants in the Arctic grow close to the ground? What would happen if they grew taller?
5. What danger do desert plants face?
6. Why aren't desert plants "designed" to cool themselves by evaporation?
7. What two advantages does the "sticklike shape" of desert plants have?

Passage 2 (page 117)

1. Why does a tumor need a supply of blood to grow? (para. 1)
2. What happens if a tumor doesn't get a blood supply? Why is this a problem? (para. 1)
3. What happens when a tumor is supplied with blood? (para. 1)
4. How do healthy cells regulate the growth of nearby blood vessels? (para. 2)
5. Explain the role of inhibitors and inducers. Which are usually more dominant? (Look up *induce* and *inhibit* in a dictionary, if need be.)
6. Explain how new vessels link the tumor with the rest of the circulatory system. (para. 2)
7. What advantage might endostatin and angiostatin have over artificially developed inhibitors? (para. 3)
8. How do experts feel about these two substances? (para. 3)

Passage 3 (page 118)

1. What does *incandescent* (lines 2-4) mean?
2. What three things can GONG scientists learn by measuring the pulsations in the sun?
3. What have scientists learned by studying the sun's "heartbeat"? What ability does this knowledge give them that they didn't have in the past?

Passage 4 (page 119)

1. What did the Earth look like in Permian times 250 million years ago? (para. 1)
2. What were the climate and the ocean like back then?
3. According to the old theory, what change occurred when sea life died and decayed in deeper water? What happened as a result of this change?
4. According to the new theory, what was to blame for the extinctions?
5. What happened to the climate when CO_2 increased in the seas and decreased in the air? (para. 2)
6. What, in turn, happened at the poles? How did this affect the nearby surface water and the CO_2-laden water at the bottom of the sea?
7. What effect did the CO_2-rich water have when it reached shallower areas?
8. Explain how the cycle stopped and eventually started again.
9. How did the Permian extinctions compare to the extinctions that eliminated the dinosaurs?

Practice Test 6

Passage 1 (page 138)

1. Describe the steps in which the original gem became the Hope. What was it called after each "cut"?
2. Describe the steps taken to prove that no other diamonds came from the original Tavernier.

Internet Follow-Up – The article fails to mention one of the most fascinating things about the Hope Diamond, and that's the "curse" that is supposedly attached to it. Search the Internet for "curse of the Hope Diamond" and report your findings to the class.

Passage 2 (page 139)

1. What does moyamoya mean, and why is the disease called that?
2. What are some of the early symptoms of moyamoya?
3. Why is the disease so difficult to diagnose?
4. According to the passage, how does moyamoya cause artery blockages? How does atherosclerosis cause artery blockages?
5. List some of the early, unsuccessful methods that doctors used to treat moyamoya.
6. Describe the procedure that surgeons use to treat adult patients with moyamoya.

Internet Activity (Optional): Search the Internet for information in English about one or more of the following and report your findings to your classmate. Your reports can focus on a basic description of the disease, its symptoms, and treatment.

beriberi
brucellosis
Dengue fever
Munchausen syndrome
Legionnaire's disease
leishmaniasis
Lyme disease
onchocerciasis
SARS
SID syndrome
Tourrette's syndrome
trypanosomiasis

Passage 3 (page 140)

1. According to the passage, what will future historians be most likely to remember FDR for?
2. List four reasons why FDR was loved.
3. Why was he hated?
4. Is he still hated today? Why or why not?
5. Does the writer suggest that FDR's faults outweighed his strengths, or vice versa?
6. Why does the author mention the fact that FDR "fought his own way back from polio"?

For Further Discussion – What leaders in your own country do you think future historians will single out? What were the circumstances in which they led and what contributions did they make? What 20th-century leaders internationally do you think will be singled out for special recognition by historians?

Passage 4 (page 141)

1. What did Europeans unintentionally bring with them to the New World? (para. 1)
2. What effect did this have on native populations? Why? (para. 1)
3. Where was the effect especially disastrous? (para. 2)
4. Left without a native work force, how did the Spaniards find people to work the land? (para. 2)
5. How did the Spaniards further "break the spirit and health" of the natives? (para. 3)
6. How did native populations in Canada hold up against the Europeans? (para. 4)

Practice Test 7

Passage 1 (page 160)

Note: Alzheimer's disease is a disorder characterized by loss of recent memory and a progressive loss of an individual's capacity for thought, learning, planning tasks, and focusing on what is happening.

1. Is the passage about a harmful or beneficial effect of nicotine? Describe the effect in your own words.
2. What process is described in the first four sentences of para. 2?
3. How does nicotine help this process?
4. What have studies shown about the link between smoking, nicotine, and Alzheimer's disease?
5. What does the writer imply about the "transdermal patch" mentioned in the last paragraph?

For Further Discussion – The passage puts a rather interesting twist on the old expression, "One man's meat is another man's poison." Nicotine has been shown to cause lung cancer, heart disease, and early death, and yet it may be one of the keys to an eventual cure for Alzheimer's disease. Below are some other potentially harmful things that medical science has put to good use. Discuss what you know about the medical use of each:

radiation mold germs/viruses

Can you think of other examples that illustrate the truth of the old expression?

Passage 2 (page 161)

1. The first sentence in para. 1 suggests that the writer has woven together two main themes. Briefly explain both.
2. After archaeologists found the crocodile cemetery at Tebtunis, why did their initial excitement die down?
3. What was the significance of what they eventually discovered (paras. 2-3)?
4. How did conservators try to protect the manuscripts when they were first brought back to Berkeley?
5. What eventually went wrong with what they had done?
6. Describe the machine that eventually solved the problem.

For Further Discussion – What great archaeological discoveries have been made in your country during the past century? Were the discoveries aided in any way by modern technology?

Passage 3 (page 162)

1. How would you describe the tone of para. 1? What phrases support your answer?
2. The phrase "in lockstep" means "in unison or in close conformity." Explain the relationship it refers to in para. 2?
3. What are the three methods of data collection used by Quirk (para. 3)?
4. What is the passage ultimately about: skunks? ducks? or the interrelationship between them? Explain.

Passage 4 (page 163)

Internet Link - If you'd like to see and read more about the painting referred to in para. 2, go to:
http://en.wikipedia.org/wiki/The_Gross_Clinic

1. What underestimated and underappreciated medical diagnostic tool does the writer refer to in para. 1?
2. How does Jefferson Medical College hope to train better doctors?
3. What three specific practical benefits to such courses are mentioned in para. 3?
4. What other areas are medical colleges requiring their students to study for similar reasons?

Practice Test 8

Passage 1 (page 182)

1. What do college career centers do? Scan each paragraph and list the services mentioned.
2. Judging from clues in the passage, what do you think an internship is?
3. According to the passage, what benefits do students gain from doing an internship?

For Further Discussion – What resources exist in your country to help students find jobs? What can graduates do to improve their chances of landing a job? If you were an official for the Department/Ministry of Labor, what recommendations would you make to improve a person's employment prospects?

Passage 2 (page 183)

1. Why were there many more male iguanas than female iguanas before the mid 1970s?
2. What caused the balance to shift back to normal?
3. What happened to the balance of the sexes as ecotourism began to catch on on? To what did researchers first attribute this change?
4. Why were the researchers surprised when they found tagged males on nearby islets?
5. Why were they upset about this development?
6. The writer alludes to several other problems that might arise from ecotourism. What are they?

Passage 3 (page 184)

1. Skim the passage quickly, then go back and take a closer look at para. 1. Which of the four people mentioned is the passage mainly about? Find the sentence that supports this.
2. What two scientific phenomena were explained in 1953? Who won a Nobel Prize as a result?
3. What made Franklin uniquely qualified to study and try to explain the structure of DNA?
4. What role did Franklin's work play in Watson and Crick's success?
5. Can you think of a simple reason why Franklin was not awarded a share of the Nobel Prize?
6. What conclusion does the writer draw about Franklin in the final paragraph?

For Further Discussion – Discuss what you know about DNA and the field of genetics and genetic engineering. Why was it so important that scientists discover the structure of DNA? What other medical advances have become possible as a result of science's growing knowledge of DNA? How may scientists' ability to "engineer" the genes within DNA be put to good use? Why is genetic engineering so controversial?

Passage 4 (page 185)

1. What facts does the writer say you should know about methane and how it relates to global warming?
2. Where did the methane in the northern hemisphere come from, and where has it been up to now?
3. According to information in para. 2, where else does methane come from?
4. Why are scientists so concerned about methane and the condition of the permafrost?
5. On balance, does the information in the last paragraph leave you feeling optimistic about the future?